# Selected
# Readings
# in Public
# Speaking

# Selected
# Readings
# in Public
# Speaking

edited by

**Jane Blankenship**

Mount Holyoke College

**and**

**Robert Wilhoit**

Drury College

DICKENSON PUBLISHING COMPANY, INC., BELMONT, CALIFORNIA

L. C. Cat. Card No.: 66–12868

Printed in the United States of America

# Preface

This collection of readings was prepared with a twofold purpose in mind: (1) as a core of materials around which the teacher can design a course in public speaking, and (2) as a collateral reader to be used in conjunction with a textbook on public speaking. The collection attempts to present a consistent point of view—that of the public speech as a dynamic, persuasive force in our contemporary society.

The material included in this book ranges in chronology from the writers of antiquity to contemporary writers in rhetoric and public speaking, philosophy, linguistics, and communication theory. From their various orientations, most of these writers view communication as persuasion, designed to elicit predetermined responses from listeners.

Since we believe the student, even the beginning student, should be exposed to as wide a range of materials as possible, we have included various types of readings. Some tell the student "*How* to do—" and some provide insights into "*Why* this is the way to do—" Some reveal a humanistic approach to rhetoric and public speaking; others, a scientific approach.

The book includes an introduction in which we discuss the rhetorical point of view around which the essays are centered, and seven sections, each with a brief introduction pointing out the relationships among the articles in that section, and an extended bibliography.

Although both editors have selected the articles in this text, primary responsibility has been divided in this way: Professor Blankenship—Introduction, The Nature of Communication, Language and Style, and Speech Criticism; Professor Wilhoit—Organization, Delivery, and Ethics. Both editors are equally responsible for the section on Invention.

Jane Blankenship
Robert Wilhoit

# Contents

# Introduction

When one person speaks to another, he is trying to share a piece of information, an attitude, or an opinion. For communication means *sharing*. This implies (1) that the speaker has something to share, that is, something to say, (2) that he knows how to say it so that it will be clear to the listener, and (3) that he can say it effectively, so that it will gain the listener's attention and assent.

This book is concerned with that species of communication called public speaking. What is a speech? According to our definition, a speech is a verbal communication limited generally to a certain kind of subject matter, a certain kind of intent, and a certain form. Let us discuss the implications of this definition.

*A certain kind of subject matter*. What do we give speeches about? Karl Wallace answers in this way: "Probably most thoughtful persons will at once agree that foundation materials of speeches are statements that are evoked by the need to make choices in order that we may act or get ready to act or to appraise our acts after their doing."[1] He goes on to maintain that the speaker's preeminent concern is the giving of *good reasons*, which are "a number of statements, consistent with each other, in support of an *ought* proposition or of a value-judgement."[2]

Today this emphasis on *good reasons* as the substance of oral discourse is perhaps more important than ever before. As a catalytic agent in the nurture of human values, the speaker activates the "principles we believe in, the substance of things for which we live."[3]

*A certain kind of intent*. All speeches are given to elicit response. Few people give speeches to empty rooms. Even when we describe an event or show somebody how to do something, we want him to agree that our description is accurate or that the method we are recommending is efficient. In short, even in exposition, we are *seeking agreement*. We are attempting, at a very basic level, to persuade—to get the audience to accept the speaker as a good source of information.

---

[1] "The Substance of Rhetoric: Good Reasons," *Quarterly Journal of Speech* (October 1963), p. 241.

[2] *Ibid.*, pp. 247–48.

[3] Richard Murphy, "Preface to an Ethic of Rhetoric," in *The Rhetorical Idiom*, ed. Donald C. Bryant (Ithaca: Cornell University Press, 1958), p. 141.

In some speeches, the persuasive intent is still more clear. We ask people to vote for a certain candidate and to reject others; we ask people to take a certain course of action and to reject others. When we ask someone to accept our opinions as valuable, to follow the courses of action we propose, we are trying to persuade them. Thus, speeches are verbal means of inducing cooperation in our society.

"Men want reasons to reconcile their minds to what is done, as well as motives originally to act right," said Edmund Burke. This "reconciling" goes on over the labor-management bargaining table, and over the vegetable counter at the local grocery store, as well as in the United States Congress and the Supreme Court.

This giving of good reasons is, according to Donald C. Bryant, the act of "adjusting ideas to people and . . . people to ideas."[4] But whether it is called adjusting, or reconciling, or seeking agreement, or persuasion, when the public speaker gives a speech he is presumably asking his listeners to become somehow different than they were before. They will go away from his speech knowing something new, considering new courses of action, reconsidering old courses of action and ways of doing things, reaffirming old values or developing new ones. They have somehow been moved to action.

A certain kind of form. Although a speech does not have a rigidly prescribed form, it does have a general form. In large measure, speech form is dictated by the fact that it is addressed to an audience. Before determining what speech form is, let us explore more fully the concept of speech as addressed. The discussion we shall present rests on the work of Kenneth Burke.[5]

When any verbal communication takes place, it involves two or more separate beings. The speaker and the listener are different people who know different sets of facts, who hold different attitudes, who possess different "property," in the sense of both physical and intellectual goods. But by the very act of saying anything we are attempting to overcome these differences. We use words to allow us to coexist, to cooperate in the building of society.

Communication requires formally at least three elements: the speaker, the speech, and the spoken-to (listener). If the speaker is to induce cooperation, he has to shape his speech so as to communicate with the spoken-to. Unless he does so, communication, whether one sentence or an hour-long speech, has little chance of succeeding.

---

[4] "Rhetoric: Its Functions and Its Scope," *Quarterly Journal of Speech* (December 1953), p. 413.

[5] *A Rhetoric of Motives* (Englewood Cliffs, New Jersey: Prentice-Hall, Inc., 1950).

Cooperation (communication) is possible because the listener identifies himself in some way with the speaker. This "identification" allows the speaker and the listener to remain different individuals but recognize that they are alike in some ways. Through speech, then, the sharing of ideas, attitudes, and opinions is possible.

A speech, however, derives its special form from the fact that it is *addressed* to someone. As Wilbur Schramm points out (see pp. 227–233), a speech must be designed to gain the attention of the listeners. It must employ "signs" which refer in some way to experience common to both the speaker and the listeners. A speech must arouse personality needs in the listeners and suggest some ways to meet those needs. And lastly, a speech must be in a form appropriate to the speaker's situation.

In short, a speech is a response to a given situation, and although a speaker can talk "directly" to an increasingly large number of people via TV and radio, he has a conception of "audience" in his mind as he prepares the speech. Even the public lecturer who often gives the same speech over and over generally gives that speech to audiences which share certain characteristics. And, in any event, it could be argued that national audiences have a certain character. For example, televised speeches which the President of the United States addresses to an American audience differ somewhat from those he addresses to a world audience.

The great speeches, which endure in our literature because they appeal to basic human values to which every generation can respond, have all been shaped by the occasion and audience for which they were intended. Churchill and Lincoln spoke to national audiences in times of crisis; Burke and Chatham, to arouse the British Parliament to the rights of the American colonies when few in the Parliament would acknowledge those rights.

Thus, speeches give good reasons for acting, for determining the ways of acting, and for deciding how well or how poorly people have acted. Speeches are governed largely by the attempt to elicit a certain response from those who hear them. They are organized not only according to the logical principles of internal consistency of materials, but also according to psychological principles of audience analysis.

Since a speech usually grows out of a given social need, to judge its effectiveness the critic judges how well or how poorly the speaker has selected materials that are appropriate to his audience and the situation which prompted him to speak. The critic raises these questions: Out of all the possible *means of persuasion* which the speaker could have used, which ones did he choose? Were these the best ones? Generally speaking, the means of persuasion are all of the means by which the speaker can get the audience to listen to him, to agree with him: his evidence and arguments, the integrity of his ideas, the way in which he presents his materials (organization, style, delivery).

Aristotle noted ". . . men have a sufficient natural instinct for what is true, and usually do arrive at the truth."[6] And, as he observed, public speaking as a force for the good is a useful subject of inquiry for four reasons:[7]

1. Things that are true have a natural tendency to prevail over their opposites, so if decisions are not what they should be, the defeat must be due to the speakers themselves.
2. Audiences, being human beings, do not, even when they possess exact knowledge, always feel moved to action and therefore need to be persuaded by speakers.
3. Public speaking (of the best kind) involves thorough preparation through vigorous search and inquiry into the nature of things. This allows a man to see all sides of the question so that he can more clearly know *why* one side is better than another.
4. A man ought to be able to develop one of the most characteristically human qualities—power of speech—as a means of achieving the best kind of life he can.

Because we live in a liberal democracy, as free men making free choices, the public speaker contributes to the number of decisions society is capable of making and to the quality of those decisions. His is a great opportunity indeed.

[6] *Rhetoric*, 1335a 15–17.
[7] *Ibid.*, 1355a 22–1355b 8.

# 1 The Nature of Communication

In the Introduction, we suggested that verbal communication is linguistic "sharing." But just what does this sharing involve? Speech is generally considered one of the basic abilities that sets man apart from animals. The ability to transmit knowledge, exchange ideas, and share experiences is essential to the development of civilization. Perhaps because we learn to talk without conscious effort at a very early age, we tend to think of speaking as a relatively simple process. It is actually quite complex.

Consider this "chain" of events. First the speaker decides what ideas he wants to convey. Then he selects the words he thinks will express his meaning and places these words in an order based upon the required grammatical rules of the language—articles before nouns, for example. This linguistic process is carried out by activity in the speaker's brain. The brain sends appropriate instructions to the tongue, lips, and vocal cords by means of impulses along the motor nerves. These nerve impulses set the muscles of the vocal organs into motion, producing changes of pressure on the surrounding air. These changes of pressure are called sound waves. These sound waves travel through the air between the speaker and the listener. The hearing mechanism of the listener, activated by these pressure changes, produces nerve impulses that travel to the listener's brain. There, in the already active brain, still more activity takes place, permitting recognition of the speaker's message.

Thus speech consists of "a chain of events linking the speaker's brain with the listener's brain."[1] There is at least one important side link in this "speech chain." As he talks, the speaker listens to his voice through a process called "feedback." He responds to his own message by making any adjustments which he thinks will increase its effectiveness.

In "A Model of the Communication Process," David K. Berlo offers a more detailed description of this process. He asks some very basic

---

[1] Peter B. Denes and Elliot N. Pinson, *The Speech Chain: The Physics and Biology of Spoken Language* (Bell Telephone Laboratories, Inc., 1963), p. 5. The entire book is worthwhile reading for those especially interested in the physics of sound, the acoustics of speech production, the anatomy and physiology of hearing, and the measurement of speech intelligibility.

questions: "What does it mean when we call communication a 'process'?" and "What are the essential ingredients of communication?" Berlo's communication model can be applied not only to public speaking but to all kinds of communication, for he is attempting "to isolate certain elements that all communications have in common."

Richard Murphy, in "The Speech as a Literary Genre," a portion of which is reprinted here, helps to isolate some of the elements of *a speech*. Although writing about speeches which are preserved as literature, he provides further insights into the nature of one form of communication—the public speech.

# A MODEL OF THE COMMUNICATION PROCESS

## DAVID K. BERLO

Every communication situation differs in some ways from every other one, yet we can attempt to isolate certain elements that all communication situations have in common. It is these ingredients and their interrelationships that we consider when we try to construct a general model of communication.

We attach the word "process" to our discussion of communication. The concept of process is itself complex. If we begin to discuss a model of the communication process without a common meaning for the word "process," our discussion might result in distorted views about communication.

## The Concept of Process

At least one dictionary defines "process" as "any phenomenon which shows a continuous change in time," or "any continuous operation or treatment." Five hundred years before the birth of Christ, Heraclitus pointed out the importance of the concept of process when he stated

Chapter Two of *The Process of Communication,* by David K. Berlo. Copyright © 1960 by Holt, Rinehart and Winston, Inc. Reprinted by permission of the publisher.

The author is Chairman of the Department of Communication at Michigan State University.

that a man can never step in the same river twice; the man is different and so is the river. Thomas Wolfe's novel of the 1940's, *You Can't Go Home Again*, makes the same point.

If we accept the concept of process, we view events and relationships as dynamic, on-going, ever-changing, continuous. When we label something as a process, we also mean that it does not have *a* beginning, *an* end, a fixed sequence of events. It is not static, at rest. It is moving. The ingredients within a process interact; each affects all of the others.

The concept of process is inextricably woven into the contemporary view of science and physical reality. In fact, the development of a process viewpoint in the physical sciences brought about one of the twentieth-century revolutions that we mentioned earlier. If we analyze the work of physical scientists up to and including Isaac Newton, we do not find a comprehensive analysis of process. It was believed that the world could be divided into "things" and "processes." It was believed also that things *existed*, that they were static entities, that their existence was independent of the existence or operations of other "things."

The crisis and revolution in scientific philosophy brought about by the work of Einstein, Russell, Whitehead, and others denied both of these beliefs in two ways. First, the concept of relativity suggested that any given object or event could only be analyzed or described in light of other events that were related to it, other operations involved in observing it. Second, the availability of more powerful observational techniques led to the demonstration that something as static or stable as a table, a chair, could be looked on as a constantly changing phenomenon, acting upon and being acted upon by all other objects in its environment, changing as the person who observed it changes. The traditional division between things was questioned. The traditional distinction between things and processes was broken down. An entirely different way of looking at the world had to be developed—a process view of reality.

Communication theory reflects a process point of view. A communication theorist rejects the possibility that nature consists of events or ingredients that are separable from all other events. He argues that you cannot talk about *the* beginning or *the* end of communication or say that a particular idea came from one specific source, that communication occurs in only one way, and so on.

The basis for the concept of process is the belief that the structure of physical reality cannot be *discovered* by man; it must be *created* by man. In "constructing" reality, the theorist chooses to organize his perceptions in one way or another. He may choose to say that we can call certain things "elements" or "ingredients." In doing this, he realizes that he has not discovered anything, he has created a set of tools which may or may not be useful in analyzing or describing the world. He recognizes that certain things may precede others, but that in many cases the order of precedence will vary from situation to situation. This is not to say that we can place no order on events. The dynamic of process has limitations; nevertheless, there is more than one dynamic that can be developed for nearly any combination of events.

When we try to talk or write about a process, such as communication, we face at least two problems. First, we must arrest the dynamic of the process, in the same way that we arrest motion when we take a still picture with a camera. We can make useful observations from photographs, but we err if we forget that the camera is not a complete reproduction of the objects photographed. The interrelationships among elements are obliterated, the fluidity of motion, the dynamics, are arrested. The picture is a representation of the event, it is not the event. As Hayakawa has put it, the word is not the thing, it is merely a map that we can use to guide us in exploring the territories of the world.

A second problem in describing a process derives from the necessity for the use of language. Language itself, as used by people over time, is a process. It, too, is changing, on-going; however, the process quality of language is lost when we write it. Marks on paper are a recording of language, a picture of language. They are fixed, permanent, static. Even spoken language, over a short period of time, is relatively static.

In using language to describe a process, we must choose certain words, we must freeze the physical world in a certain way. Furthermore, we must put some words first, others last. Western languages go from left to right, top to bottom. All languages go from front to back, beginning to end—even though we are aware that the process we are describing may not have a left and right, a top and a bottom, a beginning and an end.

We have no alternative if we are to analyze and communicate about a process. The important point is that we must remember that we are not including everything in our discussion. The things we talk about do not have to exist in exactly the ways we talk about them, and they certainly do not have to operate in the order in which we talk about them. Objects which we separate may not always be separable, and they never operate independently—each affects and interacts with the others. This may appear obvious, but it is easy to overlook or forget the limitations that are necessarily placed on any discussion of a process.

To illustrate the point, let us take an example other than communication. Education is a process. In discussing education, we can list certain ingredients. We have students, teachers, books, classroom lectures, libraries, discussion, meditation, thought, etc. We can order the ingredients. We can say that, in education, a teacher lectures to students (50 minutes at a time, three days a week, for $x$ years). We can say that a student reads books (6 books, 119 books, any number of books). We can say that the library has 100,000 volumes, or 1,000,000 volumes, or 6,000,000 volumes. We can say that students will hold $x$ discussion sessions, spend $y$ hours meditating, and write $z$ papers or examinations.

When we put all this together, we can say that if all of these ingredients are available and have been used, the student has received "an education." We *can* say this, but if we do we have forgotten the concept of process, the dynamics of education. As any good cook knows, it is the mixing process, the blending, that makes a good cake; ingredients are necessary, but not sufficient.

For an example in the communication field, take the theatre. What is "theatre"? Again, we can list ingredients: a playwright, a play, directors, actors, stage hands, audiences, scenery, lighting, an auditorium. Add them, and the total is theatre? Definitely not. Again, it is the blending, the dynamic interrelationships among the ingredients developed in the process that determine whether we have what we would call "theatre."

We need to remember that the dynamic of movement which relates the ingredients is vital. The concept of dynamic also implies that factors that we may overlook in any single listing of the ingredients also determine what is produced.

The dynamic of theatre is in part related to whether the play is produced for an audience before or after they have eaten dinner, or whether they had a heavy or a light meal, whether they enjoyed it or disliked it. The dynamic of education is in part determined by whether the student has just come from another situation in which he learned something which still excites him or whether he is fresh and has an "uncluttered" mind, whether he is taking an elective course he chose himself or a required one, whether his classmates make comments which stimulate him, or whether he has only his own thinking to help him, and so on.

Much of the scientific research in communication attempts to isolate factors which do or do not make a difference in the development of the process. Obviously, all the ingredients have not been determined—in fact, there is considerable basis for doubt as to whether they ever will be determined.

In any case, we need constantly to remember that our discussion of a process is incomplete, with a forced order and possibly a distorted perspective. Discussion is useful; it can lead to greater insight about a process. But it is not a complete picture, it can never reproduce the process itself. We cannot list all the ingredients nor talk adequately about how they affect each other. We can provide some suggestions, some hints about both the ingredients and the dynamic of the process.

There have been approaches to analyzing communication that have not been process-oriented. Such approaches might be labeled as "hypodermic needle" concepts of how communication works, or "click-click; push-pull" points of view. Such descriptions of communication are restricted to saying that first the communicator does A, then he does B, then C happens, and so on.

Much of the early discussion of the effects of the mass media of communication were of the "hypodermic-needle" variety. Critics as well as advocates of the print or electronic media (radio, TV) talked about how these media would affect the American public. Their concept of effects implied that a radio broadcast or a television program could be viewed as a hypodermic needle. If we would just stick these messages in the minds of the public, learning or entertainment or greater participation in civic affairs would be produced. The research conducted on the effects of the media indicates otherwise; whether or not these sources of communication are effective depends on a complex of factors, some of which the media can control and some of which they cannot.

Much of the debate over the effects of comic books on children, the effects of the movies, advertising, or political campaigns on the public is of this variety. Critics and commentators often overlook the effect of children on the contents of the comics, the effect of the public on movies, etc. It certainly is true that newspapers affect public opinion, but a process point of view argues that it is equally true that public opinion affects the newspapers.

With the concept of process established in our minds, we can profit from an analysis of the ingredients of communication, the elements that seem necessary (if not sufficient) for communication to occur. We want to look at elements such as *who* is communicating, *why* he is communicating, and to *whom* he is communicating. We want to look at communication behaviors: *messages* which are produced, *what* people are trying to communicate. We want to look at style, how people *treat* their messages. We want to examine the means of communication, the *channels* that people use to get their messages to their listeners, their readers. In short, we want to list the elements in the communication process that we must take into account when (a) we initiate communication, (b) we respond to communication, or (c) we serve as communication observers or analysts.

## The Ingredients of Communication

The concern with communication has produced many attempts to develop models of the process—descriptions, listing of ingredients. Of course, these models differ. None can be said to be "right," or "true." Some may be more useful than others, some may correspond more than others to the current state of knowledge about communication.

In the *Rhetoric*, Aristotle said that we have to look at three communication ingredients: the speaker, the speech, and the audience. He meant that each of these elements is necessary to communication and that we can organize our study of the process under the three headings of (1) the person who speaks, (2) the speech that he produces, and (3) the person who listens.[1]

Most of our current communication models are similar to Aristotle's, though somewhat more complex. One of the most-used contemporary models was developed in 1947 by Claude Shannon, a mathematician, and explained to the nonmathematician by Warren Weaver.[2] Shannon and Weaver were not even talking about human communication. They were talking about electronic communication. In fact, Shannon worked for the Bell Telephone Laboratory. Yet behavioral scientists have found the Shannon-Weaver model useful in describing human communication.

The Shannon-Weaver model certainly is consistent with Aristotle's position. Shannon and Weaver said that the ingredients in communication include (1) a source, (2) a transmitter, (3) a signal, (4) a receiver, and (5) a destination. If we translate the source into the speaker, the signal into the speech, and the destination into the listener,

[1] W. Rhys Roberts, "Rhetorica," in *The Works of Aristotle*, ed. W. D. Ross. Oxford University Press, 1946, Volume XI, p. 14.

[2] Claude Shannon and Warren Weaver, *The Mathematical Theory of Communication*. University of Illinois Press, 1949, p. 5.

we have the Aristotelian model, plus two added ingredients, a transmitter which sends out the source's message, and a receiver which catches the message for the destination.

There are other models of the communication process, developed by Schramm,[3] Westley and MacLean,[4] Fearing,[5] Johnson,[6] and others. The suggested readings at the end of the book list several of these. A comparison will indicate the great similarities among them. They differ partly in terminology, partly in the addition or subtraction of one or two elements, partly in the differences in the point of view of the disciplines from which they emerged.

In developing the model presented here, I have tried to be consistent with current theory and research in the behavioral sciences. It has been changed many times in the past few years, as a result of using it with students in the classroom, with adults in extension courses, and with workshops and seminars in industry, agriculture, and government. It is similar to other communication models and is presented only because people have found it a useful scheme for talking about communication in many different communication situations.

## A Communication Model

We can say that all human communication has some *source*, some person or group of persons with a purpose, a reason for engaging in communication. Given a source, with ideas, needs, intentions, information, and a purpose for communicating, a second ingredient is necessary. The purpose of the source has to be expressed in the form of a *message*. In human communication, a message is behavior available in physical form—the translation of ideas, purposes, and intentions into a code, a systematic set of symbols.

How do the source's purposes get translated into a code, a language?

[3] Wilbur Schramm, "How communication works," in *The Process and Effects of Mass Communication*, ed. Wilbur Schramm. University of Illinois Press, 1954, pp. 3–26.

[4] Bruce Westley and Malcolm MacLean, Jr., "A conceptual model for communication research," *Journalism Quarterly*, 34: 31–38, 1957.

[5] Franklin Fearing, "Toward a psychological theory of human communication," *Journal of Personality*, 22: 71–78, 1953.

[6] Wendell Johnson, "The fateful process of Mister A talking to Mister B," in *How Successful Executives Handle People*, Harvard Business Review, 1953, p. 50.

This requires a third communication ingredient, an *encoder*. The communication encoder is responsible for taking the ideas of the source and putting them in a code, expressing the source's purpose in the form of a message. In person-to-person communication, the encoding function is performed by the motor skills of the source—his vocal mechanisms (which produce the oral word, cries, musical notes, etc.), the muscle systems in the hand (which produce the written word, pictures, etc.), the muscle systems elsewhere in the body (which produce gestures of the face or arms, posture, etc.).

When we talk about more complex communication situations, we often separate the source from the encoder. For example, we can look at a sales manager as a source and his salesmen as encoders: people who produce messages for the consumer which translate the intentions or purposes of the manager.

For the present, we shall restrict our model to the minimum complexity. We have a communication source with purpose and an encoder who translates or expresses this purpose in the form of a message. We are ready for a fourth ingredient, the *channel*.

We can look at channels in several ways. Communication theory presents at least three meanings for the word "channel." For the moment, it is enough to say that a channel is a medium, a carrier of messages. It is correct to say that messages can exist only in *some* channel; however, the *choice* of channels often is an important factor in the effectiveness of communication.

We have introduced a communication *source*, an *encoder*, a *message*, and a *channel*. If we stop here, no communication has taken place. For communication to occur, there must be somebody at the other end of the channel. If we have a purpose, encode a message, and put it into one or another channel, we have done only part of the job. When we talk, somebody must listen; when we write, somebody must read. The person or persons at the other end can be called the communication *receiver*, the target of communication.

Communication sources and receivers must be similar systems. If they are not similar, communication cannot occur. We can go one step further and say that the source and the receiver may be (and often are) the same person; the source may communicate with himself—he listens to what he says, he reads what he writes, he thinks. In psychological terms, the source intends to produce a stimulus. The receiver responds to that stimulus if communication occurs; if he does not respond, communication has not occurred.

We now have all the basic communication ingredients except one. Just as a source needs an encoder to translate his purposes into a message, to express purpose in a code, the receiver needs a *decoder* to retranslate, to decode the message and put it into a form that the receiver can use. We said that in person-to-person communication the encoder would be the set of motor skills of the source. By the same token, we can look at the decoder as the set of sensory skills of the receiver. In one- or two-person communication situations, the decoder can be thought of as the senses.

These, then, are the ingredients that we will include in our discussion of a model of the communication process:

1. the communication source;
2. the encoder;
3. the message;
4. the channel;
5. the decoder;
6. the communication receiver.

We will mention many other communication factors; however, we will return to these six ingredients again and again, as we talk about communication at various levels of complexity.

## The Parts of the Model

What do we mean by a source, an encoder, and so on? Our preliminary discussion has given us the beginnings of a meaning for each of these terms—but only the beginnings. At this point, precise definitions of each term might not be as useful as a set of examples which include all the ingredients.

Let us start with a common communication situation: two people talking. Suppose it is Friday morning. We find Joe and Mary in the local coffee shop. There is a picnic scheduled for Sunday afternoon. Suddenly, Joe realizes that Mary is *the* girl to take on the picnic. Joe decides to ask her for a Sunday afternoon date. Joe is now ready to act as a communication source—he has a purpose: to get Mary to agree to accompany him on Sunday. (He may have other purposes as well, but they are not our concern.)

Joe wants to produce a message. His central nervous system orders his speech mechanism to construct a message to express his purpose. The speech mechanism, serving as an encoder, produces the following message: "Mary, will you go to the picnic with me on Sunday?"

The message is transmitted via sound waves through air, so that Mary can receive it. This is the channel. Mary's hearing mechanism serves as a decoder. She hears Joe's message, decodes the message into a nervous impulse, and sends it to her central nervous system. Mary's central nervous system responds to the message. It decides that Friday is too late to ask for a Sunday date. Mary intends to refuse the date, and sends an order to her speech mechanism. The message is produced: "Thanks, Joe, but no thanks." Or something somewhat more polite.

This is a very elementary and oversimplified treatment of the nature of the communication process, but it includes, at least superficially, all six ingredients we have introduced. Let us try another example.

Take the communication situation in which you are now engaged: reading this chapter. In this communication situation, I served as the source. I had a purpose in producing this manuscript—this message. My writing mechanisms served as an encoder (of course, typewriters, typists, and printing presses also served as encoders). The message includes the words on this page, and the way that the words are arranged. The message is transmitted to you through the medium of a book, by means of light waves. Your eye is the decoder. It receives the message, decodes it, retranslates it into a nervous impulse, and sends it to your central nervous system. Your central nervous system is the receiver. As you read, you will make responses to the book.

Let us take another example, and look at it more closely. Suppose Bill and John are at the dinner table. Bill has a problem. He is ready to eat a sandwich. He likes salt on a sandwich. The salt is at John's end of the table. Bill wants the salt. What does he do? He could reach from his end of the table to John's end and get the salt himself; however, this not only would be rude, it would be work. More likely, Bill asks John to pass the salt. Being a congenial sort of fellow, John passes Bill the salt. Bill puts it on his sandwich. All is well.

Again, what has happened, in terms of our communication model? Bill's central nervous system served as a communication source. He had a need, *salt on sandwich*. He had an intention, a purpose, to get John to pass him the salt. Bill relayed this purpose as a nervous impulse to his encoder, his speech mechanism. His encoder translated and expressed his purpose in code—English—and produced a message. The message: "Pass me the salt, please."

Bill transmitted this message via sound waves, through the air, in such a way that John could receive the message. John's hearing mechanism caught the message, decoded it, and sent it on to John's central nervous system. John had meaning for the message, responded to it, and passed Bill the salt. Mission accomplished.

This is communication. These are elementary examples, but even here communication is quite complex. The process we have just described occurs in only a small fraction of the time it took to talk about it—and we oversimplified our description at that. What were some of the things that could have gone wrong?

Suppose Bill did not have a clear idea of his purpose. He knew he needed something for his sandwich but he did not know what he needed. How could he have instructed his encoder to transmit a message?

Suppose Bill did not like John, or thought that John was inferior to him. This information might get through to his encoder, and the message might come out something like "Hey, you, gimme the salt—now." John might pass the salt—or he might say, "Get it yourself."

Suppose Bill was a new clerk in the company, and John was a Vice-President. Bill might not feel that he should start any communication with John—and Bill eats a sandwich without salt.

Suppose wires get crossed between Bill's nervous system and his encoder, and he produces an embarrassing message such as "Sass me the palt." Suppose his encoder is deficient, and it substitutes an "m" for an "s"; the message becomes "Pass me the malt." Either John gives Bill something Bill doesn't want or he doesn't give him anything at all.

Suppose the coffee shop is crowded and noisy. John does not hear Bill because the communication channel is overloaded. Result—John does not respond, and Bill never eats with John again. Finally, suppose John and Bill come from different cultures. In John's culture people do not eat salt on meat, or John might even disapprove of anyone using salt on meat. Result—he might not understand Bill, or he might not think as well of him.

These are only a few examples of the kinds of things that can go wrong, even in a simple two-person communication situation. You might like to return to our example of Joe asking Mary for a date or of your reading of this manuscript. What kinds of things could have happened at one or another stage of the process to cause those two communication situations to break down?

Our examples have been confined to relatively uncomplicated communication situations. The model is equally useful in describing the communication behavior of a complex organization. In such a situation, the encoding and decoding functions often are separable from source and receiver functions. Correspondingly, certain people in the organization occupy roles as both sources and receivers.

Take a large-city newspaper as an example. The operation of the newspaper involves a complex network of communication. The newspaper hires people whose prime job is decoding—reporters who observe one or more kinds of events in the world and relay them to the "central nervous system" of the paper, the "desk" or "slot" or central control office.

When these messages are received, some decision is reached by the editorial staff. As a result of these decisions, orders are given from the control desk to produce or not produce a given message in the paper. Again, the encoding function becomes specialized. The paper employs rewrite men, proofreaders, linotype operators, pressmen, delivery boys. They all are responsible for one or another part of the encoding and channeling functions, getting the message out of the control office on to the pages of the newspaper, and thence to a different set of receivers, the reading public.

The communication model can be used to describe the personal behavior of any member of the newspaper staff. At the same time, it can be applied at a different level of analysis, and used to describe the workings of the organization as a communication network.

Within the paper, elaborate subdivisions of communication responsibility are made. Some people decode only certain kinds of messages: police work, society behavior, sports, etc. Others are assigned to a more general beat. Some people do not feed information into the paper, but are responsible solely for encoding messages which get this information back out. Still others neither decode nor encode (at the network analysis level), but are responsible for receiver-source behaviors; in other words, for making decisions about the messages they receive and giving orders about messages they want sent out.

The newspaper is one example of a communication network. Others might include the behaviors of any information organization, the operations of the Department of State, and the structure of a large industrial organization. Communication analysis can be performed on communicative institutions or on a specific person. The model is equally applicable to both. It represents a point of view, a way of looking at behavior, whether the behavior is individual or institutional.

The examples given have several implications for further discussion. One is the varying nature of communication purposes. To a large extent, the modern newspaper is not an "original" source of communication. It specializes in interpreting information it receives from one set of sources and transmitting this information, as interpreted, to another set of receivers. It works as an intermediary in communication.

At the same time, through the editorial page, the newspaper does originate messages, does transmit "original" information to its reading audience. It both originates and interprets. One of the canons of responsible journalism is the requirement that the newspaper keep these two functions separate—that it avoid originating material while pretending to be interpreting material received from outside its own system.

There are other examples of the originator-interpreter distinction. The New York Stock Exchange is a good illustration. The operation of the market can be analyzed as an intricate communication network, in which the behaviors allowed to people performing various roles are explicitly defined and rigorously enforced. Some brokers on the floor are primarily encoders. They transmit the intentions of the main office or of customers who may live far from the exchange itself. Other brokers are both encoders and decoders. They transmit their employer's purposes and decode messages from others about the state of the market, the price of a particular stock. They send these messages to their office, where a decision is made. Still others are allowed to make decisions by themselves. They may buy or sell on their own initiative, for their firms or their personal holdings.

A second implication of the examples given concerns the way in which we should interpret the concepts of source, encoder, decoder, and receiver. These should not be viewed as separate things or entities or people. They are the names of behaviors which have to be performed for communication to occur. More than one person may be involved in the same behavior-form (multiple sources, encoders, etc.). One person may perform more than one set of behaviors. The same person may be both a source and a receiver, even simultaneously. The same person may—and usually does—both encode and decode messages. This illustrates the earlier point that the ingredients of communication, or of any process, are not separable, cannot be divided into independent or nonoverlapping entities.

The examples also can be used to illustrate the principle of relativity referred to earlier. At one level of analysis, we can describe a reporter as a decoder. At another, he is both a source and a receiver and perfoms both encoding and decoding behaviors. What we call him depends upon our own purposes, how we view him, in what context we place him, and so on.

Finally, the examples demonstrate the meaning of process, the interrelationship of the ingredients of communication. Within the newspaper, we cannot order communication events as (1) reporting, (2) decision-making by the central office on the value of messages received, (3) orders to put certain articles in the paper, and (4) encoding of those articles. It is hard to say which comes first.

Clearly, the reporter is affected by what he believes his editors want him to report, by the deadlines he faces in order to meet the requirements of the encoding process, etc. The central office is limited by what it receives from its reporters. It also is affected by what it believes to be the editorial policy of the publisher, his political beliefs, the space available in the paper, the time and costs of encoding, etc. And, of course, all employees are affected at all times by their assumptions as to the purposes of the reader who eventually will consume the paper. What they believe the reader wants affects what they report, what they interpret, and what they encode.

The communication of news is a process. All the ingredients of the process affect each other. A dynamic peculiar to that specific process is developed. A journalism student can quickly become familiar with the ingredients of journalism: events, typewriters, articles, city desks, printing presses, distribution systems, etc. It is the dynamic which is hard to learn, and which usually has to be experienced before it is understood.

The ingredients discussed are essential to communication. Whether we talk about communication in terms of one person, two persons, or an institutional network, the functions labeled as source, encoder, decoder, and receiver have to be performed. Messages always are involved and must exist in some channel. How they go together, in what order, and with what kinds of interrelationships depend on the situation, the nature of the specific process under study, the dynamic developed.

It is useful to use these ingredients to talk about communication. It is dangerous to assume that one comes first, one last, or that they are independent of each other. This denies the concept of process, and communication is a process. The importance of process might best be typified by the traditional argument of the relative priority of chickens and eggs. One useful deterrent to forgetting about interrelationships within a process is to remember the following definition: a chicken is what an egg makes in order to reproduce itself.

## THE SPEECH AS LITERARY GENRE

### RICHARD MURPHY

. . . A speech as a literary form, then, is a prose composition of varying length, fashioned for a specific or generic audience, usually but not necessarily spoken and listened to, written or recorded in some way on brain, paper, or tape for permanence, in which are inter-related author, reading or listening audience, theme, and occasion; it has ethical appeal and universality, moving force and fluency; its design is artistic, and its purpose is to direct the reader or listener to a conclusion selected by the composer.

1. *A speech is a prose composition,* although passages may be poetic, as in Burke or Ingersoll. Systematic rhythm patterns do not occur in the literature of speeches, except as parts of a poetic whole, as in Shakespeare. When Dionysius of Miletus chanted his speech, his teacher, Isaeus, rebuked him with, "Young man from Iona, I did not train you to sing."[1] And the imagery in a speech differs, as Longinus observed, from that in poetry. In a speech that imagery is best which not only has energy and reality, but is "mingled with the practical, the argumentative."[2] A typical poetic image is "Ruth among the alien corn"; it is self-sufficient. Daniel Webster's figure of the mariner storm-tossed at

From the article "The Speech as Literary Genre," *Quarterly Journal of Speech* (April 1958). By permission of the Speech Association of America and of the author. In a paper, "Problems in Speech Texts," read at the University of Iowa Conference on Rhetoric and Poetic, November 1964, Professor Murphy adapted his original definition to read like this: "A speech is a composition (usually in prose, but there are mediaeval sermons in verse) of variable length, fashioned for a specific or a generic audience, usually but not necessarily spoken and listened to, in which are inter-related author, reading or listening audience, theme, and occasion, for the purpose of directing the reader or listener to a conclusion selected by the composer. In its practical form, such as salesmanship or soul-saving, a certain amount of success in effect is anticipated. If the speech is to achieve status as literature, it must be written or recorded in some way on brain, paper, or tape for transmission and examination, and it should have qualities of ethical appeal and universality, moving force and fluency, an artistic design, and humane value. In speeches which have become literature, a certain amount of failure in immediate practical effect has been traditional."

The author, a former editor of the *Quarterly Journal of Speech,* is Professor of Speech at the University of Illinois.

[1] Philostratus, *The Lives of the Sophists,* 513.

[2] *Longinus on the Sublime,* XV, 9.

sea[3] is a typical speech image; it directs attention to his purpose, the immediate reading of the resolution; the image is subordinated to an end.

2. *Varying length*. Edward VIII eloquently abdicated, assisted by some stylistic touches by Winston Churchill, in a page broadcast to the world. Burke could fill a small book with his discourse. Senators have been known to talk around the clock, not always, of course, in Attic Style.

3. *Specific or generic audience*. Russell Conwell's *Acres of Diamonds* was designed for and delivered to thousands of audiences. The President frequently talks to no one assembled group, but to scattered millions around the world. This practice, admittedly, is contrary to much current theory. The textbook says: "There is no such thing as a speech in and for itself. There is only a speech on a specific subject, for a specific purpose, delivered by a specific person, before a specific audience, at a specific time and place."

4. *Usually, but not necessarily, spoken and listened to*. The natural destiny of a speech is to be delivered, of course. Delivery imparts an actuality, an authenticity to a speech. But it does not determine the speech; form must do that. Isocrates' *Areopagiticus* was not delivered, was not intended to be delivered, but it has served as a model speech for 2300 years. In the work-a-day world of speeches, frequently a speech text never gets delivered. Senator Joseph R. McCarthy, when under consideration for censure by the Senate, released a speech which was front-paged across the country. He was so busy he did not actually speak it, but had it "inserted in the RECORD."[4] Whatever merits the speech may have, whether it is a speech at all, will have to be determined by something other than a study of the Senator's voice and gesture. The Earl of Buchan labored well and long on a speech for a meeting of the Scottish Peers. The meeting never occurred. Undaunted, Buchan had the speech handsomely printed, and dedicated it to his brother, Thomas Erskine.[5]

5. *Written or recorded in some way*. Unless there is some recording there can be no permanence; the speech cannot become literature. Some of the great speeches have been recorded in memory, and recol-

---

[3] Reply to Hayne.

[4] *Congressional Record*, 83d Cong., 2nd sess., Nov. 10, 1954, pp. 14820–14823.

[5] *Speech of the Earl of Buchan, Intended to Have Been Delivered at the Meeting of the Peers of Scotland, For the General Election of Their Representatives*, Oct. 17, 1780 (Edinburgh, 1780).

lected in tranquility; William Wirt recalled what Patrick Henry said, and Dr. Johnson reconstructed Chatham.

6. *In which are inter-related author, reading or listening audience, theme, and occasion.* Always the speech grows out of some social occasion. One does not give a speech when he is impressed by the sun, moon, or stars. He writes a lyric or a sonnet, or a personal essay.

7. *Having ethical appeal and universality.* There is no great speech on the values of holding fellow humans as slaves; there are a great number on the rights of free men. To be literature, the speech must transcend the immediate occasion, and have a certain timelessness. Lincoln dedicated Gettysburg, it is true, but he did it in timeless values of democratic belief. To design a speech which will have universal appeal, and yet meet the demands of a social setting, is a colossal job. All those little local flourishes—who is on the platform, acknowledgments to the committee on arrangements—so dear to a specific audience have to be cast aside if the speech is to be recorded as literature. Lincoln managed it, but it is quite a feat to appeal to the day and to the ages in one effort.

8. *Moving force and fluency.* The speech is a dynamic form. It must have direction. It must approach, establish, and conclude. There must be a flow, a stream of rhetoric to convey the ideas past obstructions of misunderstanding, ignorance, and lethargy. The historical term for this is eloquence. A poem, a letter, an essay may be eloquent, also, but not necessarily so. Unless the speech is eloquent, it is not literature.

9. *Artistic design.* Although there is no absolute form prescribed for a speech, such as in the sonnet, there is rather general agreement that in a speech the author starts with an audience where it is and tries to end where he thinks it ought to be. Aristotle allowed for no more than an introduction, statement, argument (including refutation), and epilogue.[6] What is now known as the classical plan is more elaborate: exordium, narration, statement, partition, proof, refutation, peroration. Textbooks have various designs for speeches, but they are all alike in that they provide for taking an audience along to a conclusion. And they are forms for speeches in that they are not fitting for a short story, novel, or ode.

10. *Purpose.* "All the ends of speaking are reducible to four," wrote Campbell, "every speech being intended to enlighten the understanding,

[6] *Rhetoric,* 1414b.

to please the imagination, to move the passions, or to influence the will."[7] Campbell's psychology has been somewhat modernized, but his definition still remains as the classic, although it may be translated into such terms as "to inform, to impress, to entertain, to persuade," or "to interest, to make clear, to induce belief, to influence conduct." Some of these purposes may be achieved, of course, in other literary forms. The distinctive element in speeches is that one, some, or all of these are attained in relation to an audience. In the lyric or the letter, the purpose may be no more than to express oneself.

[7] George Campbell, *The Philosophy of Rhetoric* (London, 1776), I, 1.

# 2 Invention:
## The Search for Ideas

Invention, the search for ideas to use in the speech, includes (1) selection of a topic appropriate to the speaker, the audience, and the occasion, and (2) determination of the particular position which the speaker will take with regard to his topic and the best evidence and arguments to support this position. Evidence and arguments are selected not only because they are intrinsically worthwhile, but because they may be especially valuable before a particular audience.

In "Choosing a Subject," William Norwood Brigance points out the care that must be taken with this first step of speech preparation. (Originally published in 1932, the article also demonstrates that although topics may change, ways of evaluating topics have remained very much the same.)

Next, Charles S. Mudd and Malcolm O. Sillars discuss ways of finding the basic issues in topics concerning policy, fact, and value.

In the third selection, Aristotle points out that the speaker who is to be in command of the means of persuasion must "be able (1) to reason logically, (2) to understand human character and goodness in their various forms, and (3) to understand the emotions." Traditionally, the modes of persuasion related to these three abilities have been termed logical proof, ethical proof, and emotional proof. Today we understand that these modes of persuasion are not independent in the mind of the speaker as he prepares his speech or in their effect on his audience;[1] however, it can be useful to discuss them separately, as in the articles on logical proof (Thonssen and Baird) and ethical proof (Haiman).

Thonssen and Baird, writing as critics in their article "Testing the Argumentative Development," explore the concepts of evidence and argument. They suggest some of the ways logical proof can be examined and tested to determine how well it supports the speaker's point.

Although logical proof should form the core of support for a speaker's main points, "We might almost affirm that the speaker's *ethos*

---

[1] See, for example, Randall C. Ruechelle, "An Experimental Study of Audience Recognition of Emotional and Intellectual Appeals in Persuasion," *Speech Monographs* (March 1958), pp. 49–58.

is the most potent of all the means of persuasion," as Aristotle has said.[2] The speaker's *ethos* here means his character, his good sense, and his good will toward his audience. Contemporary experiments concerning ethical proof have explored many and varied topics. They have attempted to establish the various "dimensions" of *ethos*, such as prestige, credibility, and likeableness, and to determine the effect of *ethos* on persons of different sex, age, and educational group. Franklyn S. Haiman's "Experimental Study of the Effects of Ethos in Public Speaking" is one of the most interesting of these studies. Although it contains statistical data, the article can be read meaningfully without prior knowledge of statistics. Haiman concurs with the almost universal finding that "the ethos of the source is related in some way to the impact of the message."[3] Only further experimentation can reveal the exact nature of this relationship.

The third kind of proof, emotional proof, requires that the speaker know something about the predispositions of his audience—their needs and motives. We cannot, however, separate thought and feeling, as some older schools of psychology do. Listeners respond to the speaker's message as *total* human beings, in whom thought and feeling are connected in many ways.

As the speaker seeks to analyze his audience, he is confronted by such questions as "What is the nature of attention?"[4] and "What is the nature of motivation?"[5] The answers to these and many other general questions will help him to understand and know what proofs to offer his particular audience. We have therefore included two articles providing general insights, which the speaker can apply to his own particular situation: "The Anatomy of Attention" by Wilbur Schramm and "Toward an Analysis of Motivation" by Otis M. Walter.

[2] *Rhetoric*, trans. Lane Cooper (New York: Appleton-Century-Crofts, Inc., 1932), p. 9.

[3] Kenneth Andersen and Theodore Clevenger, Jr., "A Summary of Experimental Research in Ethos," *Speech Monographs* (June 1963), p. 77.

[4] See, for example, Nicholas Brown, "Attention: A Theoretical Note," *The Journal of General Psychology* (1960), pp. 103–11, and J. H. Deutsch and D. Deutsch, "Attention: Some Theoretical Considerations," *Psychological Review* (1963), pp. 80–90.

[5] See, for example, Jon Eisenson, J. Jeffrey Auer, and John V. Irwin, *The Psychology of Communication* (New York: Appleton-Century-Crofts, Inc., 1963), pp. 245–46, for a treatment of the basic, unlearned drives present in all people.

## CHOOSING A SUBJECT

WILLIAM NORWOOD BRIGANCE

Perhaps the most difficult of all phases of speaking for a student is to choose a suitable subject. Whether entering a speaking contest, making a classroom speech, or being invited to speak at a banquet, or upon any occasion, his first question is, "What subject shall I choose?" This, in a large part, is due to the lack of opportunity that any young speaker has had to lay the general foundation which we have been discussing heretofore, but it is also inherent in the nature of speaking, and many speakers of long experience also confess difficulty in selecting a suitable subject. The canons of a good subject are often violated by speakers, both young and old. Almost every teacher of speaking has heard entrants and even winners of intercollegiate oratorical contests, whose subjects were as remote as Neptune from the interest of their audience. And what college student is there who has not listened to assembly or chapel speakers who seemingly tried to cut the Gordian knot by never choosing a subject at all, but, like an idle grasshopper, hopped from compliment to anecdote and anecdote to paternal advice and so on *ad infinitum* and *ad nauseam!* In contrast, consider the lasting and almost miraculous appeal of such subjects as DeWitt Talmage's "Big Blunders," William Jennings Bryan's "Prince of Peace," and Russell Conwell's "Acres of Diamonds,"[1] of which the latter alone was given six thousand times to all kinds of audiences and under all imaginable conditions.[2]

What makes a subject fitting and how may one be guided in its selection? Four suggestions may be offered.

From *The Spoken Word* by William Norwood Brigance, 1932. Copyright 1927 by F. S. Crofts and Co. Reprinted by permission of Appleton-Century-Crofts.

The author, one of the founders of the Speech Association of America, was Professor of Speech at Wabash College.

[1] These speeches are worth a careful study. Talmage's may be found in James N. O'Neill's *Classified Models of Speech Composition* (New York: The Century Co., 1921), p. 828; Bryan's in *Speeches of William Jennings Bryan* (New York: Funk Company, 1909), II, 261; and Conwell's in Agnes Rush Burr's *Life of Russell H. Conwell* (New York: Winston Publishing Company, 1926), p. 405.

[2] Burr, *Life of Conwell*, p. 307.

## The Subject Should Be Adapted to the Occasion

In fact it is often possible, upon such occasions as Memorial Day, Fourth of July, Labor Day, Armistice Day, Thanksgiving, Christmas and Easter, to have the subject grow out of the occasion. On any occasion when this is possible it is an ideal way of securing interest in the subject. Lincoln's "Gettysburg Address" dealt purely with the occasion of dedicating a part of that battlefield as a national cemetery. Grady, when invited to address a banquet of the New England Society of New York City, seized upon the significant fact that this was the first occasion wherein a Southerner had been asked to speak there. Even more adroitly did George William Curtis, in a commencement address at Union College in 1877, draw his subject from the occasion:

> The theme of today seems to me to be prescribed by the occasion. It is the festival of the departure of a body of educated young men into the world. This company of picked recruits marches out with beating drums and flying colors to join the army. We who feel that our fate is gracious which allowed a liberal training, are here to welcome and to advise. On your behalf, Mr. President and gentlemen, with your authority, and with all my heart, I shall say a word to them and to you of *the public duty of educated men in America.*[3]

There are occasions, of course, which do not allow such adaptation, yet every occasion is worth careful consideration so that, even if it affords no suggestion for a subject, at least the speaker will not be led to choosing a subject positively out of harmony with it.

## The Subject Should Be Adapted to the Audience

Above all things, a speech involves a speaker-to-audience contact and if a speaker is to acquire that contact, he must adapt his subject to his audience. He must inquire of himself as to their religious training, their educational opportunities, their occupation and their special local or geographical interests and prejudices. There are, of course, some subjects, like the famous lectures referred to above of Talmage, Bryan, and Conwell, that are attuned to the sensibilities of all audiences, that

[3] *Orations and Addresses of George William Curtis* (New York: Harper & Brothers), I, 264.

touch the interests of the many as well as of the selective few, that reach to the level of the highest professional man yet descend to the life of the toiler, that enrich the faith of the aged yet fire the heart of the young— but these subjects are not good subjects in spite of a lack of adaptation but because of a peculiar, subtle adaptation to all audiences.

In adapting the subject to an audience it will aid the young speaker to remember that there are, broadly speaking, two kinds of audiences— *select audiences* and *general audiences*. The *select audience* is one possessing certain special interests or purposes—as one composed of members of labor unions, farmers, students, bankers, lawyers, ministers, teachers, physicians, juries, or legislatures. The strong special interests of a select audience should make it relatively easy to adapt a subject to their interests and discuss themes vital to their welfare, yet it is not unusual to find the special interests of a select audience ignored by a speaker in choosing a subject. I recall a student who, being hard pressed for a subject, chose to discuss the work of the Methodist Church in France before a classroom audience in which there was but one Methodist besides himself! But, being a student, he could be more easily forgiven than a far more experienced speaker whom I once heard speak to a college audience as if they were dear little kindergarten cherubs! Wendell Phillips paid a compliment of high order to the Irish orator, Daniel O'Connell, when he said of him: "O'Connell was . . . before the courts, logic; at the bar of the senate, unanswerable and dignified; on the platform, grace, wit, pathos; before the masses, a whole man."[4] One attribute of Roosevelt's great power as a speaker was that he knew the interests and spoke the language of many groups—of ranchers, of woodsmen, of soldiers, of farmers, of historians, of naturalists, of the East Side slums in New York, and of the city's most socially élite. To any of these groups he could adapt himself and his subject.

The second kind of audience, the *general audience*, is, as the name implies, one composed of all ages, sexes, and occupations. If it offers to the speaker a wider scope in the choice of a subject, it also offers interests that are less strong and compels a speaker to use more skill in orienting his speech to include their diverse interests.

In adapting the subject to any audience, a speaker will also do well to consider their particular *mood*. Is it an after-dinner audience seeking

---

[4] "Eulogy of Daniel O'Connell": O'Neill, *Models of Speech Composition*, p. 464.

intellectual refreshment following a heavy meal or is it a more serious minded audience, scattered with old soldiers, gathered for the purpose of remembering stirring events and sacrifices of the past? Is it a student body gathered for a few minutes between classes or is it this same student body gathered, in caps and gowns, at their own commencement exercises? Things highly appropriate for an audience in one mood would be utterly unfit for that same audience in another mood.

Finally, a speaker must consider the *timeliness* of his subject for the audience. Some subjects are possessed of *passing* timeliness and others of *inherent,* perpetual timeliness. Let us note a few subjects of passing timeliness that have arisen since the late war. A great political scandal arises out of leasing the oil reserves at Teapot Dome and it becomes, for a while, a subject of timely discussion for almost any general audience. A flood of crime sweeps the nation and a speaker who intelligently discusses the subject, finds interested hearers everywhere. Evolution, as a religious issue, is reopened at the Scopes trial, and an authority upon evolution who might have spoken to empty seats a year before, has overflowing crowds eager to hear him. These are subjects of intense interest for a time, yet they are subjects of passing timeliness, for after they have been widely discussed in the press and on the platform and public sentiment has crystallized upon them, there will doubtless come a reaction against them, and the public will turn away to other and newer themes. Any subject, however, will be timely to which a speaker can impart *interest and freshness*. There were few subjects so stale to the general audience right after the war was over and American soldiers had returned from Europe, as the war itself. People were tired of war talk and war taxes. Yet a speaker who chose as his theme, "Who started the war?" and argued that it was not Germany but Russia and France, got attention because he had given an interest and freshness to his subject.

I have said that a subject might possess two kinds of timeliness,— passing timeliness, which has just been discussed, and inherent, perpetual timeliness. In general, it may be said that any subject that comes within the deep seated *wants or needs of an audience, that is, any subject that to them is vital* possesses an inherent timeliness. Such general subjects as "success," "education," and "religion," possess this inherent timeliness. Russell H. Conwell's famous lecture, "Acres of Diamonds," dealt with "success," and Bryan's "Prince of Peace," with religion. Albert Edward Wiggam has been lecturing for years upon "heredity" because he has shown that it deals with the vital question of life itself. The Republican campaign managers in 1924 had their speakers hammer upon "economy," a theme vital to men and women and to the young and old, and scored a great political victory.

Very often a college student in seeking a subject is unaware of what possible subjects really are timely or vital. Such a student may find excellent suggestions in looking through the articles in recent issues of non-fiction and semi-fiction magazines. Editors of such magazines are keenly alive to questions of vital public interest and if a student finds different phases of some general field being discussed by different magazines, or repeatedly discussed by the same magazine, he is fairly sure of finding somewhere within that field a good timely subject. Again, college students will find a vital field often overlooked in campus topics. Some of the most effective classroom speeches I have ever heard have been upon such themes as "Evils of Fraternity Rushings," "Compulsory Chapel Attendance," "College Politics," and "Athletic Excesses." A few years ago at the Northern Oratorical League annual contest (held among the larger universities of the middle west) several of the speakers were very evenly matched, but the prize went to a young woman who spoke on the chaotic and exhausting life of a modern university.[5] I have always felt that she won, and richly deserved to win, because of the exquisite adaptation of her theme to the audience, an audience composed entirely of students and faculty members of a large university.

## The Speaker Should Be Capable of Handling the Subject

The inability of a speaker to handle a subject may arise out of several difficulties. Let us consider two of the more prominent ones.

1. *The time limit.* There is a time limit to every speech, albeit very often exceeded. Sometimes it is set by the exigencies of the occasion, as with after-dinner speeches. Too often, as with campaign speeches, it is set by the limits of a speaker's endurance—but always it should be set by the limits of the hearers' attention. "How long shall I speak?" asked a visiting minister of the regular pastor. "As long as you like," was the reply, "but rumor has it that no souls are saved after the first twenty minutes." Now there are some subjects which simply cannot be discussed in limits of time at a speaker's disposal and, for that reason, should not be chosen. I recall a student who made a failure of a five-minute classroom speech

[5] Miss Frances Killefer, University of Illinois.

because, in that short limit of time, he tried to present all the arguments for our joining the League of Nations; and another speaker at a football banquet who tried to give a full history of the origin and development of football. Both speeches were failures for the same reason—the subject and the time limit could not be made to fit. It was like trying to jam a rope through the eye of a needle.

2. *The speaker's qualifications* for handling the subject should also be considered. He chooses, let us say, to speak upon capital punishment. What are his qualifications to speak upon this subject? Probably none. For a classroom speech, or even an intercollegiate oration, his case is not hopeless if he is willing to put some strenuous hours of research and labor and make himself an authority, in a small way, upon the question. If he is not willing to do that, or if he has not within reach sufficient information on the question, he had best drop it at once. There are questions, like "States Rights" or "The Influence of Jefferson (or any other person) upon our Present Generation," which are beyond the depth of the average student, unless he should be exceptionally well informed upon American history. *Whenever possible it is far better for a student to reach back into his own experience for some theme that has touched his past life.* He may live in a mining community, and although having no personal knowledge of the causes of the latest miners' strike, yet if he will inform himself upon it, the very fact that he has resided among the strikers will command an interest and attention in his subject. A student may go to the library and learn twice as much about conditions in Europe as another who has just taken a summer trip abroad, but it is the latter who will command more interest in his topic.

It is a widely accepted fact that great periods of oratory have arisen when men have become aroused over some great injustice, or some common cause that demands leaders. Without going back into the history of other nations, we may look into our own history and see that this is true. The revolutionary era brought forth Otis, the Adamses, and Henry. The issue of constitutional interpretation brought forth Clay, Calhoun, Hayne, and Webster. The slave issue brought forth Beecher, Lincoln, Sumner, Curtis, and Phillips on the one side and Davis, Yancy, Breckinridge, Wigfall, and Lamar on the other. The underlying principle applies to any one who possesses a supreme conviction upon a subject and students are no exception. Among the very best of speeches that I recall made by college students was one by a young man preparing for law who became deeply concerned over the rise of crime in America;

another by a student who had worked among migratory workers of the west and became incensed over treatment accorded them by officials of the law; and still a third by a student whose mother and father were divorced and who chose for his theme, the evils of divorce.

## The Speaker Should Choose a Single, Definite Subject

Of all factors in selecting a subject, none is more important than this one. After a speaker has chosen the general field of his speech, it is imperative that he narrow it down to some one of its multifold phases. If the general subject be "Peace," do not stop there but bring it down to some one phase of peace—"The Influence of Newspapers on Peace," "War Dangers of Our Present Method of Teaching History," or "The Balkans as a War Explosive." These are definite phases of the peace question and by narrowing himself to one of them the speaker will save himself from that vague and meaningless treatment so often found in discussing themes of this sort. In this narrowing of the subject, there also lies the great secret of cutting a speech to any reasonably desired length. If a speech is too long for the time at a speaker's disposal, he can condense it only to a certain point. Beyond that point it will be impaired by the inevitable abstractness that attends too great a condensation. So instead of trying to pack the speech to the point of abstractness, it is far better to throw away one or more whole sections of it, then take the remaining sections and reorganize them into a whole speech.

Let us take an illustration. I recall a student who brought to class a plan for a speech upon "Post War Conditions in Europe." The outline was several pages in length, far too long to reproduce here, but the following word-sketch outline will show the extent of the field that the subject covered:

I. Conditions in England
   A. Industrial
   B. Financial
   C. Social
   D. Political
II. Conditions in Germany
   A. Industrial
   B. Financial
   C. Social
   D. Political
   E. Military

III. Conditions in Austria
    A. Industrial
    B. Financial
    C. Social
    D. Political
    E. Military
    F. Educational
    G. Religious
    H. Agricultural
IV. Conditions in France
    A. Industrial
    B. Financial
    C. Social
    D. Political
    E. Educational
    F. Agricultural
    G. Military

This for an eight minute speech! A little inquiry brought to light the real reason for so ambitious and extensive a subject. The student really knew nothing about any phase of conditions in any country in Europe except in the most general and hazy manner, and he hoped, by so grand a lay-out, to fill up the time limit! When I narrowed his theme down to "Military Conditions in France,"—exactly one-twenty-fourth of his original theme—he was forced to get out and really learn something about it. In failing to narrow his subject down to one, single, definite phase this student had failed to consider that no audience would care to hear a speaker discuss conditions in Europe who knew no more about those conditions than any one of them, but that they would listen with interest to the speaker who could tell them explicitly about things which they did not know.

When Abraham Lincoln chose to discuss the slavery question at Cooper Institute Hall in 1860, he might have rambled all over the whole question and talked of the Missouri Compromise, the Compromise of 1850 with its controversial fugitive slave law, the Kansas-Nebraska bill and the Dred Scott decision—and by covering so wide a scope, have told his audience nothing not already known to them. Had he done so he probably would barely have been known in history. Instead, he chose to confine himself to the exceedingly narrow and definite question of whether the fathers who framed the constitution thought that the federal government had the power to control slavery in territories—and by so narrowing his subject he utterly exhausted it—and made it a great stepping stone to the presidency.

## FINDING THE ISSUES

### CHARLES S. MUDD
### MALCOLM O. SILLARS

Ministers and salesmen, governors and fraternity presidents, lawyers and housewives all have ideas they want others to accept. You are barraged with efforts to persuade you: appeals and arguments of enormous variety. You try to persuade others, both individuals and groups: to accept the truth of something you believe; to value something you like; to do something you want done.

Suppose you and your friend Bob would like to take the same elective course so you can study together. You favor Anthropology. You might say:

> "A half dozen of the fellows in the fraternity are going to take Larssill's course in Anthropology next semester. Hal says Larssill's an easy grader; he doesn't even check on whether you do the reading. Last semester, he didn't call the roll half the time."

But Bob is a good student. He is not looking for a snap course; he wants one which will be worthwhile and interesting. He isn't worried about whether the professor is an easy grader. He likes to do the reading for the courses he takes. Although he recognizes that there are valuable insights to be gained from a study of anthropology, he has heard reports that the instructor is dull and fears that the course may be a bore. Therefore, while the arguments you have used seem plausible to you, they probably won't be convincing to Bob; they fail to deal with the specific questions that bother him.

## Issues Defined

Before you can expect to persuade Bob, you will need to find arguments that deal with the grounds upon which he disagrees with your

From *Speech: Content and Communication* by Charles S. Mudd and Malcolm O. Sillars, published by Chandler Publishing Company, San Francisco. Copyright © 1962 by Chandler Publishing Company. Reprinted by permission.

The authors are Professors of Speech at San Fernando Valley State College.

proposal. This means that in persuasion you must find the points at which your position comes into conflict with his. These points of disagreement are called "issues."

In the question of whether Bob should take the course in Anthropology, his position is somewhat like the following:

> "I hear that Larssill is a very dull lecturer. He just stands up in front of the room and reads from those yellow pages he hasn't revised in twenty years; he doesn't even look at the class. I don't think it would be an interesting course."

The position you should take if you are to argue effectively must be somewhat along these lines:

> "Anthropology is an interesting subject. The course has field trips to Indian burial grounds and to museums. You're already interested in sociology, and Larssill's course covers the cultural background of this very area."

The *issue* Bob raises lies in the question: "Is Anthropology an interesting course?" If you argue on any grounds other than this issue that concerns Bob, your efforts are more than likely to fail.

Notice that both you and Bob express your attitudes about the Anthropology course in the form of *argument*. Both of you give *reasons* for the attitude. Moreover, when you take the position you should, the arguments directly oppose one another. In this relation you find the issue, that is, *the question over which the opposing arguments clash.*

## Analysis—the Method for Finding Issues

The process of finding issues is called analysis. Through analysis, a speaker discovers the point of controversy which he must resolve if a speech is to be effectively persuasive.

### Analyzing Propositions of Policy

When he sets out to prove that Communist China should be admitted to the United Nations, a speaker may find it necessary to prove that Nationalist China is not a symbol of democracy in Asia. By what process does he discover that he must prove the latter proposition? It seems remote from the speaker's basic purpose, but it can be an essential point in his proof. The speaker knows that his audience opposes the admission of Communist China to the United Nations on the following grounds:

> The nations of southeast Asia consider Nationalist China to be a symbol of democracy. Admitting Communist China to the United Nations would humiliate Nationalist China, discredit the symbol of democracy, and thereby weaken the confidence of southeast Asians in democracy.

To change the attitude of his listeners, the speaker must discover and remove the basic area of disagreement between his position and theirs. In the present instance, there are three points at which an issue may arise:

1. Is Nationalist China a symbol of democracy for southeast Asians?
2. Will the admission of Communist China to the United Nations discredit that symbol?
3. Will discrediting the symbol weaken democracy in Asia?

Examining these areas of potential difference, the speaker sees that he must agree with the audience that admission of Communist China to the United Nations will cause great discredit through loss of face for Nationalist China (a grave matter among eastern nations). He recognizes further that he must agree with the audience on the importance of symbols. Consequently, neither of these two questions is the issue. On the remaining point, however, speaker and audience do not agree. The *issue* lies in the question of whether Nationalist China *is* or *is not* a symbol of democracy among the nations of southeast Asia.

*Finding the issues in propositions of policy.* An example will most easily explain the method of analyzing a proposition of policy. College fraternities have been a source of controversy on American college campuses for a very long time. From time to time, the proposal to abolish fraternities has been seriously advanced. When such a proposal is made, its discussion comprises both vigorous attack and ardent defense. If you become involved in the controversy, you will need to defend your point of view. No matter which of the opposing positions you take, here is how you can make an analysis of the proposition, "College fraternities should be abolished."

First draw a line down the middle of a sheet of paper. On the left side of the sheet list all the arguments you can find which support the proposal. On the right side, list the arguments that oppose the proposition. Match the opposing arguments by pairing them against each other:

| College Fraternities Should Be Abolished | College Fraternities Should Not Be Abolished |
|---|---|
| Standards for selecting members are poor. They are based on money, surface personality, and narrow identity of interests. | Standards for selecting members are high. Members are selected for their qualities of social adaptability, their character, scholarship, and leadership potential. |

An identical statement sometimes supports opposing views:

| College Fraternities Should Be Abolished | College Fraternities Should Not Be Abolished |
|---|---|
| Men who associate together as fraternity brothers are expected to give and receive mutual support. | Men who associate together as fraternity brothers are expected to give and receive mutual support. |

If nothing more is to be said on this point, there is no issue, and the matter should be waived—that is, left out of the discussion. There is no use taking a speaker's or an audience's time to labor a point that is not at issue. But don't forget statements of this kind; even waived matter can be useful in a speech. Save the note. (Moreover, as you may be eager to point out, the statements do clash when pertinent sentences are added, according to viewpoint: "This expectation leads to beautiful friendships" or "This expectation builds cliques and factions.")

An argument in one column or the other may appear to admit of no opposition:

| College Fraternities Should Be Abolished | College Fraternities Should Not Be Abolished |
|---|---|
| No apparent argument. | Members get jobs and make friends in strange towns through fraternity associations. |

It is unwise to assume that such unopposed arguments constitute waived matter. The offering of the argument suggests that an issue exists. To make the analysis complete, find an argument to answer the one that seems unopposed. In your reading or thinking about the controversy, you will usually find a suitable argument to clarify the issue. For example:

| College Fraternities Should Be Abolished | College Fraternities Should Not Be Abolished |
|---|---|
| This claim is a statement that fraternity members cannot verify. *Or* Fraternity membership is a false basis for selecting employees and friends. | Members get jobs and make friends in strange towns through fraternity associations. |

When you have eliminated waived matter and found opposing points of view on all the arguments, your analysis sheets will look somewhat like this:

| College Fraternities Should Be Abolished | College Fraternities Should Not Be Abolished |
|---|---|
| Fraternities discriminate against minority groups. Even where regulations no longer exist in constitutions, discrimination is practiced by "gentlemen's agreements." | Very few fraternities still have religious and racial restrictions in their constitutions. |
| Discrimination has no place on a college campus. | A man has a right to choose his friends. |
| ~~Men who associate together as fraternity brothers are expected to give and receive mutual support.~~ | ~~Men who associate together as fraternity brothers are expected to give and receive mutual support.~~ |
| The standards of selection are poor. They are based on money, surface personality, and sameness. | Fraternity members are selected for their personality, character, scholarship, and leadership. |
| Fraternity activities interfere with the study programs of the members. | Fraternities provide tutoring, require study hours, and in general watch the grades of their members. |

| College Fraternities Should Be Abolished | College Fraternities Should Not Be Abolished |
| --- | --- |
| Fraternities try to control the college activities for their own purposes. The member's first loyalty is to the fraternity, not the college. | Fraternity members are the strongest supporters of college activities. If they control, it is because they are more active than other students. |
| This is minor compared to all the damages they do the college by the actions noted above. | Fraternities do service projects for the college and the community. |
| This claim is a statement that fraternity members can not verify.<br>*Or*<br>Fraternity membership is a false basis for selecting employees and friends. | Members get jobs and make friends in strange towns through fraternity associations. |

*Phrasing the issues.* After the analysis sheet is prepared, the points at which the two opposing sides clash are more easily seen. The next step is to phrase as a question the clash implied in each of the sets of opposing arguments. This is done in the same manner that the clash was phrased in the example of the anthropology class on page 36. The questions that result are the issues. For example:

| | |
| --- | --- |
| Fraternity activities interfere with the study programs of the members. | Fraternities provide tutoring, require study hours, and in general watch the grades of their members. |

The issue that separates the opposing positions is the question: "Are fraternity activities detrimental to scholastic achievement?"

Examine each of the issues to see that all are *clearly stated.* The following issue is badly drawn:

*Issue:* "How serious is the discrimination against minority groups?"

As it is phrased, the question presents no issue between clearly opposed points of view. Moreover, it assumes that there is discrimination when the very existence of discrimination is itself an issue that must be resolved.

*Reducing the number of issues.* Not all of the issues that are discovered by your analysis of the proposition will need to be argued. The issues in any proposition should be reduced to the smallest number which will accurately identify the important elements of the clash.

Wherever possible, combine issues that seem to overlap. The following issues involve only one point of conflict:

> *Issue:* Do fraternities develop a social life restricted to their own members?
> *Issue:* Do fraternities isolate their members from the normal life of the campus?

Eliminate issues which seem trivial. The following clash is not central to the disagreement:

| | |
|---|---|
| Fraternities promote sentimentality. | No, they don't, but why waste time arguing about that? |

Eliminate issues which seem to be irrelevant:

| | |
|---|---|
| Local chapters couldn't exist without help from the national fraternity. | Many local chapters and all unaffiliated fraternities operate without financial help from a national office. |

The issue exists: "Are college fraternities financially independent?" But it has no relevance to the proposition at hand.

When the job of analyzing the proposition is done, you will have a list of issues like the following:

> *Issue 1.* Do fraternities discriminate against people because of race, color or creed? If it is admitted that discrimination is practiced, substitute the *issue:* Is discrimination desirable on a college campus?

*Issue* 2. (Apart from questions of race, color, or creed) do fraternities select members for the right reasons?

*Issue* 3. Are fraternity activities detrimental to scholastic achievement?

*Issue* 4. Is a fraternity member's first loyalty to this organization or to the college?

*Issue* 5. Are fraternity service projects significant compared with other strengths and weaknesses?

*Issue* 6. Does membership in a fraternity help a student after he leaves college? If it is admitted that membership is helpful, substitute the *issue*: Is fraternity membership a satisfactory basis for selecting employees and friends?

*Classifying the issues (general issues).* To persuade an audience to accept a proposition of policy, the speaker's proposal must meet the test of three general questions. The audience must be able to answer yes to these three questions before the proposition is proved.

1. Is the problem that underlies the proposition severe enough to warrant considering a change from our present course of action?
2. Is the proposed policy a more desirable means of meeting the problem than the policy now in operation?
3. Is the proposed policy workable?

These three questions are called the general issues of propositions of policy. They are general in that they are found in any policy clash. They embrace the specific issues, such as those listed above for the proposition that college fraternities should be abolished—the issues in the form that you hear argued in the dormitory, in the drugstore, on television programs.

The general issues are useful in two ways:

1. They help you to identify and interpret the specific issues you have discovered in your analysis.
2. They offer a means of grouping the specific issues by putting each one into a recognizable, workable class.

In an argument over the abolition of capital punishment, for example, some would contend that to abolish capital punishment would be desirable because innocent men are sometimes put to death (that is, the problem is severe). Others would say that the responsibility of determining another man's life or death is too heavy a burden for anyone to bear (again, the problem is severe). On the other side, you hear it argued that to abolish capital punishment would lead to an increase in crime (that is, the proposed policy is less desirable than the present one).

All these arguments relate to the first and second general issues. That is, each of the three arguments cited is concerned either with the severity of the problem or with the desirable or undesirable character of the proposal. Should you, then, when you take a position in the matter, press the issues of whether the proposed solution is workable? Not unless there are different views on workability: you are concerned with resolving the *issues that divide opinion*.

When you and an audience are agreed that it would be easy to abolish capital punishment simply by changing the law (the third general question), disagreement is limited to determining whether American justice is improperly maintained today (the first general question), and whether capital punishment is the most desirable means to maintain justice (the second general question). Is capital punishment visited on the innocent? Is the responsibility for taking life too serious for anyone to assume? Is the abolition of capital punishment the only way to maintain justice? Can't we change other laws? Can't we reform the judicial procedure? These and a number of other questions come into your listeners' minds. They become the basis of the specific issues, the ones which must be resolved to prove your case.

### Analyzing Propositions of Value and Fact

If you look back at the issues we have used as examples, you will recognize in them a common characteristic: in every instance, the question that states the issue must be answered with a proposition of value or fact. Then in order to resolve the issue, a speaker must be able to prove the proposition which states his position on the issue. Issues, in other words, are resolved and policy decisions are made on the basis of judgments of value and fact.

Proving a proposition of fact or value requires giving arguments to support it, arguments that will eliminate grounds the audience may have for rejecting it. Any issues that stand between speaker and audience must be resolved. The fact that there are issues in propositions of fact and value implies that they must also be analyzed before they can be proved. The same method of analysis is applied to both of these kinds of propositions.

There are two items in the statement of every proposition of value or fact. The first is the subject term, the idea, thing, or event to which reference is made. The second is the predicate term, the word or phrase or clause which says something about the subject term.

SUBJECT TERM                      PREDICATE TERM

*Fact*: The Soviet Union *is* a composite state.
*Value*: The Soviet Union *is* warlike.

The first step in finding the issues in propositions of fact and value is to formulate a successful definition of the predicate term. This definition will serve as a set of criteria for evaluating the subject term. Analyze, for example, the proposition: "The Soviet Union is warlike." Here, "the Soviet Union" is the subject term. The predicate term is the word "warlike." A warlike nation might be defined as one which:

(1) takes direct aggressive actions against others,
(2) incites others to take aggressive actions against third parties, and
(3) operates presently in preparation for the time when it will commit one or both of the first two acts.

If these criteria satisfy a speaker as a definition of a warlike power, and if he is convinced that they will be acceptable to his listeners, the next step is to apply them to the actions of the Soviet Union.

The final step in the analysis is to make a judgment. If the speaker can convince his audience that the majority of Soviet actions fit the definition, he will prove that the proposition is true.

## The Five Loci of Potential Issues

When there is disagreement on any proposition, each issue will arise at one or another of five points. These are the *loci* of the issues, the points where they are located. In analyzing a proposition he intends to prove, a speaker may expect to find in these five regions of potential issues the conflicting attitudes that identify a division of opinion. The first region applies only to propositions of policy. The last four are the sources of issues that arise from propositions of value and fact.

### Issues Located in the First General Question

The first point at which conflict may be found is in the first general issue:

Is the problem that underlies the proposition severe enough to warrant considering a change from our present course of action?

This may be the locus of an issue in a policy proposition. No proposal to adopt a *new* policy is likely to succeed unless there is agreement on the need for a change from *present* policy. Debaters generalize this issue in the question, "Does the need justify the plan?" It may be agreed, for instance, that adequate health facilities are lacking for many people in the United States; but in analyzing the proposal to establish a Federal Health Insurance program, we must ask whether the condition is serious enough to justify a change.

### Issues Located in the Criteria

There may be disagreement over the validity of the criteria. That is, an issue may arise over whether the predicate term of the proposition (of fact or value) has been defined. There are many speakers whose use of logic and evidence is good, but whose conclusions are based on standards that appear to be false. There is grave danger that issues will arise over definition unless such abstract terms as "good," "truth," "peace," and "prosperity" are defined with great care. In the 1956 political campaign, Republicans defined "peace" as the absence of Americans from active combat. The Democrats tried to apply the term to the broader base of general world conditions. No one disagreed that Americans were not fighting; they disagreed on whether this fact was a basis for saying that there was peace.

Apart from the matter of acceptable definition of terms, an issue can arise over criteria when there is a disagreement over whether a given criterion is acceptable no matter how well it may be defined. Expenditures for national defense are frequently attacked on the grounds that they consume far too great a proportion of the federal government's income. Often enough, these attacks are answered by saying, "It isn't a matter of cost." In other words, the whole idea of expense is rejected as a criterion for measuring the worth of a project.

### Issues Located in the Relative Importance of the Criteria

Even when there is general agreement on the criteria that should be used in making a judgment, and even when the criteria are acceptably defined, an issue may arise over the relative importance (a proposition of value) the criteria should have in influencing a judgment. Suppose you were to evaluate a baseball player's ability using as criteria (a) hitting, (b) fielding, (c) running bases, (d) team spirit. You might, when comparing two men, find that one was a better hitter and base runner but the other was a better fielder and had more spirit. The problem of deciding which is the better ball player can be solved only by deciding the issue of which of these characteristics (criteria) is most important.

## Issues Located in the Application of the Criteria to Evidence

A fourth area of potential issue is in the application of the criteria to evidence. Assuming that there was complete agreement at all three of the preceding points, there might very well be an issue at the point where the actual judgment of fact or value is made. The United Nations is much concerned of late with aggression. Any delegate to the United Nations will acknowledge that the elimination of aggression is a universally accepted criterion which guides that body in many of its deliberations. No issue there. You might even get markedly similar definitions of the term "aggression" from members of widely disparate political points of view. But ask several of these same members whether the Russians committed aggression in Budapest in October of 1956. There's an issue! Were the Russian soldiers aggressors, or were they neighbors come to rescue?

## Issues Located in the Evidence

At the base of all controversy is the possibility of disagreement over evidence (a proposition of fact). Such issues arise with great frequency between the Soviet bloc and the Western powers in the conflict known as the cold war. Were American planes flying over Soviet territory, or were they not? Were these planes armed, or were they not? Were they fired on, or were they not? Neither faction will agree that the other side's evidence is true.

Analyzing propositions in terms of the five points at which conflicts of opinion will arise helps you to formulate the issues. This formulation helps you to identify and deal with the doubts and contrary opinions of the audience that constitute the barriers to persuasion. These barriers can be pierced—persuasion can take place—when the doubts are resolved and the opinions changed.

It is one thing to talk about persuading but it is another thing to do the job. How many speakers can resolve the doubts and meet the arguments of the audiences they face? The answer to this question is at the core of what makes public speaking a fascinating study.

## How Issues Are Used

### To Indicate the Lines of Argument

Analyzing the proposition lays out the groundwork for a speech. Finding the issues points the direction the line of argument must follow. For if you are to resolve the doubt and opposition in an audience, the central arguments in your speech, those which are best developed and best supported, should be the arguments which deal with the issues. A candidate for Student Council Treasurer may be an honest, brilliant, and trusted member of the college community. But if his fellow students doubt his ability to keep a good set of records, that doubt is the issue his supporters need to attack.

This emphasis on issues raises a question: Does a speaker always talk about issues? Does he ever use generally accepted ideas? In one sense you do always talk about issues, but in doing so you will use noncontroversial ideas in a very helpful way:

When you analyze a proposition, you discover points of agreement as well as areas of dispute and doubt. These points of agreement are the *waived matter* described on page 38. They serve as a common ground between you and your audience; they are the base upon which you support your position on the matters at issue.

During the campaign for Student Council Treasurer, the candidate's fellow students recognize him as a trusted person, an honest person, and a person with good ideas about student government. These acknowledgments are waived matter. His supporters can use them as arguments to help minimize the fact that he has not had the training in accounting which many of the students believe a treasurer needs. Waived matter should not be used to hide or avoid an issue. The issue is there: "Does the Student Council Treasurer need to be trained in accounting?" And the issue must be resolved. But by giving a more complete picture of the contest, arguments built on waived matter help to establish the probability that as treasurer a man might do a better job than his opponent *even though the opponent is an accounting major*. In this sense, even noncontroversial waived matter should be emphasized *in relation to the issues*.

### To Group the Arguments

The practice of grouping the specific issues in a proposition of policy under the general questions is used successfully by many speakers. It is a good practice because it accomplishes several things:

1. It avoids giving the audience the impression that you have a loose collection of scattered arguments.
2. It creates the idea that you have blocks of arguments and evidence, first in one area and then in another.
3. It makes transitions easier because similar issues are annexed to one another.
4. It gives your speaking a sense of thoroughness and adds credibility to your proposition.

## Summary

In order to prove a proposition, a speaker must analyze it to find the points at which his audience disagrees with his proposal. These points of conflict are called issues.

To find the issues in propositions of policy, the propositions are analyzed by drawing out of directly opposed arguments the essential elements of clash and phrasing them as clearly stated questions. The number of these questions is reduced by combining issues that overlap, by eliminating waived matter, and by eliminating issues which seem to be trivial or irrelevant. The issues that make up the resulting list are grouped according to the general issues that embrace them. The general issues are three questions which apply to all propositions of policy and which the audience must be able to answer affirmatively before a proposition can be accepted as proved.

To find the issues in propositions of fact or value, the propositions are analyzed by defining the predicate term in the proposition. This definition is used as a criterion for determining whether available evidence warrants the judgment that the predicate term makes about the subject term.

Issues will arise at one or more of five loci:

1. The question whether a problem is serious enough to warrant a change in policy.
2. The acceptability of the criteria used to evaluate judgments of value and fact.

3. The relative importance of the criteria.
4. The judgment that is made when the criteria are applied to the available evidence.
5. The accuracy of the evidence itself.

The issues a speaker finds when he analyzes a proposition are used to help him find the lines of argument he should use in proving his proposition, and as a means of grouping his arguments for greater strength in either attack or defense.

## THE MODES OF PERSUASION

### ARISTOTLE

Rhetoric may be defined as the faculty of observing in any given case the available means of persuasion. This is not a function of any other art. Every other art can instruct or persuade about its own particular subject-matter; for instance, medicine about what is healthy and unhealthy, geometry about the properties of magnitudes, arithmetic about numbers, and the same is true of the other arts and sciences. But rhetoric we look upon as the power of observing the means of persuasion on almost any subject presented to us; and that is why we say that, in its technical character, it is not concerned with any special or definite class of subjects.

Of the modes of persuasion some belong strictly to the art of rhetoric and some do not. By the latter I mean such things as are not supplied by the speaker but are there at the outset—witnesses, evidence given under torture, written contracts, and so on. By the former I mean such as we can ourselves construct by means of the principles of rhetoric. The one kind has merely to be used, the other has to be invented.

Of the modes of persuasion furnished by the spoken word there are three kinds. The first kind depends on the personal character of the speaker; the second on putting the audience into a certain frame of mind; the third on the proof, or apparent proof, provided by the words of the speech itself. Persuasion is achieved by the speaker's personal character when the speech is so spoken as to make us think him credible. We

From Aristotle, *Rhetoric and Poetics*, trans. W. Rhys Roberts and Ingram Bywater. (New York: The Modern Library, 1954.) Reprinted by permission of Oxford University Press, Inc.

believe good men more fully and more readily than others: this is true generally whatever the question is, and absolutely true where exact certainty is impossible and opinions are divided. This kind of persuasion, like the others, should be achieved by what the speaker says, not by what people think of his character before he begins to speak. It is not true, as some writers assume in their treatises on rhetoric, that the personal goodness revealed by the speaker contributes nothing to his power of persuasion; on the contrary, his character may almost be called the most effective means of persuasion he possesses. Secondly, persuasion may come through the hearers, when the speech stirs their emotions. Our judgements when we are pleased and friendly are not the same as when we are pained and hostile. It is towards producing these effects, as we maintain, that present-day writers on rhetoric direct the whole of their efforts. This subject shall be treated in detail when we come to speak of the emotions.[1] Thirdly, persuasion is effected through the speech itself when we have proved a truth or an apparent truth by means of the persuasive arguments suitable to the case in question.

There are, then, these three means of effecting persuasion. The man who is to be in command of them must, it is clear, be able (1) to reason logically, (2) to understand human character and goodness in their various forms, and (3) to understand the emotions—that is, to name them and describe them, to know their causes and the way in which they are excited.

[1] ii, cc. 2–11.

## TESTING THE ARGUMENTATIVE DEVELOPMENT

### LESTER THONSSEN
### A. CRAIG BAIRD

In passing judgment upon the logical aspect of a persuasive address, we ask the question: "Did the speaker enforce his point?" As we have previously indicated, proof may be of several kinds; but at this moment

From Lester Thonssen and A. Craig Baird, *Speech Criticism—The Development of Standards for Rhetorical Appraisal*. Copyright 1948 The Ronald Press Company.

Lester Thonssen is Professor of Speech at the City College of New York. A. Craig Baird is Professor Emeritus, University of Iowa.

we are primarily concerned with the establishment of that measure of assent which indicates a reasonable degree of truth. Fundamentally, the constituents of logical proof are *evidence* and *argument* or reasoning. Each conforms to general rules and admits of rigorous testing.

### Examining the Evidence

Evidence is the raw material used to establish proof. It may include the testimony of individuals, personal experiences, tables of statistics, illustrative examples, or any so-called "factual" items which induce in the mind of the hearer or reader a state of belief—a tendency to affirm the existence of the fact or proposition to which the evidence attaches and in support of which it is introduced. Thus, in his attempt to establish ground for conciliation with the Colonies, Burke introduced comparative data as to the export trade of England to the Colonies in 1704 and in 1772; and he remarked: "The trade with America alone is now within less than £500,000 of being equal to what this great commercial nation, England, carried on at the beginning of this century with the whole world." Previously, he had presented figures to reveal the accuracy of this claim. And then he turned to his conclusion: "This is the relative proportion of the importance of the colonies at these two periods; and all reasoning concerning our mode of treating them must have this proportion as its basis, or it is a reasoning weak, rotten, and sophistical."[1] Likewise, in his speech of May 27, 1941, declaring an unlimited national emergency, Franklin D. Roosevelt relied upon external data when he asserted that "All freedom—meaning freedom to live and not freedom to conquer and subjugate other peoples—depends on freedom of the seas."

> Since 1799, 142 years ago, when our infant Navy made the West Indies and the Caribbean and the Gulf of Mexico safe for American ships; since 1804 and 1805, when we made all peaceful commerce safe from the depredations of the Barbary pirates; since the War of 1812, which was fought for the preservation of sailors' rights; since 1867, when our sea power made it possible for the Mexicans to expel the French Army of Louis Napoleon, we have striven and fought in defense of freedom of the seas, freedom of the seas for our own shipping, for the commerce of our sister republics, for the right of all nations to use the highways of world trade, and for our own safety.

[1] Chauncey A. Goodrich. *Select British Eloquence*. New York, 1853, p. 270.

Here are typical displays of evidence, and upon the relevance and merit of these and allied materials will depend much of the argument's claims to integrity. The critic's chief function at this point is to test the speaker's evidence to determine whether it serves as an adequate and valid substructure of reasoning. Since the principal types of evidence used by the speaker, apart from the reference to his own authority, are statistics and testimony, we shall refer briefly to the criteria governing reliability in those divisions.

Edwin A. Burtt tells us that the problem of statistics, on the critical side, must be approached in the light of two cardinal principles.[2] The statistician must discover, and subsequently the critic must examine, "some quantitative unit in terms of which he can translate the phenomenon he is studying into a magnitude whose variations are mathematical." That is, the task involved deals with *counting*; finding out "*how much* of the phenomenon is present in the locality or under the conditions which determine [the] investigation." The second principle of statistical inquiry "is that the limits of the field within which the measurements hold should be carefully determined and clearly stated." Thus, if an investigator finds that a certain group of men gives ten per cent of its time to political interests, he should not point to general conclusions regarding the public as a whole, unless he has made the necessary checks on the limitations of his study. This brings up the whole problem of sampling, of finding out whether the instances chosen represent a systematically typical segment of the group as a whole. Burtt concludes "Wherever it is possible, each single case within the field to which the conclusion is to apply should be examined. . . ." Obviously, this is not always feasible or possible. In recent years, the public opinion polls have done much to refine statistical inquiries of this sort, so that we no longer regard accuracy of judgment in generalization as an immediate function of numbers. Through systematic sampling, remarkably accurate estimates of the public's thoughts and actions are made weekly, to the end that prediction of political developments is materially facilitated.

It follows, then, that the evaluation of statistical units requires investigation into the methods employed by the statisticians in collecting, classifying, and interpreting the data. The critic of speeches, however, makes two judgments: one, of the speaker's wisdom in choosing a certain body of figures; another, of the statistician's severity and accuracy in setting forth the facts from which the inferences are drawn.

[2] *Principles and Problems of Right Thinking.* New York, 1928, pp. 315–319.

The tests applied to the statistics will accordingly fall into the following categories: (1) Are the instances from which the inference is developed sufficiently numerous to be significant? (2) Are the units included in the investigation properly and carefully defined? (3) Is there comparability between the things compared? (4) Are the instances of such a character as to provide a systematically typical sample of the field as a whole? (5) Are the facts reported and classified accurately? (6) Do the statistics furnish an index to the information desired, i.e., is the relationship clear between the conclusion derived from the figures and the conclusion sought in the subject of the discourse? These tests, it should be noted, relate closely to the ones employed in checking arguments from specific cases, or generalizations. We shall refer to them later.

Much of the evidence used by speakers in support of their ideas is of a testimonial nature. In other words, outside authorities often furnish testimony which the speaker incorporates into his speech, hoping thereby to give credence to his cause and plausibility to his claims. Or he may rely mainly on his own reputation for expertness to enforce his propositions. What is the value of such evidence? How is its validity determined? Several tests serve to orient the critic in his appraisal.

Although consistency may be the "idol of small minds," it is, nevertheless, the guiding consideration for the critic when he appraises speech compositions. Addresses must present unified, internally consistent ideas. The parts must be consonant with one another, producing, in the end, a composite that is logically harmonious. This means simply that the evidence used by a speaker must not clash; what is affirmed at one point must not be denied at another. Nor does this allow any tampering with data to fit them to the demands of the speaker's thesis. It is assumed that if the evidence does not sustain an argument, the speaker will refrain from developing the contention. The appeal must clearly be to the truth of the case, not to the whim of the speaker.

The story is told of a confused witness who was testifying in his own behalf on a charge brought against him by a neighbor. The matter at issue involved damages for the destruction of a copper kettle. The distraught witness presented the following case: "In the first place, I didn't borrow the kettle. Anyway, it had a hole in it when I got it; and, finally, it was brand new when I brought it back." Since inconsistencies of statement, or of combined facts, even though not so palpably obvious as the one in the foregoing illustration, cast suspicions upon the integrity of argument, critics will turn to some, if not all, of the following tests of evidence:

(1) Is the testimony or evidence consistent with itself and with the known laws of logical argument? (2) Is the particular authority whose testimony is used to support a contention reliable? (3) Has the authority had an opportunity to examine and observe the data from which he speaks? (4) Does he entertain any prejudices which might influence his judgment on the matter at issue? (5) Is he generally recognized as able and competent in the given field? (6) Are the facts in the testimony causally related one to the other? (7) Is the source citation or the authority specific? That is, does it indicate exactly where the testimony comes from, and whether it is first- or second-hand? (8) Does other evidence corroborate what is introduced? (9) Is the evidence recent? (10) Does the evidence satisfy the listeners?

The last test, while very important, must be considered in a specific light. It does not suggest that the speaker should use evidence, even though inadequate and faulty, provided it satisfies the hearers' demands and prejudices. On the contrary, it reminds us that evidence, however good, must be so adapted to the hearers that they will remain sensibly aware of its essential merit. The speaker alone can provide for such adaptation; he must prepare the minds of the audience for the ready acceptance of the evidence used to support the arguments. A more complete discussion of this aspect of the process of conviction will be reserved for the next two chapters.

### Appraising the Argument

We turn now to the second constituent of logical proof, namely, the argument or reasoning. Assuming that the evidence is at hand, how shall it be woven into a complete pattern? What is the nature of the elements that bind the totality of material together? The process of reasoning or argument serves as the cohesive force; through the relationships it establishes, the mind is led from the recognition of discernible facts to a conclusion.

The principal forms of discourse used by the speaker in the logical development of his ideas are exposition and argument. The distinction between them is not absolute; indeed, the two are complementary in the sense that argument depends heavily upon expository detail. Since all argument, regardless of type, must make certain ideas clear before it can lead to the fixation of belief or attitude, it follows that expositional detail is prerequisite to argumentative development.

Definition and example play important roles in exposition. Both contain power of illustration, of enlarging understanding through sharpening of verbal focus. The critic's concern with their use is limited largely to the simple inquiry: Do these instruments make the idea *clearer?*

Briefly, then, the definitions will be tested in the light of these questions: (1) Do the remarks designed to elucidate points through definition emphasize the distinguishing characteristics of the subject? (2) Do they cover the items properly included in the subject? (3) Do they exclude everything not properly included in them? (4) Do they make clear the meaning of concepts without relying upon the terms themselves or derivatives of them? (5) Do they have instant intelligibility value?

The foregoing tests represent usable instruments for determining areas of meaning. They are not to be applied with such narrow tolerances as to defeat their broader purpose. Fundamentally, definition is a process, not a fixed mould. It undergoes changes as its relationship with the general field of inquiry becomes more complex. Through definition we place a term in a series or a spectrum of meaning, and reveal how, through progressive enlargement of its relations to the field, it becomes meaningful in the unbroken continuity.

This process character of definition makes certain of the special methods of determining meaning peculiarly useful: (1) through explanation of the operational plan (how a thing works); (2) through description of function (what it does); (3) through historical exposition (how it was developed); and (4) through comparison and contrast.

As for the examples, they should conform to the spirit of these questions: (1) Do they belong in the class or form of experience which they are intended to exemplify? In other words, examples must illustrate; failing that, they lose their logical right to a place in discourse. (2) Are they described in sufficient but not too much detail to make for full and easy understanding? (3) Do they fit sensibly into the context of the speech? (4) Are they sufficiently numerous, but not so numerous as to overwhelm the listeners? Both the speaker and the critic should remember that, as a homiletician once remarked, a single lamp is worth a thousand fireflies.

When our object is not only to clarify but also to proceed from premises to conclusions through the use of issues, we use argument as the foundation of our speaking. In such cases we are resorting to inference, a process that explores proof possibilities in cases. The methods by which we conduct this process include induction and deduction.

These forms of argument are present to some extent in all thinking. To arrive at a general principle through the examination of particulars (induction), certain assumptions of a deductive sort must be used as the basis of argument. Conversely, to establish an individual truth through the medium of a universal principle (deduction), recourse must be had to induction in order to establish the universal. Consequently, these forms of argument supplement each other.

## The Process of Deduction

It is generally recognized that reasoning from a general truth to a particular conclusion (deduction) occurs most typically through the syllogism. Composed of three propositions—major premise, minor premise, and conclusion—the syllogism is not only an effective form of argument, but also a practical device for the critic in testing arguments. The principal types of syllogism are the categorical, disjunctive, and hypothetical.

The categorical syllogism defines, classifies, and asserts without qualification. Its form is represented in this example.

> All rhetoricians rely upon the classics.
> Thomas Wilson is a rhetorician.
> Therefore, Thomas Wilson relies upon the classics.

Schematically, this syllogism, with its three propositions and three terms, looks as follows:

|  |  |
|---|---|
| Middle Term | Major Term |
| Major Premise: All rhetoricians | rely upon the classics |
| Minor Term | Middle Term |
| Minor Premise: Thomas Wilson | is a rhetorician |
| Minor Term | Major Term |
| Conclusion: Thomas Wilson | relies upon the classics. |

The validity of these syllogisms can be determined through certain tests or rules which specifically relate to the categorical pattern as set forth above: (1) The syllogism must contain a major premise, a minor premise, and a conclusion. (2) It must contain three terms: major, middle, and minor. The arrangement of these terms in the propositions conforms to the scheme previously outlined. (3) The middle term of the syllogism must be distributed—i.e., used in a universal sense, meaning *all* or *every*—in at least one of the premises. (4) To be distributed in the conclusion, the term must be distributed in one of the premises. (5) Two negative premises make impossible the drawing of a valid conclusion. (6) If one premise is negative, the conclusion must likewise be negative. (7) Negative conclusions cannot be drawn unless one premise is negative. (8) The facts alleged in the premises should be true.

In a disjunctive syllogism the major premise is a disjunctive proposition, listing alternative possibilities. Its form is as follows:

> Either overproduction or underconsumption was responsible for the postwar depression.
> Overproduction was not responsible.
> Therefore, underconsumption was responsible for the postwar depression.

When testing such an argument, we usually refer to these criteria: (1) The alternative possibilities mentioned in the major premise should be as exhaustive as the case will permit. (2) The enumerated possibilities should not overlap. (3) If the minor premise affirms one of the alternatives, the conclusion must deny the other. (4) If the minor premise denies one of the alternatives, the conclusion must affirm the other.

The last basic type of syllogism is the hypothetical, in which the principal assertion is conditioned. Complex in structure, the sentence setting forth the major premise contains an antecedent (the conditional clause) and a consequent (the main clause). This illustration brings out its structure and also suggests its relation to causal patterns of reasoning:

> If world peace is to be achieved, an international federation must be established.
> World peace must be achieved.
> Therefore, an international federation must be established.

In order to test such a syllogism, care must be taken to insure compliance with these rules: (1) If the minor premise affirms the antecedent, the conclusion must affirm the consequent. (2) If the minor premise denies the consequent, the conclusion must deny the antecedent. (3) A denial of the antecedent or an affirmation of the consequent does not make possible the realization of a reliable conclusion.

The foregoing tests, chiefly of deductive reasoning, serve both the speaker and the critic by providing guides to validity in argument. Since most of the arguments used in daily life rest upon basic assumptions, and since many of the arguments are expressed enthymematically—that is, syllogistically, but with one of the premises or the conclusion suppressed—it becomes necessary and profitable for the critic, especially, to recast such reasoning in complete syllogistic form and then apply the appropriate tests to the pattern.

By their very nature the syllogisms set up a formal, "absolute" standard of logical development. Irregularities in reasoning often result from rigid adherence to such categorical, all-or-none patterns. Therefore the critic will want to ascertain the *relative*, the *probable* status of major deductive claims by checking them against determinable criteria of causation, definition, factual verification, attendant circumstance, and related inductive techniques.

### The Process of Induction

This involves movement from particulars to a general conclusion. As a result of his observation of specific instances or concrete facts, the speaker tries to formulate a general conclusion or principle deriving from observed data. Chief among the types of inductive argument are those of causal relation, specific instance, authority, and analogy.

Arguments from causal relation establish links between particulars —by noting the impact or influence of one event upon another, or by tracing the cause of an observed event. In the first instance, the direction of the reasoning is from cause to effect; in the latter, from effect to cause.

Basically, the concept of causation presupposes an interaction of phenomena. A given event is part of an unbroken series—cause and effect operate within a system, with certain forces impinging more directly upon the event than others, but all occurring within a series of happenings.

The general rules for testing causal arguments may be summed up in these questions: (1) Is there a causal connection between the two events? (2) Is a particular cause adequate to produce an alleged effect? (3) Is the alleged cause adequate to produce the known result? (4) Are there any other causes operating in such a way as to preclude the likelihood of the known cause producing the alleged effect? (5) Have the alleged facts been verified?

Arguments from specific instance, or generalization, arrive at a general conclusion through the examination of particular cases. Their validity is tested in much the same way as was previously mentioned in the discussion of statistical evidence. In other words, we determine whether the number of instances is sufficiently large to warrant the generalization; whether there are any negative instances which invalidate the conclusion; whether the instances chosen are typical; whether the generalizations conform to the demands of the causal patterns implicit in their development; and whether the facts are true as set forth.

Argument from authority proposes to establish the speaker's case by linking an expert's testimony to the allegation contained in the generalization. The tests of its reliability would be the same as those for expert testimony, previously discussed.

In testing analogical reasoning, the comparison between objects or relationships, we inquire, first, whether the points of likeness outweigh the points of difference. Granting that the analogy is useful chiefly as a reinforcer or illustrator of argument, rather than as an exacting argument in its own right, we should scrutinize penetratingly the essential features of comparability between the two objects or relationships involved in the comparison. Furthermore, we determine whether the analogy is valid by checking the related arguments from generalization and causal relation upon which analogical reasoning draws. And, finally, we ascertain whether the facts as set forth in the analogy are true.

The orator's thinking is a cardinal feature of the speaking enterprise. One of the most challenging phases of the critic's function, therefore, is to determine accurately and fairly how free the speaker's reasoning is from error, both logical and psychological. It is patently impossible to prepare an exhaustive catalog of the many forms of faulty thinking. But the contents of this chapter, supplemented by other common sense observations, should enable the critic to classify, for purposes of practical convenience, the major inquiries which will explore the adequacy and soundness of a speaker's thinking.

Questions may be put as follows: (1) Does the speaker deal with an adequate and reliably established body of facts? (2) Does he proceed from assumptions and hypotheses which are neither biased nor gratuitous? (3) Does his verbalization of ideas reveal the true significance of his claims clearly, unequivocally? (4) Does his analysis of the idea reveal unity of intention, internal consistency, and a full recognition of the important as against the unimportant elements in the discourse? (5) Does his reasoning meet the tests of validity appropriate to the various forms of argumentative development? (6) Does he substitute emotional excitation of the hearers for logical proof?

To sum up the whole matter, the thinking of the orator must be characterized by features which, according to Avey,[3] can best be suggested by this alliteration: clearness in language usage; consistency, in the sense of being free from contradiction; completeness, to the extent of providing conclusions only when adequate facts have been surveyed; consecutiveness in its order of thought presentation; and cogency, in the sense that all of the parts are held together and articulated with the main proposition.

[3] Albert Avey. *The Function and Forms of Thought*. New York, 1927, pp. 351ff.

## AN EXPERIMENTAL STUDY OF THE EFFECTS OF ETHOS IN PUBLIC SPEAKING

### FRANKLYN S. HAIMAN

It has long been affirmed by rhetoricians that much of the effectiveness of public speaking is dependent upon the character and personality of the speaker. As Aristotle put it, "We might almost affirm that the speaker's *ethos* is the most potent of all the means to persuasion."[1] Most of the great teachers of rhetoric have followed Aristotle's lead, so that today this concept of "ethical persuasion" holds a very important place in the field of speech.[2] It has therefore been thought worthwhile to examine this concept with the view of determining experimentally the part played by certain factors of *ethos* (e.g. prestige, likableness, and

Franklyn S. Haiman, "An Experimental Study of the Effects of Ethos in Public Speaking," *Speech Monographs* (September 1949), pp. 190–202. Reprinted by permission of the Speech Association of America and of the author.

The author is chairman of the Department of Public Address and Group Communication at Northwestern University.

This paper reports the essential features of a dissertation submitted in partial fulfillment of the requirements for the Doctor of Philosophy degree at Northwestern University in June, 1948. The study was conducted under the joint supervision of Dr. Kenneth G. Hance, Professor of Public Speaking, and Dr. Robert H. Seashore, Professor of Psychology.

[1] Aristotle, *The Rhetoric*, trans. Lane Cooper (New York, 1930), p. 9.

[2] For the historical development of this concept see William M. Sattler, "Conceptions of Ethos in Rhetoric," Ph.D. Dissertation, Northwestern University, 1941.

physical attractiveness) in the effectiveness of persuasive public speaking.

In recent years an increasing number of studies have applied the experimental method to the field of public speaking in an effort to measure the effectiveness of oral persuasion. One of the earliest was the work of Millson in 1932 which demonstrated that audiences do change their verbal opinions in response to student speakers.[3] The following year Chen reported a similar finding, along with other tentative conclusions, some of which concerned the role of a speaker's personality in persuasion.[4] A doctoral dissertation by Knower in 1935 established a general pattern for experimental studies of changes in audience attitudes which has been followed by many later investigators.[5] Knower, in the study referred to, was interested in measuring the effect of such variables as logical versus emotional speaking, male versus female speakers, etc. Lull has measured the effect of humor as a variable factor,[6] and Lomas sought to discover the effect of provocative language.[7] The study reported in this article follows in the same pattern, but has focused its attention on certain factors of *ethos*—variables which have not previously been investigated.

Three experiments were conducted in this study, using students at Northwestern University, 1947–48, as audience subjects. The experimenter attempted to hold constant all but certain ethical factors in speaking situations, and then to vary the factors of *ethos* in order to determine what, if any, corresponding variation this would produce in audience reaction.

As a criterion for the effectiveness of persuasive speaking, shifts of opinion to the side of a controversial question advocated by the speaker were measured. After studying the various possible methods of measur-

[3] William A. D. Millson, "Problems in Measuring Audience Reaction," *Quarterly Journal of Speech*, 18 (November 1932), 627.

[4] William Keh-Ching Chen, "The Influence of Oral Propaganda Material Upon Students' Attitudes," *Archives of Psychology*, 23 (1933), 43.

[5] Franklin H. Knower, "Experimental Studies of Changes in Attitude," Part I, *Journal of Social Psychology*, 6 (August 1935), 315–345; Part II, *Journal of Abnormal and Social Psychology*, 30 (January–March 1936), 522–532. Part III, *Journal of Applied Psychology*, 20 (February 1936), 114–127.

[6] P. E. Lull, "The Effectiveness of Humor in Persuasive Speech," *Speech Monographs*, 3 (1940), 22–25.

[7] Charles W. Lomas, "An Experimental Study of the Effects of Provocative Language on Audience Reaction to Political Speeches," Ph.D. Dissertation, Northwestern University, 1940.

ing these audience shifts, it was decided to use the Woodward ballot as the principal tool in this project. First, the conclusions of Monroe as to the reliability and validity of this instrument[8] have not yet been challenged. Second, the Woodward ballot is a brief and simple tool, both for the subject to mark and the investigator to score.

A fifteen-minute persuasive speech in which favor was sought for a program of national compulsory health insurance was written by the investigator and used in all the experiments.

Practical necessity imposed certain limitations on this project and thus on the generalizations which can be made from its results. As is so often the case, it was necessary to use only college students as audience subjects. Because of the limits of time, it was decided to work only with certain factors of *ethos* outside of the speech text, leaving experiments with the manifestations of *ethos* within the language of the text to other investigators.[9] Finally, it was necessary to work only with those factors or groups of factors which could be isolated readily from others.

It was assumed at the outset of this study that the original, pre-speech opinions of members of the audience on the controversial issue to be discussed might cause different kinds of reactions to the speaker. Experimental and control groups therefore had to be equated on the basis of original opinions. The practical limitations of the research situation and the undesirability of creating an artificial atmosphere made it inadvisable to attempt to select audiences and gather them together especially for the experiments. Rather it was decided to use college classes as they were. If any significant disparities between groups in their distribution of original opinions should appear, ballots could be thrown out at random in order to equate the groups. . . . [Here follows a detailed description of the three experiments.]

## Over-All Analysis

The data from the foregoing experiments provided raw material from which an investigation could be made of the effect that a listener's original opinion on the subject matter exerts upon his view of the

[8] Alan H. Monroe, "The Reliability and Validity of the Shift-of-Opinion Ballot, *Quarterly Journal of Speech*, 23 (December 1937), 585ff.

[9] Such a study is that by Edward L. Pross, "A Critical Analysis of Certain Aspects of Ethical Proof," Ph.D. Dissertation, State University of Iowa, 1942.

speaker's *ethos*. In an earlier study, similar to this one, Knower concluded that the arguments of a speaker did affect listeners' attitudes toward him personally.[10]

It will be remembered that in Experiment I, the listeners rated the speakers on the items of reputation and competence. On competence, the differences among the mean ratings given by the three categories of original opinion were found to be statistically significant at the 5% level, with the Original Yes voters giving the highest average rating, Undecideds next, and Original No voters giving the lowest ratings. Using the technique of epsilon-square and epsilon,[11] the strength of correlation was estimated at .14. On the factor of reputation, there was no significant correlation between original opinion and ratings given.

In Experiment II, we found a statistically significant pattern of ratings on three items—fairmindedness, sincerity, and competence—with the highest average rating again coming from favorable listeners. The correlations were .22 for fairmindedness (significant above 1% level), .12 for sincerity (significant at 5% level), and .12 for competence (significant at 5% level). On the other three items—likableness, physical attractiveness, and conceit, there were no consistent patterns discernible.

In Experiment III, only two items—fairmindedness and competence—produced the same kind of statistically significant pattern found above, but the strength of the correlation on these items was much stronger in this experiment. For fairmindedness, epsilon was .33; and for competence .24. On the items of sincerity and conceit no significant patterns were found.

Based upon these findings, we may draw some general conclusions. Certainly none of the correlations found can be considered very high. However, we can safely conclude that for *some* factors of *ethos*, such as fairmindedness and competence, original opinion on the subject matter of the speaker apparently does prejudice to some small degree the listener's concept of the speaker's *ethos*. For the factor of sincerity the evidence is inconclusive. For the other factors dealt with in this study—reputation, conceit, likableness, and physical attractiveness—there is no reason to believe that original opinion plays a part in the listener's evaluation of them.

[10] Franklin H. Knower, "Experimental Studies of Changes in Attitudes," *Journal of Applied Psychology*, 20 (1936), 127.

[11] Allen L. Edwards, *Statistical Analysis* (New York, 1946), pp. 234–235.

## Questionnaire Survey

The experimental procedures reported above were supplemented in this study with a questionnaire approach designed to gather information from the practical world of affairs. The purpose of this survey was to determine what correlation, if any, exists between the persuasive success of speakers in American public affairs and certain factors of their *ethos*, as shown by the combined judgments of a group of professional critics of public speaking.

The first step necessary in this survey was the establishment of two criterion groups—one consisting of men and women in American public life who were judged by experts to be outstandingly successful in the art of persuasion; the other consisting of a comparable group of men and women who were judged by experts to be outstandingly unsuccessful in that art. For this purpose a questionnaire was devised and distributed to 19 judges—all college teachers of public speaking. The judges were asked to name the people whom they considered to be the five most persuasive and the five least persuasive speakers whom they had seen and heard in American public life during the past eighteen years. The successful criterion group was formed by taking the names of those six speakers who were most frequently mentioned as "most persuasive" speakers, and the unsuccessful criterion group was gathered from those most frequently mentioned on the "least persuasive" lists. Obviously some persons were included simply because they happened to be best known to this group of judges. The two groups which resulted were as follows:

| *Successful* | *Unsuccessful* |
|---|---|
| Franklin D. Roosevelt | Herbert Hoover |
| Norman Thomas | *Harry Truman |
| Eric Johnston | Alf Landon |
| Ernest Tittle | Robert Taft |
| Claude Pepper | Robert McCormick |
| Harrison Brown | John Foster Dulles |

*This survey was made long before the election of 1948.

The next step was to secure judgments as to the relative rank of these 12 speakers on five factors of *ethos*—prestige, physical attractiveness, sincerity, likableness, and general competence. A questionnaire was devised for this purpose and filled out by 20 judges, 17 of whom were the same as filled out the first questionnaire. The results of the first questionnaire were not yet made available to the judges, and they were not yet told the purpose of the study.

Very few judges were able to rank all 12 speakers on all five factors of *ethos*. Regardless of the number of speakers ranked, each judge's list for each of the factors of *ethos* was divided into four equal parts. It was now possible to go back and tabulate, for each of the factors of *ethos*, the frequency with which the names in the successful and unsuccessful criterion groups appeared in each of the four quartiles.

From these tabulations inspection immediately revealed some kind of positive correlation between success in the art of persuasion and rank on each of the factors of *ethos* for which these speakers were rated. Statistical procedures were then required to determine the significance and strength of each of these correlations, and the contingency coefficient (C) was the measure of association considered most applicable to this problem.[12] Since only twelve speakers—a rather small sampling—were involved in these ratings, we must be cautious in drawing conclusions from any correlations obtained.

The results were as follows:

1. *Prestige.* The correlation of .23 found between this factor and persuasive success must be regarded as quite low, though significant (at 3% level of confidence). This finding appears to run counter to the experimental findings of Experiment I, which indicated great importance for the prestige factor. Once it is remembered, however, that all the speakers (successful and unsuccessful) in this survey—though they may have differed among themselves in the degree of prestige they possessed—were men and women who stand very high in prestige by comparison to the average citizen, this apparent discrepancy vanishes. In other words, we had only the upper end of the prestige continuum involved in this survey, and we would thus expect the differential effects of prestige to be relatively small in such a narrow range of talent.

2. *Physical attractiveness.* The correlation of .71 found between this factor and persuasive success must be regarded as quite high in terms of the conditions of the survey. This finding tends to confirm the inference made as a result of Experiment III that physical appearance is related to persuasive effectiveness. However, the relationship indicated here appears much stronger than would have been expected as a result of Experiment III.

---

[12] J. P. Guilford, *Psychometric Methods* (New York, 1936), pp. 353–360.

3.  *Sincerity*. The correlation of .46 found between this factor and persuasive success must be regarded as significant (above the 1% level), but moderately low.

4.  *Likableness*. The correlation of .87 found between this factor and persuasive success may be regarded as very high. This correlation was much higher than that obtained between persuasive success and any other factor judged in this survey. It is interesting to note that, out of 20 judges, not one rated any speaker from the unsuccessful criterion group in the upper quartile of his list for this factor; and not one judge rated any speaker from the successful criterion group in the lower quartile of his list. This would indicate an exceedingly high premium on likableness as a factor of persuasive success in American public life. It tends to confirm the inference made from Experiment III that likableness is related to persuasive effectiveness, but the relationship indicated here is very much stronger than one would be led to expect by Experiment III.

5.  *General competence*. The correlation of .43 between this factor and persuasive success must be regarded as significant (above the 1% level), but moderately low. The strength of the relationship on this factor is approximately the same as it was on the factor of sincerity—both of which findings are somewhat disturbing from an idealistic point of view.

## Summary

The conclusions of this study on the effects of *ethos* in public speaking may be summarized as follows:

1.  Variations in the prestige of a speaker, produced by varying the chairman's introductory identification of him, were found to influence significantly the effectiveness of a persuasive speech in behalf of national compulsory health insurance—as shown by audience shift-of-opinon ballots in a classroom situation.

2.  Variations in the over-all ethical appeal of speakers, produced by having persons of different ethical appeal deliver the same speech, were found to influence, in one degree or another, the persuasive effect of the speech—as shown by shift-of-opinion ballots in a classroom situation. For these college groups, an especially high premium seemed to be placed upon the factor of competence.

3. With all other factors held constant, a significant change in the likableness and physical attractiveness of a speaker talking to college students in behalf of national compulsory health insurance did not make a great deal of difference in shift-of-opinion results. However, the obtained difference was almost statistically significant.

4. As shown by analysis of variance, a significant relationship between level of original opinion and the size of opinion shift was found, with the students originally opposed to the proposition of the speaker making the greatest shifts, and the students originally in favor of the proposition making the smallest shifts.

5. Although female students did not differ significantly from males in the average size or distance of opinion shift, a significantly higher proportion of females shifted their opinions.

6. Female students were significantly more generous than males in rating the *ethos* of speakers, regardless of the speaker's sex.

7. A combined analysis of all the experiments revealed that the original opinions of listeners on the topic of national compulsory health insurance affected their judgment of certain factors in the speaker's *ethos*:

(a) Judgments as to the speaker's fairmindedness and competence were influenced in a small degree by the listener's initial attitude toward the topic.

(b) Evaluations of the speaker's reputation, conceit, likableness, and physical attractiveness were not influenced by the listener's initial attitude toward the topic.

(c) For the factor of sincerity the evidence was not conclusive either way.

8. As shown by the ratings of expert judges, a positive correlation was found to exist between several factors of *ethos* and success in the art of persuasion by nationally known speakers in American public life. The factor of likableness correlated most highly with success; physical attractiveness correlated quite highly with success; sincerity and general competence correlated positively, but only moderately, with success.

Undoubtedly there are many more aspects of *ethos* and of the part it plays in public speaking which would lend themselves profitably to such research. Many of the findings of this study need to be refined and qualified by additional work. Many areas which were neglected or passed over lightly here should be investigated more thoroughly. It is hoped that this study will serve to arouse the curiosity and stimulate the interest of other research workers in the field.

## THE ANATOMY OF ATTENTION

### WILBUR SCHRAMM

Communication is a buyer's market. Far more stimuli come to us than we are able to attend to. When we drive downtown, we notice very little about the houses and people on both sides of the street. Yet they are all the time offering stimuli to our senses. In other situations—for example, if we are looking for an address along the street—we may pay close attention. But when we drive downtown we are probably attending only to the traffic lights, automobiles, pedestrians at crossings, and other signals that help us drive safely where we want to go.

The signs of communication have to compete for an audience. You can see how this works for the mass media, and a little reflection will show you that it operates also in face-to-face conversation. How often, for example, do you have the undivided attention of the person you are talking to?

There is good reason to think that we scan our communication environment like an index, selecting among cues and concentrating our attention on the signs associated with the cues that specially attract us. You can see this operate when we scan the newspaper headlines, and sometimes when we use tables of contents. It seems also to be operative when we listen to voice radio. For example, experiments indicate that we habitually listen to a newscast at a relatively low level of attention until a cue word or phrase awakens our attention and invites us to respond to the group of signs associated with the cue.

Furthermore, we tend to perceive the message in terms of the index cue. For example, the meaning we perceive in a picture often depends greatly on the caption. Two different newspaper headlines can result in two different impressions of the story. A word like "but" (as an experiment with public discussion indicates) can apparently index the material that follows it as "negative" regardless of the nature of the material.

Experimental work on this index function is in very early stages, and

From Wilbur Schramm, ed., *The Process and Effects of Mass Communication* (Urbana: University of Illinois Press, 1954). Reprinted by permission.

The author is Director of the Institute for Communication Research and Janet M. Peck Professor of International Communication at Stanford University.

the process is not wholly understood as yet. Nevertheless, the idea promises to have important implications for encoders, who may find they should spend more effort devising index systems, spacing out and weighting their index cues.

The principles that determine whether a cue will attract attention may be described simply as follows:

1. *Availability*. The first requisite is to deliver the signal, to make it easy to pick up. Other things being equal, you are more likely to tune in a program where the signal is strong and clear than one which fades and blurs and requires you to strain to hear. Other things being equal, you are more likely to look at a large billboard placed where you can conveniently see it as you stop for a traffic light, than you are to see a small placard on a house past which you drive at 60 miles an hour. Other things being equal, you are more likely to read the newspaper available when you are home and relaxed for the evening. *Other things being equal.* Of course, things are not always equal. During the Nazi occupation, Frenchmen who had radios were willing to strain to hear, if by so doing they could hear the BBC in place of the official Nazi radio. The few people in occupied Seoul during the summer of 1950 who had radios were willing to risk their lives in order to hear the UN radio for a few minutes a day, instead of the much more easily available Communist radio. But these things were done because of other motivations. Except for these motivations, the principle of least effort would have applied in those cases as it applies in the everyday commonplace act of discriminating among broadcasting stations, newspapers, theaters, and advertising signs.

2. *Contrast*. Your attention is likely to be attracted to any signal which contrasts notably with the rest of your environment, providing that signal is readily available. Something that is noticeably louder, or brighter, or larger; a sudden movement in a static field; a sudden change in tone, intensity, pace, mass—all these things will serve to draw attention to themselves. Within the limits of ready availability, the converse will also hold. That is, a few seconds of silence in the midst of continuing sound, an autumn pastel in the midst of bright summer landscapes, a runner who suddenly stops in the middle of a race—these too will attract attention. This is one of the most valuable principles for the construction of advertising materials, and it has many implications.

But let us here record one point of caution in using the principle. It is easy to overdo loudness and size contrast and "novelty." It is easy for radio announcers and commentators, for example, to enter into an impossible competition for attention through loudness and excitement. The attention-drawing effect of loudness seems to operate on a kind of Weber's Law which, as you remember, is the psychophysical principle that constantly *increasing* differentials are required for discrimination among weights as the weights are increased. In other words, in a competition to attract attention through loudness, as the voices grow louder and louder, the intervals which separate the loudness of the speakers must be made greater and greater, if any difference is to be perceived. Low in the scale, the difference may be only one decibel; it may be 10 decibels, high in the scale of intensity. If loudness and excitement were the only tools with which radio commercials could compete, then soon radio announcers would be reduced to screaming. If intensity were the only means of attracting attention, then size would soon become impracticable, sound unsupportable, and brightness merely garish. Contrast must be attained by other means as well. A very good reason for using other means is the fact that if an intensity cue, once selected, does not adequately reward the selector, then the selector will be much less likely to respond to a similar cue the next time. The sensitivity, that is, may be decreased. Experiments have shown, for example, that words like "Flash!" and "Bulletin!" used indiscriminately, will at first raise the attention, but quickly lose their attention-gathering effect if the rewards are not proportional to the strength of the cues.

Repetition should also be mentioned under this head. Not only does it make a cue statistically more readily available, and in contrast with non-continuing cues; but also it seems to have the power of accumulating attention power—as a series of very small stimuli, for example, will finally trigger a nerve current.

3. *Reward and threat.* This is perhaps too simple a way of trying to state the fact that the relation of a cue to a receiver's needs, wants, motivations, interests, habits, roles, frames of reference—however we want to codify his personality—will have a great deal to do with determining whether it attracts attention. A familiar name in a headline, a picture of one's own street, a story about the university football team in which one feels an almost personal pride, a story about a polio epidemic which may affect one's children, a story about a subject which has previously rewarded us and been remembered—cues like these will certainly attract attention. Similarly, we tend to be attracted to some cues because they fit the roles we play in society; they are the things that

are "done," the things that are "read," the things we ought to be informed on. We respond to many cues simply because of habit (e.g., to turn on a certain radio program). In a sense, all this activity can be explained in terms of the reward or threat which the cues offer an individual scanner, or the habits that have grown out of rewarded responses.

A communicator is in the position of trying to arrange his index cues so that they will appeal to the personality needs of his audience. Some of these will be individual and personal; others will be widespread and general. For example, stories about Lindbergh in 1927 would have a personal-acquaintance appeal to a few hundred or thousand people, but vast numbers could enjoy the conflict situation of a man against an ocean, and could identify with the American boy who had that adventure and won the victory. The face-to-face communicator will therefore draw on all he knows about his listener, all that he can find out by feedback, in order to cue his message to the personal interests of the listener and thus get as much of the attention as possible. The mass communicator, on the other hand, will consider the general interests and needs of his audience, and try to cue his messages to the interests of large groups. This fact has been responsible for much of the dissatisfaction with mass communication, which, as it has grown larger, has been forced in the interests of economy to appeal to the interests of groups as large as possible, and thus to adopt what has been called a "lowest common denominator" approach, and ignore many specialized interests and needs.

The communicator tries to encode his material so as to give two dimensions of index information about it: intensity and subject matter. This is a delicate business, because if he gains attention by an intensity cue and then does not suitably reward the attention, or if he indicates (for example, by a scarehead) that a story has great reward or threat for the audience and the story does not live up to the head, he is in danger of extinguishing that response in his audience. Furthermore, if his headline does not accurately represent the story content, he may cause a misperception of the whole story. Therefore, the acts of indexing which seem most obvious to us—such as placing and headlining stories in a newspaper—are actually delicate problems in balancing intensity cues (headline size and blackness, position on the page, page in the paper, length of story, relation to pictorial material, etc.) against the predicted importance of the story to readers; and also constructing the headlines so as to indicate accurately what the content has to offer in response to the interests and needs of readers. If the signs of the story are themselves a kind of shorthand, then the headlines are shorthand for shorthand, and the weight of responsibility on the editor is very great indeed.

The audience, on its part, discriminates amongst the cues at hand, in terms of their relative availability (including economic availability), their contrast with environment, and the apparent reward or threat they offer. To a certain extent, as we have said, role and custom enter into the selection of an audience, but these also may be explained in terms of reward and learned habit.

We know something about how audiences organize themselves around the index cues of mass communication, although our information is better on gross problems (e.g., media audiences) than on finer questions (e.g., response to different kinds of cues). We know, for example, that in the United States two mass media (radio and newspapers) reach practically everyone, except the very young. Magazines reach about two-thirds of the people, motion pictures about one-half, books about one-fourth. Television is still not generally enough available to permit a fair comparison, although it seems destined to belong to the newspaper-radio group. There are great differences between countries of the world in respect to availability of mass media and therefore the size of audiences. In the United States, the circulation of daily newspapers is about 54 million, considerably more than one per average home. In Greece, where the population is about 8 million, the circulation of daily newspapers is about 800,000 or a little less than one paper for every two homes. In Burma, where there are 18 million people, the total daily circulation is about 100,000. In the United States there are about 95 million radios, or more than two per average home. In France, where the population is 41 million, there are 7.5 million receivers, a little less than one per home. In Ethiopia, where there are 17 million people, there are only 5,000 receiving sets.

In the United States, where our most detailed audience figures have been compiled, book reading and motion picture attendance fall off sharply after the teen years. After these years, school-motivation to use books is gone, and the social motivation to go to the movies is in competition with the more easily available entertainment at home. Newspaper reading seems to increase from the early teens through middle age, and radio listening appears to be on a high plateau during the middle years. People with more money or more education are likely to spend more time than others on mass media in general (except radio). And except for radio, and perhaps television, a kind of all-or-none law seems to be operative: that is, on the average, if an individual is above average in his communication time, he will also be above average in the amount of time he gives to each of the individual media.

If now we ask what materials different kinds of individuals select *within* the media, we come to a more complex situation. The first thing to be noted is that an individual selects only a small part of the mass communication material available to him. The average U.S. reader reads only one-fourth to one-third of the contents of a daily newspaper, chooses only a few per cent of the radio programs available to him. A very large proportion of attention to the mass media is to material which indexes itself as entertainment, or to pictures and other spectacular material which offers relatively easy going and a high level of excitement. The so-called "serious" use of mass communications (once past the textbook years) appears to be learned slowly, and to correlate highly with education and with pressing individual needs. Foreign political news, for example, is read by small percentages of U.S. newspaper audiences unless it is couched in terms of conflict (as the 1952 Olympic Games were described, and as we tend increasingly to write of international diplomacy) or in terms that offer strong threat or reward to the reader or his family (for example, the threat of war or the promised reward of war's end). However, foreign political news will be read by larger percentages of college graduates than others, and by higher percentages of persons past the age of 30 than younger persons. Role differences account for some reading patterns, as for example the heavy male reading of sports, the heavy female reading of society news and fashion material. Likewise, the frame of reference is a powerful determinant, as can be seen in the heavy reading of local news in weekly newspapers, and in farmers' selection of agricultural material. However, it should be remembered that pictures and comics have highest readership in newspapers, comedians and thriller programs on the radio, a digest magazine and a picture magazine among periodicals.

Lest all this talk of mass communication throw perspective awry, we should mention here that the average person in the United States seems to devote only a little over four hours a day, about one-fourth of his waking hours, to mass communication. Most of his other waking hours are used, or are available, for individual communication—for conversations, telephone calls, letters, etc. If we then ask about the average person's *focus* of attention, we can assume that it decreases swiftly as it goes out from his primary group. That is, the greater part of his attention is given to communication with his family and close friends. Another part is devoted to business and acquaintances; a smaller part to the affairs of his town and state; a still smaller part to national and world events. Within his mass communication time, a considerable part of his attention is focussed on "escape" materials, which temporarily take him away from the threat or decision situations which surround his vote, his business, his health, or his home. There must be great individual differences, however, about which we know all too little, in the attention patterns of different individuals, and in different cultures. Actually this is a very important kind of knowledge, not only in the study of personality growth and communication practices, but also in the comparative study of cultures and the study of international relations. It is a matter of considerable importance to us at this moment, for example, to know what signals from the outside world come to the attention of the ordinary Russian or Chinese, Indian or Arab.

## TOWARD AN ANALYSIS OF MOTIVATION

### OTIS M. WALTER

### I

For over two thousand years, rhetoricians have attempted to develop an understanding of the forces that impel the human being to act. Various concepts of "emotion," "drive," "need," "desire," and "motive" have been evolved. A recent textbook in psychology states what seems to be the most common contemporary division of these springs of action when it classifies them into primary forces and those forces derived from the primary ones:

> Since man is an organism before he becomes a person, and since physiological homeostasis must be maintained if he is to live at all, it is common usage to speak of his physiological needs as primary, his social, ethical, and religious needs as secondary, as derived. . . .[1]

Otis M. Walter, "Toward an Analysis of Motivation," *Quarterly Journal of Speech* (October 1955). Reprinted by permission.
Otis M. Walter is Professor of Speech at the University of Pittsburgh.
[1] Lawrence E. Cole, *Human Behavior* (New York, 1953), p. 199.

Brembeck and Howell have adapted this kind of analysis to rhetoric and list such physiological drives as hunger, thirst, sex, and security from bodily injury.[2] The same authors include such socially derived impulsions as subsistence motives, social approval motives, conformity motives, and mastery motives. A similar treatment is found in Monroe's more elementary book when he says:

> Fundamentally, there are four primary motives which influence human beings. Behind every act, belief, or emotion will be found one or more of these basic desires:
> 1. Self-preservation and the desire for physical well-being.
> 2. Freedom from external restraint.
> 3. Preservation and increase of self-esteem (ego expansion).
> 4. Preservation of the human race. . . .[3]

Monroe lists eighteen motives derived from these primary ones, such as acquisition and saving, adventure, companionship, creating, curiosity, and destruction.[4]

Such lists of motives have been common to Speech textbooks since the time of Phillips.[5] Examples of them can be found in Parrish,[6] Sarett and Foster,[7] and Oliver,[8] to mention only a few. We could assume that, because so many rhetoricians use these lists, they are considered of practical value in the teaching of speakers. It is not my aim here to suggest otherwise, but instead to show that motivation may be analyzed in a somewhat more detailed and perhaps more useful way.

A major reason for developing a more thorough analysis of motivation in rhetoric is that lists of motives together with discussions of the nature of motives furnish the student of rhetoric with only an incomplete analysis of the process of motivation. Such motives as the desire for security may be looked upon as "generalized goals" toward

---

[2] Winston L. Brembeck and William S. Howell, *Persuasion* (New York, 1952), Pt. iii.

[3] Alan H. Monroe, *Principles and Types of Speech*, 3rd ed. (New York, 1949), p. 194.

[4] *Ibid.*, p. 196.

[5] A. E. Phillips, *Effective Speaking* (Chicago, 1908), Ch. 5.

[6] Wayland Maxfield Parrish, *Speaking in Public* (New York, 1947), Ch. 14.

[7] Lew Sarett and William T. Foster, *Basic Principles of Speech*, rev. ed. (New York, 1946), pp. 494–500.

[8] Robert Oliver, *The Psychology of Persuasive Speech* (New York, 1942), pp. 167–8.

which the organism moves. The generalized goal of security may be gratified by securing a specific goal such as a better job. Thus it is that motivation, as treated in rhetoric, hardly involves more than a consideration of certain kinds of general and specific goals. Yet the process of motivation is more complex than a movement toward goals. For example, what is the effect on motivation of a goal from which the individual is restrained by a barrier? It will be shown later that such a situation significantly conditions the problem of persuasion. What implications are there for persuasion when one attempts to appeal to a motive and the process of gratifying that motive will subject one to danger or the possible loss of other goals? What are the implications for persuasion when goals, motives, or desires are in conflict? Most treatments of motivation ignore these significant and complicating variations. Furthermore, attitudes, sentiments, stereotypes, opinions, and the like, though related to motivation, are commonly treated as separate entities. It is possible, however, to integrate them into a theory of motivation. If motive situations involve barriers, threats, conflicting attitudes, sentiments, stereotypes, opinions, etc., how do these matters affect what Aristotle calls "the available means of persuasion?" Certainly no mere list of motives, however long, can make clear all the possibilities and implications of these problems to the student of rhetoric. The simple situation in which the individual is motivated toward a goal is by no means the only situation in which motivation operates. We must develop a theory that will include and utilize these complicating features of motivation. The purpose of this paper is to explain a coherent system by which these variations of motivational behavior may be utilized by the rhetorician.

## II

It may be possible, paradoxically enough, that the study of motivation would be advanced if we, temporarily at least, abandoned the search for motives. To begin with, we could describe motivational behavior by studying motivational *situations* in which the human being behaves. Kenneth Burke offers a suggestion in this direction. He says that the concept of "motive" is nothing but a shorthand term for a situation. In his description of what he calls the "dramatistic view" of behavior, he holds:

In a rounded statement about motives, you must have some word that names the *act* (names what took place, in thought or deed), and another that names the *scene* (the background of the act, the situation in which it occurred); also, you must indicate what person or kind of person (*agent*) performed the act, what means or instruments he used (*agency*) and the purpose. . . .[9]

Thus, according to Burke, the explanation of a situation lies in the act, the scene, the agent, the agency, and the purpose involved. He believes that his analysis is so fundamental that it may serve as a means of integrating the studies of the social sciences and as a perspective for the analysis of history as well.[10]

Let us examine the utility of the "dramatistic view" of man for rhetorical theory. It is apparent from this synopsis of the dramatistic view that Burke includes in it all facets of the rhetorical act. Thus, all rhetorical matters can be classified under the five elements found in every situation. Under "agent," for example, could be classified, among other things, discussions of ethos. Under "scene" would fall audience analysis, the nature of the occasion, and the like. Under "agency" could be classified matters of style, organization, and in sum, the speech itself. The usefulness of such a system for the study of motivation is limited because it includes *all* factors of influence in human behavior. Rather than a description of factors in *motivation*, it is an outline of the *entire* rhetorical process. As such, it is parallel to the Roman classification of Invention, Arrangement, Style, Memory, and Delivery—it excludes nothing. Its defect is not a failure to subsume under its headings all manifestations of human behavior; its defect is simply that it includes much more than what is commonly considered to be motivation. To be sure, life occurs in this kind of milieu, but it can only be analyzed and studied if a more *limited* view of the total situation is taken. A scientist, for example, cannot study "cancer," but *only one kind of reaction* of cancer at a time. A psychologist cannot study the whole human being, despite the desirability of such an attempt, but must limit his view to some aspect of the human being. The nature of the human being is such that the scientist has no choice in this matter. It is true that errors are often made in limiting one's view. The history of science and philosophy abounds with "wrong" questions in which a mistaken limitation was placed on the observer. In fact, the great error in the contemporary

[9] Kenneth Burke, A *Grammar of Motives* (New York, 1945), p. xv. See also Marie Hochmuth, "Kenneth Burke and the New Rhetoric," *Quarterly Journal of Speech*, 37 (1952), 141.

[10] Hochmuth, *op. cit.*, p. 143.

analysis of motivation in rhetorical theory is precisely this kind of error. The study of motivation has revolved about the question: "What are the most basic tendencies that move the human being to act?" This kind of definition of the problem has led directly to the oversimplifications and inadequacies dealt with above. But like it or not, if we mean to study something, we must take a limited view of it. We can only try to be careful to take a view that will not presuppose erroneous answers.

The problem before us is that of searching for a question other than "What are the most basic tendencies that move the human being to act?" In order to evolve such a question, we have first suggested that we examine motivational *situations* rather than "motives." We have further implied that we restrict ourselves by suggesting that the question be limited to motivational behavior per se, and that, so far as possible, unrelated behavior be omitted. With these matters as background we are now ready to raise fundamental questions, the answers to which may provide material of interest to the student of rhetoric. Let us ask: "*What are the situations in which an individual is moved to act?*" And further ask: "*What implications do these situations have for rhetorical theory?*" If we have asked the right questions, the answers should provide us with a scheme for systematically treating the concept of motivation in rhetoric without oversimplification and with the possibility of integrating into a theory of motivation the concepts of attitude, sentiment, opinion, and stereotypes.

## III

Let us examine some basic motivational situations and explore their rhetorical implications. It seems to me that there are five basic situations.[11]

The *Difficulty Situation* is the most fundamental of all. The prerequisite for it is that an individual or group of individuals perceives a difficulty.

[Before he moved his arm,] the baby was subjected to . . . an annoying pressure, or he was attracted by a stimulus-object not

[11] The writer is obviously indebted to a number of men for the analysis that follows. The basic motivational situations were suggested to the writer by a similar analysis of behavior made by John Dashiel, *Fundamentals of General Psychology* (New York, 1937), Ch. 2, who ultimately based much of his analysis on the psychology of John Dewey. In exploring the rhetorical implications of these five basic structures, it is apparent that the writer has relied heavily on Aristotle's *Rhetoric*. Also stimulating and of help has been Spinoza's analysis of the emotions in *The Ethics*.

readily within his grasp; the troubled children were restrained from
. . . a high school grade . . . ; the would-be solver was challenged
by the puzzle. Something was wrong in every case, some thwarting
of the normal processes of the individual. . . .[12]

Dewey stated that no man ever thinks unless he is first confronted with a
"felt difficulty."[13] Freud has pointed out that even such apparently
unmotivated actions as slips of the tongue, mistakes in typing, and
dreams come about as a result of frustrations.[14] Thus the *sine qua non* for
a motivational situation is a condition in which the audience feels,
vaguely or precisely, that something is wrong. They may not know what
exactly the problem is, but they must feel that somehow "things are not
as they should be." The man with the pain in his stomach may not know
the cause of his difficulty, but if the pain is severe enough, it will surely
motivate him. The felt difficulty may be vaguely defined as "the mess in
Washington" or may be as hidden as the neurotic's complaints. This
kind of problem seems to be the starting point of motivation and the
simplest motivational situation.

Let us explore some of the rhetorical implications of this motivational situation. By "rhetorical implications" I mean the possible lines of
argument a speaker may take with an audience. The implications given
here will be only suggestive of the vast number of possibilities that might
occur. But among other things, here are a few of the rhetorical possibilities:

A. To deny that there is a difficulty, to belittle the importance of the
difficulty, to point out that yielding to the difficulty is unworthy, or
to point out that others in similar situations paid no heed to the
difficulty.

B. To cause the audience to realize the importance and pressing nature
of the difficulty as something deserving or requiring their attention.

C. To locate and define the difficulty, to urge the audience to define
the difficulty and locate the causes of the problem, or to set up procedures by which such definitions could be evolved and such causes
located.

D. To attack any particular formulation of the difficulty as irrational,
unjust, unworthy.

[12] Dashiel, *op. cit.*, p. 35.

[13] John Dewey, *How We Think* (New York, 1910), p. 9.

[14] Sigmund Freud, "The Psychopathology of Everyday Life," *The Basic Writings of Sigmund Freud*, trans. A. A. Brill (New York, 1938), pp. 35–181.

E. To direct attention to other difficulties on the grounds that they are more significant, more pressing, more possible of solution.

The *Goal-Oriented Situation*, which I place second in my list of five, arises when individuals are considering the possibilities of certain rather well-defined goals as solutions to the difficulty. The rhetorical possibilities of this kind of situation are significantly different from those in the previous motivational situation. Here are a few suggestions of these possibilities:

A. To urge the audience to achieve a certain goal, the speaker argues that:
   1. The goal is one that can produce benefits for the audience: pleasure, wealth, security, prestige.
   2. The goal is one that is deserved by the members of the audience.
   3. The goal is easily obtainable.
   4. The goal will bring benefits for those with whom the audience is identified: family, friends, socio-economic class, occupational group.
   5. The goal will be taken by those less in need or less deserving unless the audience responds quickly.
   6. The goal is necessary for survival or well-being, or it will, at least, remove the difficulty that began the problem.
B. To urge that the audience give up a certain goal, the speaker argues that:
   1. The reverse of the above in "A" is true, namely, that the goal is in no way necessary or that it could not remove the original difficulty.
   2. An entirely different approach to the problem is needed, or other goals than those desired at the moment are superior in several ways in removing the difficulty.
   3. There is no Difficulty Situation, and hence no need for any concern about goals.
   4. The goal is not what the individual or group wants as a solution to their difficulty; or it would be injurious if they possessed it; or it produces benefits of a questionable nature; or it cannot be obtained as easily as other goals; or there are more worthwhile goals.

It is immediately apparent that the rhetorical development of motivational situations is nothing new. Within the framework of certain emotions, Aristotle made explicit for speakers the lines of argument that have been repeated in a less thorough manner by other rhetoricians. However, the basic relation between Aristotle's analysis of emotion and his *topoi*, on the one hand, and the problem of motivation, on the other, has never been stressed sufficiently. This relation is even more important when we begin the consideration of the more complex and, I believe, more common motivational situations that follow.

The *Barrier Situation* arises when goals become complicated by the interposition of a barrier between the individual and a desired object. To a small child, for example, the goal may be a piece of candy and the barrier the glass case. Or the goal to the college student may be a good grade and the barrier the amount of work required to obtain the grade. In such cases, the individual is *restrained* from a goal. Such situations are extremely common. No student becomes a lawyer without years of study, no runner a champion without patience and effort, no wife a good cook without long trial and error. It could be said, in fact, that we are always separated from unachieved goals, even if the separation be one of time alone. In the world of communication, more speaking is probably done in the context of motivation modified by restraint or blockage of individuals from goals than in any other context under consideration here. Let us consider the rhetorical possibilities in this kind of situation. Again, the implications are markedly different from those in the two preceding kinds. Among them are the following:

A. To urge the audience to achieve the goal, despite the barrier, the speaker argues that:
   1. The goal is worth achieving (See "A" under Goal-Oriented Situation).
   2. The barrier is contemptible, unintelligent, unnecessary, or unjust.
   3. The barrier works to the advantage of our enemies.
   4. The agent that raised the barrier is contemptuous, unintelligent, or unjust.
   5. The agent that has raised the barrier has harmed us or treated us with indifference or with disparagement.
   6. The agent that raised the barrier acts as if he were doing us a favor.
   7. The agent that raised the barrier has given to others that which we deserve.
   8. The agent that raised the barrier has tried to make us feel shameful when we do not deserve to feel so.

9. The agent that raised the barrier has injured or treated with indifference or disparagement those with whom we identify ourselves (family, friends, home, country, occupation, class).

10. The agent that raised the barrier has slighted us, or those with whom we are identified, in regard to our strongest virtues.

11. The agent that raised the barrier has received good treatment at our hands but has not returned it, or has returned less than he received, and has done so deliberately.

B. To urge the audience to give up the goal, the speaker argues that:
1. There is no basic difficulty that requires the goal or the goal is not worth obtaining. (See "A" under Difficulty Situation.)
2. The opposite of the factors in "A" above are true.
3. There are extenuating circumstances such as these: The barrier is a necessary one, or was placed there because of our own desires, or was raised inadvertently by some act of our own, or those who raised it did so for our own good, or did not mean to cause us harm.

C. To urge the audience to detour to a substitute goal, the speaker attempts to do one of the following:
1. Weaken the desire for the goal and the desirability of surmounting the barrier by the material suggested in "B" above.
2. Emphasize the value of a substitute goal as being superior, or easier to obtain, as in "A" under *Goal-Oriented Situation.*

D. To urge the audience to a further study of the barrier and goal-situation, the speaker attempts to do one of the following:
1. Point out that the barrier is not understood properly and does not have the nature, strength, and characteristics usually attributed to it.
2. Urge the audience to study further, or set up a procedure for studying, the means of eradicating, reducing, out-flanking this goal, or finding ways of changing to other goals.

The rhetorical implications of the Barrier Situation are far more extensive than those detailed above. Our attempt here can be only to suggest a few ways in which motivational situations will affect rhetorical analysis.

The *Threat Situation* appears when we find that we are moved to action because of a threat that may harm us. Thus, the young man may wish a good-night kiss, but may fear that the young lady may slap him too hard to make the attempt worth while. Entire nations may be motivated by a threat and give up the pursuit of certain goals in favor of protecting themselves. This situation differs markedly from the simple Difficulty Situation in that, in the latter, the need or difficulty is relatively vague and not yet located, whereas in the former there is no doubt as to the identity of the alleged threat. The Threat Situation differs from the Barrier Situation somewhat as follows: In the latter, the barrier is interposed between the individual and a goal and is a relatively inactive barrier—it does not have the power of doing more than to prevent the individual from attaining the goal; the Threat Situation, however, is of such nature that it can be alleged that the threat has the power to harm the individual by removing achieved goals or introducing new difficulties. These differences make an enormous change in the rhetorical implications of each situation. Notice the difference in the rhetorical possibilities of the Threat Situation from other situations. The following possibilities are suggestive:

A. To urge the audience that the threat is strong enough to merit their attention, the speaker argues that:
   1. The threat has the power to harm or destroy the audience.
   2. The threat has the power to harm or destroy those identified with the audience: family, friends, institutions, occupational group, class, country.
   3. The threat is unscrupulous, immoral, merciless.
   4. Others who have been in a similar position have considered the force formidable, or if not, they were harmed or destroyed by it when they did not expect it.
B. To urge the audience to give up the goal, inhibit its desire for the goal, or expend its energies toward a different goal, the speaker argues that:
   1. The threat is too strong:
      (a) The threat has the power to destroy or harm the audience, or is superior to the audience's power to resist, and is close at hand.
      (b) The threat will harm or destroy those with which the audience is identified: home, family, friends, institutions, country, occupational group, class.
      (c) Others who are like the audience consider the force formidable, or have been defeated by it although they did not expect to be.
      (d) The threat is unscrupulous, immoral, merciless, unjust.

(e) The weaknesses rather than the strength of the audience have been attacked.

(f) Help is far away, we have no allies and no one to share our fate.

2. The goal is not worth seeking (or keeping):

(a) The goal is not worth the effort or pain required to get it; it would be injurious if we possessed it; it could not be enjoyed if we had it; it produces benefits of questionable nature, or benefits that would not be outweighed by the threat.

(b) Other goals that can be obtained more easily are more worth while or are as good, or are satisfactory substitutes.

(c) Others of as great nobility as the audience have accepted other goals in similar circumstances, or have given up the ones threatened.

C. To urge the audience to resist and combat the threat, the speaker seeks to do the following:

1. Minimize the power of the threat by refuting any of the ideas in "B" above. (In certain cases, however, the opposite procedure should be used. When the audience fails to comprehend the magnitude of the threat, it is often sound to build up the perception of the ideas mentioned in "A" above by dramatizing some of them.)

2. Support some of the following ideas that are most appropriate:

(a) Great effort can reduce the threat, has done so in similar circumstances.

(b) Justice and morality are on the side of those combating the threat; the audience must join them, or must resist alone.

(c) There is a plan by which the threat may be successfully combated or circumvented.

(d) The audience is characterized by courage and greater power than is commonly believed or than can be defeated or harmed by the force.

(e) Others less able than the audience have combated a similar force successfully and have done so courageously.

The last of the five basic motivational situations is the *Identification Situation*. It arises when human beings act for the sake of other groups. Charity drives, heroism, and much self-sacrifice come about in situations of this kind, where the individual who is acting is often concerned primarily with the welfare of another person. The hero did not jump into the water in order to pull out the drowning boy to increase his prestige, but because he felt identified with the boy and felt the boy's welfare to be his own. Let us examine the rhetorical implications of this kind of situation:

A. To urge that one group extend help or otherwise identify itself with another group, the speaker argues thus:
   1. The individual or group of individuals who are to feel this identification must feel that those on behalf of whom help will be given are similar to those who will help. Similarity may be in aims, background, attitudes, methods of facing life, education, status, hopes, plight, foibles.
   2. The group to be aided is in need, or is facing difficulties not its own fault, or has been strong in the face of a threat.
B. To urge that sympathy or sympathetic acts awarded a given individual or group should not be given, the speaker argues thus:
   1. The individuals in the group to be given help are different in basic ways from those in the audience.
   2. Their problem is not a great one, has been exaggerated by them, is their own fault; or they are able to solve it alone.
   3. The granting of aid at this time would expose the audience to danger or would weaken them; or the granting of aid is unnecessary.

## IV

The attempt here has been to point out that the most basic tendencies in human motivation resolve into a question that has not yielded enough knowledge about the process of motivation. It is my hope that an examination of situations may lead to more productive data on the nature of motivation. Five basic motivational situations have been described. The premises of many arguments that may be used in these situations have been outlined in order to bring us closer to the possibility of analyzing the available means of persuasion. Matters involving the audience's attitudes, stereotypes, sentiments, and opinions have been included in this development of rhetorical implications. This kind of analysis will, perhaps, provide the rhetorician with a useful approach to the analysis of motivation.

# 3 Organization: The Arrangement of Ideas

How often have you heard fellow students say that although a speaker sounded as if he knew what he was talking about, gave interesting examples, and delivered his speech fluently, they could not follow him? An audience requires that a speaker so assemble his materials that they can see the relationship of each part of the speech to the major thesis or contention and to every other part. Such a concern is an expression of man's unique desire to reduce disorganization through organization. This desire is satisfied when he sees the interrelationships between ideas, discovers what matters are important and which subsidiary, and realizes the overall chain of reasoning. To be able to "follow" a speaker is a prime requisite for an effective communication.

Classical rhetoricians early recognized the importance of structure and arrangement. Plato remarked that a speech should be put together like "a living creature," with head and feet, middle and extremities, all present and in proportion.[1] In other words, a speech should have a beginning, a middle, and an end which are organically related and proportionate to each other and to the whole. Later rhetoricians have enlarged upon his suggestion and added their own divisions of the parts of a speech. Aristotle, for example, believed that the only important parts were a statement of the case and its proof, but he added that if other parts were necessary, the total number should not exceed four: the exordium, the statement of the case, proof, and the peroration or conclusion.[2] The exordium was intended to enlist the attention and interest of the audience, to render them well-disposed toward the speaker, and to prepare them for the ideas to come. The statement set forth the nature of the subject to be developed. The proof supported the main ideas by elaboration of the subject matter. The peroration inspired the audience with a favorable opinion of the speaker, and excited the emotions of the audience to recall the facts of the speech. With relatively minor revisions, such a division is still useful today.

[1] *Phaedrus*, 264.
[2] *Rhetoric*, Book Three, Chapter Thirteen.

John Black and Wilbur E. Moore, in "The Organization of Speech," point out that the speaker must thoughtfully consider what kind of pattern his ideas and materials are best suited to. They suggest a variety of potential patterns of arrangement and point out that ultimately the pattern selected by the speaker should be the one which best suits his subject, his audience, and the occasion for which the speech is prepared.

In "Speech Introductions and Conclusions," Edd Miller examines what modern-day speakers have included in two of the divisions of a speech, the introduction and the conclusion. From such studies of contemporary practice we can gain further insight into what has proven effective in present-day speechmaking.

## THE ORGANIZATION OF SPEECH

JOHN W. BLACK
WILBUR E. MOORE

At all levels of life, the structuring or organization of parts into wholes follows relatively well-established designs. The colloids of the human body, the molecules of steel, the human beings within a stable society, although constantly in changing relationships, still move in highly predictable patterns. In abnormal conditions, such as cancerous diseases, structural flaws, and revolutions, the breakup of established designs may be followed by chaotic and unpredictable changes and end in the destruction of a particular structure. On the other hand, dynamic alterations of pattern often are followed by new alignments of parts and by a revitalized and stronger organization.

Although social structures are no longer thought to be as rigid as Alexander Pope's "An Essay on Man" suggested, still society, to be at all

---

From *Speech: Code, Meaning, and Communication*, by John W. Black and Wilbur E. Moore. Copyright © 1955 McGraw-Hill Book Company. Used by permission of McGraw-Hill Book Company.

John W. Black is Professor of Speech and Director of Speech and Hearing Science at Ohio State University. Wilbur E. Moore is Vice-President for Academic Affairs, Central Michigan University.

cohesive, must impose forms of organization upon its members. But either to persuade and coerce its members into desirable behavior on the one hand or to dissuade and restrain them from undesirable activity on the other, a society must first of all group and classify individual human responses.[1] The principal tool by which society classifies is, as we have seen, articulate speech. If you will reflect but a moment upon organizing groups like the home, the church, the school, the state, and upon regulative terms like *good* and *bad*, *clean* and *unclean*, *smart* and *dumb*, *brave* and *cowardly*, *lawful* and *unlawful*, *successful* and *unsuccessful*, *religious* and *irreligious*, you will sense the tremendous organizing effects speech has upon your own personality and upon your relations with other members of any social group. Edward Sapir, who was a distinguished anthropologist, wrote that even such highly personal activities as ways of breathing fell into categories of polite and impolite and, therefore, became organized physiological responses partly as a result of social forces.[2]

The very act of learning involves perception of patterns, *Gestalten* (shapes), configurations. More and more, the authorities on the psychology of learning emphasize the importance of this organizing function of the mind and of speech. In fact, much research indicates that learning is painfully slow and inferior in quality if organization is not also present. In learning which involves symbols, the organizing function is even more important. If this theory is true, as it now seems to be, it means that if you have learned to talk, you have also learned to organize. The simplest human act, the simplest kind of speech involves organization to some degree.

It is urgent that beginning students of speech understand the full significance of this view. If they do, they will lighten their labor in organizing not only their speeches but all their work. If they understand that the real question, then, is not whether they should organize ideas, but which one of a number of correct patterns of organization they wish to apply to a given problem, much of their uncertainty can be eliminated.

[1] George Zipf, *Human Behavior and the Principle of Least Effort*, pp. 275–276. Addison-Wesley Publishing Co., Cambridge, Mass., 1949.

[2] Edward Sapir, "The Unconscious Patterning of Behavior in Society," *Selected Writings of Edward Sapir in Language, Culture and Personality*, p. 545. University of California Press, Berkeley, California, 1951.

## Organization and Meaning

So that you may more fully understand the relationship between organization and meaning, let us look at the following sentence, which is made up of words quite familiar to you.

| s | t | o | d | e | y |
|---|---|---|---|---|---|
| y | u | t | a | c | a |
| a | o | s | e | n | w |
| s | e | i | r | e | e |
| t | s | e | e | t | h |
| i | n | n | b | n | t |
| t | e | o | d | e | s |
| a | s | y | l | s | i |
| h | e | n | u | s | s |
| w | k | a | o | i | i |
| f | a | f | h | h | h |
| o | m | i | s | t | t |

Before reading further, look at the sentence again. Have you understood its meaning? How have you tried to organize the letters? Have you persistently tried to organize them from left to right and from top to bottom? We suggest now that you forget the left-to-right pattern imposed by your culture and look at the lower right-hand corner first. Read up four letters and draw a light horizontal line. Proceed by reading up each column of letters. Do the letters now fall into recognizable patterns?

As one further simple illustration of the fact that organization yields meaning, look at the three ways of arranging the simple words "he," "only," "her," "watched." Those words may be arranged in one of the three following sequences: (1) "Only he watched her," (2) "He watched her only," (3) "He only watched her." The same words have quite different meanings according to their order.

Language is inevitably an orderly arrangement of symbols, so much so that some aspects are predictable. The order of letters is relatively fixed and may call to our minds spelling. The order of sounds is one aspect of pronunciation. The order of words is less rigid and a matter that allows the speaker considerable latitude. Again, though, some arrangements of the words are more natural than others. In contrast to the sentences suggested above, the sentence "Mary held a rose" has no alternative arrangements of words which would make sense to us; however, we could add or insert "between her index finger and thumb" after "rose," after "held," or before "Mary," and we seem to have complete freedom to interchange the words "index finger" and "thumb." This somewhat oversimplified introduction to the problem of organizing our knowledge has, we hope, served to clarify the principle that "knowing," or "having meanings," depends upon perceiving the structure, the relatedness of the parts, in a whole. In brief, we may summarize by stating that having meanings implies some organization of details.

Much of the structure, or organization, of the universe is still unknown. Much is only hypothesized or guessed at. A great deal, however, is "known." As human meanings have evolved, they have fallen into organized patterns in biology, chemistry, physics, geology, psychology, history, religion, ethics, etc. The very development of man's complex patterns of symbols has given man the power to perceive and to express many types of relations between objects and events. In addition to relations of space and time, he has formulated symbols for expressing relations of cause and effect, linear and nonlinear relationships between events, and the dynamic relations of objects in motion expressed by modern calculus. These make possible new observations and open up new sources of meanings and stimulate still newer patterns of organization. Similarly, the very fact that there exist terms for various racial, religious, psychological, social, economic groupings of people, and terms for expressing interactions between groupings, leads scientists to develop ways of measuring quantitatively such relations.

As college students, you will find it necessary to remember much that has been reported by experts. If you will remember that remembering depends largely upon perceiving the organization as well as the details of any subject area, your efficiency will increase. Your training in this course should help you understand the chronological, economic, and psychological structure of history, the imaginative and ideational relations in literature, and the operational, functional, and quantitative designs of science. As your powers of observing and thinking develop, and as you study for classes in science, in the humanities, and in the arts, you will develop abilities in perceiving and formulating more and more intricate symbolic patterns. You will, thereby, increase your understanding of the intricate structure of the universe in which you live. Your development of your own speech will contribute much to your general education.

At times, your thinking may seem to be without a pattern or

organization of any kind. Your daydreaming, your reflections upon tasks at hand, your conversation with close friends may seem to lack the organization which we have said is inherent in speech. This type of association has been called "free association" by psychologists and psychiatrists, who have studied it both in individuals and in groups. The lack of structure, however, is more apparent than real. For in free association there is an unconscious pattern. Ideas have submerged, or unconscious, interrelations. For example, a college student who was very fearful of speaking, particularly to older men, responded in a series of words to stimulus words. The first word was "blue." Each response word, in turn, was used as a stimulus to evoke another oral response. The sequence of responses was as follows: "Lake Michigan," "holiday," "beach," "swimming," "accident," "spit-it-out," "embarrassment," "father." The student insisted that for 12 years, at least, an incident involving the need to speak quickly while on a holiday with several friends had remained buried in his memory. His oral responses, at first apparently without organization, developed a chronological pattern which brought to consciousness his bitter childhood experience.

The discovery of the structural pattern of our own ideas may be as informative about *us* as the discovery of the structure of the outside world is informative about *it*.

## Organization and Communication

The fact that the free association of words or images has an unconscious organization and that the discovery of that structure is beneficial to the speaker makes possible the therapeutic use of speech for students who suffer stage fright or any other mild anxieties. However, except in groups whose individual members are working together on mental hygiene, the free-association type of talk, with its hidden structure, becomes a barrier to communication. Listeners generally expect to understand quickly and easily. They cannot grasp the hidden structure of free association and become confused and irritated. It is for this reason that many of the very loosely organized public speeches, which resemble free association, create tensions and send the listeners away talking both inwardly and overtly about their frustrations instead of about the speaker's speech. The public speaker, therefore, is compelled to discover the more clear-cut patterns that audiences prefer.

The speaker has many types of patterns to choose from when he talks. Whatever one he selects, however, he should choose on the ground that it is the best to attain his purpose in speaking. If the purpose is to while away the time, little organization is required. If, however, busy people are meeting for a serious purpose, a quickly perceived design is essential. In any case, the organization of a talk emerges from the speaker's perception of his goal in relation to the audience, topic, and occasion. That organization which leads listeners to have images and ideas similar to those of the speaker will most likely achieve the speaker's purpose, while that pattern which has hidden or ambiguous relations between parts confuses and annoys listeners. If a person hopes to communicate well, he must choose his plan of organization carefully.

## Patterns of Arrangement

If you will review for a few moments the books you have read, the movies you have seen, or the lectures you have heard, you will be aware of the widely different patterns the communicators used to present their ideas. Even when the topics or ideas are very similar, their shapes, their arrangements, are quite different. As a student you will have the opportunity to observe that many different patterns may be, so far as we can judge, equally satisfactory. You will also observe that within a speech you may vary the patterns somewhat, but that the over-all plan must be logically and emotionally consistent. To help you with your early planning, we suggest that you study the following plans carefully, modifying and combining them to suit your own purposes and materials. The important consideration is to think about each one in relation to your subject, your audience, and the occasion.

### Imaginative Patterns

Centuries before printing was invented, when speech was the principal means of communication, philosophers speculated about the types of discourse. They observed that poetry and drama had a different form, a different pattern, from history and public speeches. To the former two types of discourse they applied the general term *poetic*, while the latter two, they said, belonged to *rhetoric*. The arrangement of materials in poetic was from image to image and was determined emotionally. The progress in rhetoric was from idea to idea and was based on logic. A modern speaker does not need to be bound by these arbitrary distinctions. Story tellers, travel lecturers, book reviewers, and even some public speakers have developed their discourses largely by images rather than by ideas. Robert Greene Ingersoll's vision of war and vision of peace, both parts of his "Decoration Day Oration of 1888," draw heavily upon the imaginative structure of Percy Bysshe Shelley's "Queen Mab." Compare the imaginative progression of a part of Shelley's poetry with one short passage of Ingersoll's oratory, and you will see how a skillful orator piled image upon image much as the poet did.

*From* QUEEN MAB

"The Present and the Past thou
        hast beheld:
It was a desolate sight. Now,
        Spirit, learn
The secrets of the Future. . . ."
"Here now the human being stands
        adorning
This loveliest earth with taintless
        body and mind; . . ."
No longer now the wingèd habi-
        tants,
That in the woods their sweet lives
        sing away,
Flee from the form of man; but
        gather round,
And prune their sunny feathers on
        the hands
Which little children stretch in
        friendly sport
Towards these dreadless partners
        of their play.
All things are void of terror: Man
        has lost
His terrible prerogative, and stands
An equal amidst equals: happiness
And science dawn though late upon
        the earth;
Peace cheers the mind, health reno-
        vates the frame;
Disease and pleasure cease to
        mingle here,
Reason and passion cease to com-
        bat there;
Whilst each unfettered o'er the
        earth extend
Their all-subduing energies, and
        wield

The sceptre of a vast dominion
        there;
Whilst every shape and mode of
        matter lends
Its force to the omnipotence of
        mind,
Which from its dark mine drags the
        gem of truth
To decorate its Paradise of peace.

PERCY BYSSHE SHELLEY

## From DECORATION DAY ORATION OF 1888

A vision of the future rises:

I see our country filled with happy homes, with firesides of content—the foremost land of all the earth.

I see a world where thrones have crumbled and where kings are dust. The aristocracy of idleness has perished from the earth.

I see a world without a slave. Man at last is free. Nature's forces have by Science been enslaved. Lightning and light, wind and wave, frost and flame, and all the secret, subtle powers of earth and air are the tireless toilers for the human race.

I see a world at peace, adorned with every form of art, with music's myriad voices thrilled, while lips are rich with words of love and truth; a world in which no exile sighs, no prisoner mourns; a world on which the gibbet's shadow does not fall; a world where labor reaps its full reward, where work and worth go hand in hand, where the poor girl trying to win bread with the needle—the needle that has been called "the asp for the breast of the poor"—is not driven to the desperate choice of crime or death, of suicide or shame.

I see a world without the beggar's outstretched palm, the miser's heartless, stony stare, the piteous wail of want, the livid lips of lies, the cruel eyes of scorn.

I see a race without disease of flesh or brain,—shapely and fair, —the married harmony of form and function,—and, as I look, life lengthens, joy deepens, love canopies the earth; and over all, in the great dome, shines the eternal star of human hope.

ROBERT GREENE INGERSOLL

Young speakers will find it difficult to sustain throughout a whole speech the image-by-image arrangement. However, they can do much to break the regularity of speeches otherwise organized if, in parts that permit it, they will weave in descriptive patterns. They need not strive for the "purple patches" of an Ingersoll or a Henry W. Grady. They may merely use simple images to give life and warmth to abstract ideas.

Observe Woodrow Wilson's vivid description of the frontiersman's westward march and how it gave warmth and life to the subject, "The Course of American History."

> . . . But, until they [the American people] had turned their backs once for all upon the sea; until they saw their western borders cleared of the French; until the mountain passes had grown familiar, and the lands beyond the central and constant theme of their hope, the goal and dream of their young men, they did not become an American people.
>
> When they did, the great determining movement of our history began. The very visages of the people changed. That alert movement of the eye, that openness to every thought of enterprise or adventure, that nomadic habit which knows no fixed home and has plans ready to be carried any whither,—all the marks of the authentic type of the "American" as we know him came into our life. The crack of the whip and the song of the teamster, the heaving chorus of boatmen poling their heavy rafts upon the rivers, the laughter of the camp, the sound of bodies of men in the still forests, became the characteristic notes in our air. A roughened race, embrowned in the sun, hardened in manner by a coarse life of change and danger, loving the rude woods and the crack of the rifle, living to begin something new every day, striking with the broad and open hand, delicate in nothing but the touch of the trigger, leaving cities in its track as if by accident rather than design, settling again to the steady ways of a fixed life only when it must: such was the American people whose achievement it was to be to take possession of their continent from end to end ere their national government was a single century old. The picture is a very singular one! Settled life and wild side by side: civilization frayed at the edges,—taken forward in rough and ready fashion, with a song and a swagger,—not by statesmen, but by woodsmen and drovers, with axes and whips and rifles in their hands, clad in buckskin, like huntsmen.

### Spatial Patterns

Talks on astronomy, geography, military tactics, football strategy, and weather often necessitate some use of spatial patterns. If care is taken to group the spatial details which are contiguous, instead of merely enumerating a long list of items, and if they are connected by transitional phrases, then the audience will visualize, understand, and remember more easily. Walter Orr Roberts's lecture "Stormy Weather on the Sun," given under the auspices of the Smithsonian Institution on March 22, 1951, contains many such phrases as the following:[3]

[3] Walter Orr Roberts, "Stormy Weather on the Sun," *Annual Report of the Smithsonian Institution*, pp. 163–174, 1952.

The sun is a gaseous sphere. As you go down toward the center . . . There near the nucleus . . . It is here in the depths . . . Lying directly on the surface . . . The transition layer between the spotted surface . . . At the edge of the sun . . . The intercession of the moon between the earth and the sun . . . The corona . . . surrounds the eclipsed sun . . .

## Temporal Patterns

One important determiner of arrangement is time, the sequence in which events occurred. The first-grade child, in recounting the events of a birthday party, is likely to say "and then" often. The party is a sequence of events, and the sequence is the order in which they occurred. The influence of time pervades all human experience. It is continuous and nonrecurrent, facts that are exploited currently by funeral directors as they place clocks on the fronts of their establishments. The effect of time sequence on our composition is marked. The student's weekly letter home may narrate the events from Monday through "today." The account of a trip may progress from "when we left" to "when we returned." The recipe book explains the ingredients of the cake in the order in which they are added. The directions on the can of polish go from "first" to "finally." The argument for the city income tax may run chronologically. The award of a distinctive prize may begin with "This girl has always been outstanding" and include references to successive accomplishments. In short, time is a great common denominator among speakers and listeners and provides a natural genesis for ordering ideas. Time influences the verbal accounts of children who have never given a passing thought to "organization," of persons who have no formal education, as well as eminent scholars who write series of volumes on world civilization.

In recounting the past, a speaker wishing to use a time arrangement need not always arrange the events in the order in which they occurred, from first to last. Successful dramatists like Kaufman and Hart have begun with a significant late event and have retraced scene by scene the occurrences leading up to it. Short-story writers often use the "flashback." Eulogies and character sketches, too, may begin with an individual's latest and most significant contributions and retrace the two or three main streams of influence upon the character.

## Topical Patterns

Another grouping of ideas is a view of the parts that comprise the whole. This may include the notion of sequence that we discussed in the preceding paragraph, but having treated time order, we shall not include it here. We look at a shelf of books and may see red covers, blue covers, etc. We take another view and may see history books, English books, etc. In either instance, with possibly no conscious deliberation on our part, the books fall into categories that when summated account for all the books. Such *classes* of events, ideas, objects, or attributes give us the basis for many of our groupings of ideas or orderings of sequential portions of our composition, oral or written. Books are principally classified by topics in libraries. Botany and zoology include systems of elaborate classifications. The yellow pages of the telephone directory classify business houses by topics (although we also need the *sequential* alphabet in order to locate a particular firm). In discussions of such topics as "We Need Sidewalks," "Public Parks Are Beneficial," "The Student Body Should Support Our Activity," groupings of ideas come to mind, possibly with a single word as the common denominator, for example, "safety," "property values," "health"; with parks, "juvenile delinquency"; with sidewalks, "adult recreation"; with our activity, "attract students," "meet the competition," "improve morale," "put classwork into operation," "get more for our tuition." These three, two, or five groups (there is no fixed number) when summated should equal the *point, topic, central idea,* or *thesis* that we are interested in developing.

The topical method is useful because many of our meanings are extremely general. Even when we attempt to bring those meanings down to specific instances they are still somewhat elusive. About the best we can do is to relate them to other somewhat less general ideas. Let us suppose, for instance, you were trying to explain an American college to someone who was not familiar in any way with one. Would you begin with the buildings and campus? The curricula? The students? The faculty? The athletic program? How would you proceed? You would probably do the best you could by talking about major aspects of college, knowing full well that some topics would have to be omitted. The order in which you took up the topics might not matter.

This method is easy, perhaps too easy, since it does not always require rigorous thinking and complete classification. It has been used by popular speakers and writers under various disguises. Thomas Dewitt Talmadge, under the topic "Big Blunders," amplified five actions which he called blunders. Logically there could have been ten or twenty. The only limits would be the audience's staying powers. On the other hand, the method permits even rigorous thinkers to treat an obviously limited number of aspects of complicated problems. The statement of the topics gives the listeners the mental pegs from which Macaulay, the historian, thought a speech should be suspended. Many examples of the excellent use of this type of organization appear in the scientific speeches printed in the *Annual Report of the Smithsonian Institution.*

## Graphical Patterns

Walter Lippmann, columnist and author of books on politics and social philosophy, when speaking before a medical association, chose the subject "The Living Organism of Our Society." His patterns of thought were drawn from a living human, which the medical men could quickly visualize. A geologist talking on oil in Michigan used the familiar pattern of a mitten with a free little finger and a free thumb suggestive of the map of Michigan. The oil fields were "placed" in relation to the thumb, the palm, and the base of the imaginary mitten. Scientific, philosophical, theological, and other types of highly abstract talks may be more easily followed if a graphic pattern to relate the parts can be used. At the same time, as we pointed out in Chap. 7, the graphic or metaphorical pattern should not be permitted to induce false or inaccurate relations. A state may roughly resemble a hand, but there are differences which cannot be forgotten. A society may seem roughly to resemble a body, but there would be confusion about what part was the "head" and what part the "tail." If care is taken to avoid metaphorical fallacies, however, and if the graphic analogy is selected judiciously, a graphic organization of parts greatly facilitates the communication of meaning. In reality, the graphic method makes use of the fact that visual experience involving spatial relations makes up our most common thought patterns and that visualization, although oversimplified, is quick and easy.

## Logical Patterns

The arranging of ideas according to some logical pattern is a common one when the speaker's purpose is to prove his main idea. The subordinate thoughts stand as proof for the primary or main idea. The logical pattern may be a deductive one in which a general truth is brought to bear upon a particular case in question. If, for instance, in Chap. 6 you believed Mrs. Montoya died first, your general knowledge of fingerprints, of the manner of springing between jammed cars, etc., would be used to prove the particular statement: "Mrs. Montoya died first." Each subheading might be proved by the specific facts observed.

Obviously, this is the method used most frequently in debate, both legal and legislative.

The pattern may be an inductive one in which a number of particular occurrences are adduced to prove a general rule or theory. For instance, proof that yellow fever was carried by the mosquito was accumulated by observing the specific instances in which individuals who were exposed to mosquitoes which had fed on yellow fever victims caught the disease, while other individuals not exposed did not catch it. This method may be developed along relatively simple designs which lead to a general rule, true only part of the time. Or it may be extended into intricate experimental designs involving refined statistical procedures and yielding rather close measurements of probability. This method is well suited to talks before scientific groups who demand rigorous logical procedures. It is poorly suited to general audiences, since they find the procedures somewhat difficult to follow.

### Psychological Patterns

Although all the patterns thus far suggested should be used only in terms of their suitability to a particular audience, and should, therefore, be evaluated for their psychological effectiveness, still their characteristic forms do not depend upon psychological considerations alone. There are, however, other patterns of organization, which are primarily formed around points of interaction among the speaker, the subject, the audience, the time. These patterns evolve primarily from psychological considerations. Speeches before hostile audiences, speeches on topics foreign to listeners' interests, speeches on intricate and complex subjects before uninitiated audiences need an organization that proceeds from the known to the unknown, from the accepted to the unaccepted, from the interesting to the less interesting. Of course, in some situations, the speaker must recognize that the entire speech may be only a preparation for later, more advanced developments.

## Preparing the Detailed Pattern

After the speaker has selected his speech topic, he needs to plan the development of his speech. What he includes, of course, is determined by what he knows and by what is suitable to the audience. Methods of analyzing the audience will be explained in Chap. 9. For the present, let us say that if the speaker expects to hold the attention of the audience, he must be sure to have a variety of ideas, illustrations, examples, comparisons, instances, etc., to develop each division of his speech. Beginning students have found the following outline of procedure helpful.

1. Write out concisely what you expect to achieve by your speech. How do you hope the audience will react?

2. Whether you express it at the beginning of the delivered speech, at the end, or whether you only imply it, phrase carefully the statement that you think will motivate the audience to do what you wish.

3. Select your pattern of organization.

4. Divide your ideas into two, three, or four principal parts, according to the patterns you have selected.

    a. If imaginative, what are the three or four large pictures you wish to paint?

    b. If spatial, sketch the broad outlines of each division.

    c. If temporal, what are the main units of time or stages of development?

    d. If topical, what is the basis of division? Have all important topics been covered? Do any of the topics duplicate one another? Is any one topic as comprehensive as the whole subject? The main partitions of your speech should follow only one principle of division. If they do not, they will be likely to overlap.

    e. If graphical, are the comparisons consistent throughout? Are they more familiar and vivid than the ideas themselves?

    f. If logical, does each of the main arguments support the statement of purpose, theme, or thesis?

    g. If psychological, are the motives carefully analyzed? Are they strong and important enough to justify their use?

5. Without too much concern at first for order, write down all your ideas and facts, using a plan similar to that suggested below.

*Materials Chart*

Main idea:

  I. Specific instances

    1.

    2.

    3.

II. General illustrations
   1.
   2.
   3.
III. Comparisons or analogies
   1.
   2.
   3.
IV. Anecdotes or incidents
   1.
   2.
   3.
 V. Quotations
   1.
   2.
   3.
VI. Statistics
   1.
   2.
   3.

6. Organize the ideas and facts given under Project 5 into the pattern you have selected. The following outline form is suggestive:

*Organization Chart*

   1. Statement of specific response wanted from the audience:
   2. Statement of theme or central idea:

Introduction

 I. Type              Purpose
II. Materials

Body

Main idea I.
  Division A.
    Materials 1.
          2.
          3.
  Division B.
    Materials 1.
          2.
          3.

Main idea II.
  Division A.
    Materials 1.
            2.
            3.
  Division B.
    Materials 1.
            2.
            3.

*Conclusion*

I. Type                     Purpose
II. Materials

7. Prepare an appropriate introduction and conclusion. Introductions should arouse interest in the subject and establish friendly relations between the speaker and the audience. A conclusion should show that the speaker knows he has completed his treatment of the subject. It should clinch matters or ask for future consideration.

## SPEECH INTRODUCTIONS AND CONCLUSIONS

### EDD MILLER

Although texts in speech nearly always emphasize the importance of introductions and conclusions to the general effectiveness of a speech, there have been few objective studies made of the proportionate length of the introduction and the conclusion to the rest of the speech; and there have been few inductive studies of types of introductions and conclusions actually used by contemporary speakers.

This article is a brief report of a study of contemporary practice by British and American speakers in their use of introductions and conclusions. An attempt was made to determine (1) the average length of

---

Edd Miller, "Speech Introductions and Conclusions," *Quarterly Journal of Speech* (April 1946), pp. 181–183. Reprinted by permission of the Speech Association of America and of the author.

Edd Miller is Professor of Speech and Assistant to the Vice-President for Academic Affairs, University of Michigan.

introductions and conclusions in contemporary speeches in proportion to the total length of the speech, and (2) the types of introductions and conclusions used in contemporary speeches. The study was not concerned with the purposes of the introductions and conclusions considered, nor did I attempt to judge the effectiveness of particular introductions and conclusions in the speeches studied.

For the study fifty speeches by contemporary British and American speakers were studied. These speeches were fifty consecutive ones as they appeared in Vital Speeches of the Day from June 15, 1943, to September 1, 1943.[1] Some speakers were represented more than once, with a total of forty-four speakers presented.

Each of the fifty speeches was studied with a view to finding the following data: (1) the type of speech, (2) the length of the speech, (3) the percentage of the speech devoted to the introduction, (4) the percentage of the speech devoted to the conclusion,[2] (5) the type of introduction, and (6) the type of conclusion.

## Length of Introductions and Conclusions

Of the fifty speeches, there were twenty to convince, twelve to inform, and eighteen to stimulate. The average percentage length of introductions and conclusions and the range in percentage length for each of the three types of speeches can be seen in Table I.

**TABLE I.**    Length of Introduction and Conclusions[3]

| Type of Speech | Introductions | | Conclusions | |
|---|---|---|---|---|
| | Range | Average | Range | Average |
| 1. Convince | 2%–17% | 7.5% | 1%–15% | 4.9% |
| 2. Inform | 2%–29% | 8.9% | 3%–8% | 5.3% |
| 3. Stimulate | 1%–38% | 13.0% | 2%–13% | 9.4% |
| 4. All Speeches | 1%–38% | 9.8% | 1%–15% | 5.4% |

[1] Vital Speeches of the Day, 9, Nos. 17–22 (June 15–September 1, 1943), 514–699. In this period there were a few speeches of other countries. These speeches were omitted from the study.

[2] Determining exactly where the introduction ended and the main discussion began or where the discussion ended and the conclusion began was sometimes difficult. In such cases the author relied on his own judgment as to the exact dividing line. Usually, however, the division was easily seen.

[3] All figures in Tables I and II represent percentage of total length of speech.

From this table it can be seen that there is a difference in length of introductions and conclusions among various types of speeches, with the speech to convince having the shortest introductions and conclusions and the speech to stimulate having the longest. The type speech with the shortest introduction also has the shortest conclusion; the type speech with the longest introduction also has the longest conclusion, and so on. The average length of the speech introduction in the speeches studied was 9.8 per cent of the speech length, and the average conclusion was 5.4 per cent of the speech. These figures compare closely with those found in other studies. Table II shows the findings of studies made by Hayworth,

**TABLE II.** Comparison with Other Studies

| Study | Length of Introductions | Length of Conclusions |
|---|---|---|
| Hayworth | 9.00% | 5.10% |
| MacVaugh[4] | 15% (21.69%) | 4% (3.75%) |
| Runion | 8.55% | 9.12% |
| This Study | 9.80% | 5.40% |

MacVaugh and Runion[5] as compared with the findings of this study. It will be noticed from Table II that, in general, the percentage of a speech devoted to introduction and conclusion was found to be about the same in each of the four studies. There is one significant variation in the length of introductions[6] and one in the length of conclusions. However, it seems safe to say that on the basis of these findings, the introduction of a speech usually occupies about 9 per cent of the total length of the speech, and the conclusion usually takes up about 5 per cent.

[4] The first figure represents the average length as found in thirty random speeches from Beecher to 1932; the figure in parenthesis shows the average length for eighteen random sermons of Fosdick.

[5] For a complete report on these studies see: Donald Hayworth, "An Analysis of Speeches in Presidential Campaigns from 1884 to 1920," *Quarterly Journal of Speech*, 16 (1930), 35–42; Gilbert Stillman MacVaugh, "Structural Analysis of the Sermons of Dr. Harry Emerson Fosdick," *Quarterly Journal of Speech*, 18 (1932), 531–546; and Howard L. Runion, "An Objective Study of the Speech Style of Woodrow Wilson," *Speech Monographs*, 3 (1936), 75–94.

[6] The speeches studied by MacVaugh would be classified as speeches to stimulate; bearing that in mind, the 15% (21.69%) figures come closer to the 13% length found here for speeches to stimulate. The difference, then, may not be significant.

## Types of Introductions and Conclusions

Eleven different types of introductions were found in the speeches studied, and ten different types of conclusions. As in the lengths of introductions and conclusions, there were variations in the types of introductions and conclusions among the three types of speeches. Table III shows the frequency of use in each type of the eleven kinds of introductions found in the fifty speeches.

**TABLE III.**    Types of Introductions

| Type | Convince | Inform | Stimulate | Total |
|---|---|---|---|---|
| 1. Reference to Subject | 6 | 4 | 3 | 13 |
| 2. Reference to Audience | 3 | 2 | 2 | 7 |
| 3. Reference to Occasion | 0 | 0 | 6 | 6 |
| 4. Quotation | 2 | 1 | 2 | 5 |
| 5. Reference to Current Events | 5 | 0 | 0 | 5 |
| 6. Historical | 2 | 2 | 0 | 4 |
| 7. Anecdote | 1 | 0 | 2 | 3 |
| 8. Startling Statement | 1 | 1 | 1 | 3 |
| 9. Question | 0 | 1 | 1 | 2 |
| 10. Humor | 0 | 1 | 0 | 1 |
| 11. Personal Reference | 0 | 0 | 1 | 1 |

The kinds of conclusions found in the examination of these fifty speeches can be seen in Table IV.

Textbook classifications of the types of introductions and conclusions are generally sound; the types given here show no significant deviation from the normal listing of the types of introductions and

**TABLE IV.**    Types of Conclusions

| Type | Convince | Inform | Stimulate | Total |
|---|---|---|---|---|
| 1. Challenge | 5 | 2 | 7 | 14 |
| 2. Quotation | 4 | 0 | 6 | 10 |
| 3. Summary | 5 | 1 | 1 | 7 |
| 4. Visualizing the Future | 2 | 3 | 2 | 7 |
| 5. Appeal | 1 | 3 | 1 | 5 |
| 6. Inspirational | 1 | 1 | 1 | 3 |
| 7. Advice | 0 | 1 | 0 | 1 |
| 8. Proposal of Solution | 1 | 0 | 0 | 1 |
| 9. Question | 1 | 0 | 0 | 1 |
| 10. Reference to Audience | 0 | 1 | 0 | 1 |

conclusions to be found in any accepted text on speech composition. The fact that many different kinds of introductions and conclusions were used in the fifty speeches examined would seem to indicate that introductions and conclusions do not automatically fall into pre-determined categories; too much seems to depend upon the type of speech, the audience, the occasion, and the speaker himself. Wherever lists of types of introductions and conclusions are given, it should be made clear that they are merely guides, not rigid patterns, and the lists should be inclusive enough to indicate the wide differences in practice.

# 4 Language and Style

In this section we shall be concerned primarily with three questions: (1) What is language? (2) What is style? and (3) What are the characteristics of effective oral style?

## Language

Language has sound, system, and symbolic meaning. By becoming more aware of these *resources* of language we can improve our style.

*Language has sound.* All sounds have certain fundamental attributes: loudness, pitch, duration, and quality. The speaker's voice is not limited to any one given pitch, loudness, duration, or even to one quality; the vocal mechanism with its set of complex neuromuscular controls is capable of a range of variations for each attribute. Our primary interest is not so much the actual characteristics of sound as the relationships between sound and meaning. The two relationships most helpful for the speaker are onomatopoeia and "sound suggestion." Onomatopoeia depends upon direct imitation ("buzz," "swish," "flash," "thump"), while "sound suggestion" implies a much more subtle relationship between sound and meaning. Here, rather than being imitative, sound is suggestive. Consider the sounds of the English language: some are long and fluid, some are harsh and short. Winston Churchill, for example, called Hitler a "bloodthirsty guttersnipe" and Mussolini a "jackal."[1] This kind of relationship between sound and meaning needs much further exploration before we are sure of the exact nature of the relationship.

*Language has structure.* Every language has some system—a complex pattern which every speaker must follow to be understood. Certain sound combinations, for example, are never found in English. Although we do have words with initial sound combinations such as *tr* (traffic), *thr* (through), and *dr* (drama), we do not have words which begin with the sound combinations *tl, thl,* or *dl. Th* may be followed by *a, e, i, o, u, r, w,* or *y,* but not by *l.*

---

[1] Jane Blankenship, *Public Speaking: A Rhetorical Perspective* (Englewood Cliffs, New Jersey: Prentice-Hall, Inc., 1966). See especially the chapter "Style: Some Theoretical Considerations."

The arrangement of words, too, follows certain patterns. We never say, "Children the are playing," because articles must precede nouns—"The children are playing." Parts of speech must also agree: one girl walks, many girls walk.

Words fall into categories with certain formal characteristics. English nouns have a plural form; adjectives do not. We can change an adjective to an adverb by adding *-ly*, but we cannot do this with a noun. Robert A. Hall, Jr., discusses this point further:

> The reason we say that *reflection* is a noun is, not that it refers to a person, place or thing (for *reflection, light, matter* and many other nouns do not), but that it fits into the system of the English language in the same way as do other words which we call nouns. The word *reflection* can take the suffix -'s (reflection's); it can, if necessary, be used in the plural (*reflections*); it can have the word *the* used before it (*the reflection*). Those things are true of all English nouns; and they are all features, not of the nouns' meaning, but of their form.[2]

Order is functional, as the following sentences reveal:

Ted struck Jim.
Jim struck Ted.

Although the words have remained the same in these sentences, the order of the words has changed and so has the meaning of the sentence.

This concept of "structural meaning" is further developed in John V. Irwin's article "How Linguistic Forms Acquire Meaning." This selection introduces some of the central terms of language study: phoneme (the basic acoustic element of oral language), morpheme (the basic grammatical element of language), and semantic meaning (the relationship of a word to the object which it represents).

Every decision the speaker makes about the structure of his sentences has far-reaching consequences. For example, Rulon Wells discusses the differences between nominal and verbal style and shows how the simple fact that some people prefer verbs to nouns (or vice versa) helps determine such factors as sentence length and diversity of sentence patterns. Although Wells is concerned primarily with writing in this selection, his point holds true for speaking as well.

[2] From *Linguistics and Your Language,* by Robert A. Hall, Jr. Copyright 1950 by Robert A. Hall, Jr. Permission of Robert A. Hall, Jr.

*Language has symbolic meaning.* That words are symbols for things or concepts is the attribute of language of which we are most aware. Yet that very attribute is the one which gives us the most difficulty. We know what words mean to us, but we cannot always be sure what they mean to others. And even if we do agree what thing or concept a word symbolizes (its *denotation*), we may have different ideas about the attitudes and feelings which the word suggests (its *connotations*). There have already been some journeys into "semantic space" in order to determine why we fail and succeed in trying to communicate with one another,[3] but much further study is needed to give us full insight into meaning in language.

## Style

Now that we have discussed briefly the resources of language, let us explore the ways in which an individual speaker can manipulate those resources to achieve an effective oral style. But perhaps we should pause first to raise the question: What is style?

*Toward a definition.* The usual Greek word for style, *lexis,* had the triple connotation of thought and word (*logos*) and speaking (*legein*). Since the time of the ancient Greeks there have been literally hundreds of definitions for the term "style," varying from Jonathan Swift's "proper words in proper places" to Buffon's "Style is the man himself." The first, perhaps, tells us what good (proper) style is, but it does not tell us what style itself is. The second definition, while much more interesting, is so broad that it provdes us with no real starting place.

An individual's style is his unique way of using the resources of the English language. Words, as we have said, represent objects or concepts; therefore, a man's choice and arrangement of words—his style—reflects his unique way of looking at the world. Style is not just some kind of peripheral ornament, added to a speech when it has already been thought through. Just as *what* a man sees influences and is influenced by *how* he sees, so style and content cannot be separated; each influences the other.

*Qualities of effective style.* Generally style can be considered under two main heads: choice of words and arrangement of words. In "Rhetorical Qualities of Words," Richard E. Hughes and P. Albert Duhamel discuss what they term "the most important single factor in determining . . . effectiveness"—the speaker's choice of words. Al-

---

[3] See Charles E. Osgood, "An Exploration into Semantic Space" in *The Science of Human Communication,* ed. Wilbur Schramm (New York: Basic Books, Inc., 1963).

though written for "the writer" and often illustrated from poetry as well as prose, their article is usually applicable to the public speaker as well. Both speaker and writer must ask some of the same questions: Is my language clear? Is it appropriate? Is it effective?[4]

We can find the answers to these questions by learning to analyze the works of others to see how they have achieved certain effects, and by applying the principles derived from that analysis to our own speaking. Only then can we use style effectively as a *means of persuasion*. Speeches can be transcribed from tape or studied from manuscript and considered in terms of these questions: (1) What did the speaker hope to achieve? (2) By what linguistic strategies did he try to achieve his purposes? (3) How else could it have been done? (4) Which alternative suggestions are better? (5) Why?[5]

[4] A number of rhetoricians have treated of the differences between oral and written style. One of the first such studies was by Gladys Borchers, "An Approach to the Problem of Oral Style," *Quarterly Journal of Speech* (February 1936), pp. 114–117. See the Bibliography for other studies of oral style.

[5] Jane Blankenship, "On the Teaching of Style," *The Speech Teacher* (March 1964), pp. 99–102.


## HOW LINGUISTIC FORMS ACQUIRE MEANINGS

### JOHN V. IRWIN

## Language Unity

Leonard Bloomfield (1926) in a frequently cited statement describes an act of speech as an utterance. As has been repeatedly recognized, both in common-sense, day-to-day observation and in rigidly controlled scientific investigation, the standard utterances within a given speech community tend to be essentially alike. The particular concern of this chapter is the study of (a) those oral linguistic forms which are essentially alike and (b) those stimulus reaction features which are respectively alike in two or more successive utterances. In this sense any

From *The Psychology of Communication* by Jon Eisenson, J. Jefferey Auer, and John V. Irwin. Copyright © 1963 by Meredith Publishing Company. Reprinted by permission of Appleton-Century-Crofts.

John V. Irwin is Professor of Speech at the University of Wisconsin.

community that uses like—or nearly like—utterances is a speech community. The complete sum, the totality, of utterances that can be made in a speech community is the language of that speech community.

Bloomfield (1926) suggests that the language act may be conveniently analyzed under the following three headings:

A. A person reacts to certain stimuli.
B. This reaction may be in the form of speech.
C. This speech in turn stimulates his hearers (or himself) to certain reactions.

Within a given language community, the A, B, and C of the above break-down acquire a close intracorrelation. Social habits beginning in infancy and continuing throughout life ensure the development and maintenance of these relationships. Bloomfield (1926) emphasizes that the stimuli classified as A, and the reactions, classified as C, are very closely linked, as each person acts differently as a speaker or as a hearer. On the other hand, the linguistic features, classified as B, must be treated separately. As noted by Weiss (1918), the significant item in the above analysis of the speech process is that the reaction, C, may be either the adequate *reaction* to the total *situation*, or, on the other hand, may become the adequate *stimulus* for either another speech reaction or, for that matter, some other type of reaction.

Perhaps it may be well to make these concepts more specific. A given individual, John, may be exposed to the stimuli from his daily newspaper. As a result of these stimuli, John makes an utterance. Hearing this utterance, Jim reacts. Jim's reaction may be another utterance or may consist of some action such as walking out of the room. Whether Jim replies verbally or non-verbally, new stimuli have been presented to John, who may now react verbally or non-verbally himself. Or he may go back to his newspaper.

It follows that the linguistic forms of a language must have common significance to the users of a language if the A-B-C type of relationship is to prevail predictably. Unless the linguistic forms used by John and by Jim have a high common core of significance, A-B-C type relationships cannot be continued cooperatively. Of course, the degree of identity of significance is never 100 per cent. Yet this lack of completeness of identity should not blind us to the highly significant core of agreement that does obtain among the members of a language community. The important question then becomes: How do linguistic forms acquire their common meaning? Or, somewhat rephrased: What is the process that enables symbols, whether auditory, visual, or tactile, to function with such predictability? This is the question that this chapter will seek to answer.

Later we shall attempt to develop a more complete explanation of this predictability. For the moment, it may be worth noting that the social acts of man probably provide the essential basis for predictability of significance. Mead (1934, p. 7) defines a social act as one which involves "the cooperation of more than one individual, and whose object is defined by the act." It is, therefore, quite possible that the significant symbol—the symbol with predictable significance to users within a language community—arises primarily within such cooperative social acts. On the other hand, it has been strongly urged that symbols can arise also from competitive behavior. Morris (1946, p. 33), for example, defines the comsign in the following terms: "A sign which has the same signification to the organism which produces it that it has to other organisms stimulated by it will be called a comsign." He stipulates, however, that "it is by no means clear that comsigns can arise only in cooperative social behavior. Competitive and even symbiotic social behavior may be sufficient to account for the genesis of some comsigns."

Certain design features in communication have been discussed on pp. 108–9 [of *The Psychology of Communication*]. Here, for purpose of emphasis, it is convenient to recognize two elements in the linguistic expression system, that is, in the B of the A-B-C analysis of Bloomfield. The two elements usually recognized in this expression system are *phonemes* and *morphemes*.

The phonemes are the basic elements of the expression system. Each phoneme, actually, consists of a *class* of very similar (but by no means identical) sounds. Each phoneme—or class—is usually treated as one sound and represented in phonetic transcription by one symbol. Each phoneme class tends to be distinctive, in the sense of differentiating one word from another. Phonemes, then, are the acoustical building blocks of the language. Depending upon the system of classification used, and upon the narrowness of transcription, the number of phonemes recognized in English will vary. In general, however, we may say that in English there are approximately 45 or 46 essential phonemes (Van Riper and Irwin, 1958).

These phonemes or sound-building blocks of a language may be put together in different sequences. The sequences within a given language are not randomly determined; certain sequences occur with much greater frequency than do others. Indeed, as pointed out in Kantner and West

(1941), certain sequences are incompatible and do not occur at all. *Phonology* is the study of phonemes and of the sequences of phonemes (Gleason, 1955).

Since a phoneme is regarded as the minimum acoustic element of oral language, it follows that the phoneme is the element in the sequence that differentiates one thing as having been said from another thing that was not said. Thus the words *bit* and *bat* are differentiated from each other by their respective vowel phonemes.

Phonemes are features of the oral language, of the language as spoken. Phonetic transcription attempts to represent the phonemes of spoken language. A crudely analogous basic unit of the written language is the grapheme. But, from the standpoint of the present analysis, it must be kept in mind that the written language is really not an independent entity; it is a dependent extension of the spoken language.

As indicated earlier, the second division in the expression system of a language is the morpheme. Morphemes enter into a close, significant, predictable relationship with the content of language. In linguistics a morpheme is defined as a word (or stable part of a word) that conveys meaning. Morphemes are typically composed of one phoneme—as in the word *a*—or several phonemes—as in the word *encyclopedia*. *Grammar* is the term applied to the study of morphemes and their combinations.

From the standpoint of the present chapter, the importance of the distinction between morphemes (grammar) and phonemes (phonology) is that morphemes typically have meanings and phonemes typically do not.

Some partial exceptions to this distinction must be noted. Since it is the phonemic sequence that determines the particular morpheme, it may be argued that the phoneme does contribute to meaning. But this argument does not contradict the notion that the isolated phoneme is essentially meaningless, and that the isolated morpheme is essentially meaningful. In this connection, it should be recognized that an occasional phoneme acquires permanent morphemic characteristics. For example, "sh" has come to mean "Be quiet." But the meaning thus acquired is as a morpheme and not as a phoneme.

It should also be mentioned that sequence in and of itself is a heavy-handed determiner of meaning. Phonemes by themselves, as already developed, are essentially meaningless. Phonemes in proper sequence become morphemes. Isolated morphemes have some meaning. Morphemes in accepted sequence have considerably more meaning. Meaning, then, is in part a function of the symbol: that is, the morpheme; it is also in part a function of the sequence in which the morpheme appears.

To carry the idea of sequence somewhat further, Stewart (1946) insists that not until the appearance of nouns was real language possible. Stewart contends that nouns and nouns alone make propositions possible. Actually, it is not desirable to push Stewart's distinction too far, because even ancient grammarians quite clearly recognized that adjectives and substantives are closely connected. The classical terms for the two classes, nouns and adjectives, indicate the closeness of this relationship. The *nomen adiectiuum* (adjective) is simply the noun that is added to the *nomen substantium* (noun) in order to suggest some special quality which the noun displays in the particular situation to which the speaker refers: thus, black hair as opposed to gray hair.

Nevertheless Stewart's insistence on the importance of propositionality is well taken. Eisenson (1957) has repeatedly stressed the importance of propositionality as opposed to non-propositionality in the speech of the stutterer and in the speech of the aphasic. Thus, to the extent that propositionality is proportionate to meaning, to that extent does the difficulty of the stutterer with fluency increase, to that extent does the difficulty of the aphasic exist.

Lerea (1958), writing partly as a speech pathologist, partly as a psychologist, and partly as a linguist, comments that it is possible to explain linguistic meaning as the sum of at least two components: lexicon and structure. Lerea adds that "the lexical meaning" of the word may be found in any dictionary. This lexical meaning, in the sense that Lerea is using the term, is the significance of the isolated word symbol. Of more importance, in the present context, is the term "structural meaning." Usually the term structural meaning refers to the relationship between the lexical elements in a particular utterance. Many examples of the effect of such relationships occur in English. In the example given by Lerea, the following statements occur:

1. The man found the black boot.
2. The bootblack found the man.

Obviously, the above sentences contain identical morphemes. Yet the two sentences would suggest to most users of English two entirely different meanings. Why? Simply because meaning in English is partly a function of morpheme and partly a function of morpheme sequence. The example here given is contrived to show the importance of sequence.

Although contrived, it is not isolated in principle. The example, in short, should be considered as representative rather than as exceptional.

In oral language, variation in the use of stress also makes frequent and important contribution to meaning along with choice of morpheme and morpheme order. For example, note how the meaning of the following sentence changes, depending on the stress that is employed. In the examples as printed, the word parts to be stressed are shown in italics.

1. We like light *house*keeping.
2. We like *light*house keeping.

Clearly, the morphemes in sentence No. 1 and sentence No. 2 are identical and in the same order. Yet, in oral usage, the stress pattern tells the listener that No. 1 refers to a form of conventional residency and No. 2 to an occupation with marine overtones. On the printed page, differences in morpheme division may also give a visual clue.

Another example follows. The same code will be followed as in the above example. But, in this instance, the reader may make his own interpretation.

1. I saw a *black*snake pit.
2. I saw a black *snake*pit.

## Symbols: What They Are and What They Do

*Semantics* is concerned with the relations between the symbols of a language and their meaning. This definition should be carefully set apart from the definition of *general* semantics which is related to the many ways in which the meanings of words and other symbols change the reponses of human beings to their environment and to each other.

It is probably desirable to review the distinction between symbols and signs. Whatmough (1956, p.19) states: "Of symbols there is nothing in the nature of things that gives them the meaning stated; that is something *we* have given them, by agreement or convention, so that the symbol acquires a certain arbitrary character." Whatmough is here stressing the arbitrary nature of the true symbol. We must re-emphasize that there is no essential, basic, fundamental, necessary, inherent relationship between a symbol and its meaning. The relationship is arbitrary. It is a "created-by-man" relationship. It is a relationship that exists only among the users of a given language, among the speakers of a given language community.

Oddly enough, once a symbol has been designated by a language community, it tends to sound right. A table is called a table because a table is a table. Of course, if a table had been called a *glomph* by early speakers of our language, the argument would run that a glomph is called a glomph because a glomph is a glomph.

As indicated, once a symbol-referent pattern is established, it tends to be both accepted and relatively permanent. Yet language is not static. And one strong factor making for change is a linguistic form that is truly confusing to the users of a language. In such instances, one can predict that over sufficient time either the symbol or its referent will be changed.

Now a sign is something different from a symbol. Of signs, Whatmough (1956, p. 19) says: "A sign has a direct relation to its object, like water dripping from the trees is a sign of rain; but the *word* rain (which obviously is not rain or a sign of rain, for I can say it indoors or for that matter I can say it repeatedly even outdoors without getting wet) is a symbol of 'rain' or 'raining.'" Whatmough here stresses the basic difference between a sign and a symbol. The symbol has no inherent relationship to the meaning; the sign has a direct relationship to its object or its meaning. It follows, then, that it is extremely important to keep separate the symbol and the sign as one examines the ways in which linguistic forms acquire meaning. The symbol acquires its arbitrary meaning in a variety of arbitrary ways. The sign reveals its meaning in a series of non-arbitrary situations. The recognizer of a sign and the recognizer of a symbol have both achieved a learned experience. Essentially identical principles of learning, as developed in chapter 6, have made these experiences possible. But, although the learning principles are similar, that which is learned is quite dissimilar. The symbol-meaning is arbitrary; the sign-meaning, inescapably determined.

Morris (1946, p.50) makes somewhat this same distinction, in his case using the terms *signal* and *symbol* as somewhat analogous to *sign* and *symbol*. Morris first quotes from Susanne Langer: "A sign (that is, a signal) indicates the existence—past, present, or future—of a thing, event, or condition. . . ." Thus a term which is used as a sign evokes appropriate action in the presence of its object; a term that is used as a symbol need not evoke such action.

Morris then continues this discussion by stating that signals [signs] announce their objects while symbols lead their interpreters to conceive their objects. He concludes, on the basis of this distinction, that the symbol is on the whole a less reliable term than is a sign. He further points out that when a term is not reliable, behavior becomes naturally hesitant. In summary, then, (a) signs indicate existence more closely than do symbols, (b) signs are likely to be less general than symbols, (c) signs and behavior are more closely tied together, and (d) the effect of both signs and symbols depends upon motivation. Having drawn this distinction between the sign and the symbol, and recognizing that in linguistic form we are dealing primarily with the symbol rather than with the sign, we must also recognize the danger of concentrating on what Morris calls the spoken-heard sign.

It is probably true, as many linguists have insisted, that the spoken language is the basis of symbolic function. It is also true, however, that in our age, an age in which such visual media as cinematography and still photography, television, printing, and painting flourish, it is extremely important not to neglect the visual sign. Fortunately, the analysis here presented, although framed in terms of the spoken-heard symbol, appears to be equally true of all symbols. The printed word, the trade-mark, the arbitrary tonal or visual symbol of the radio or television show—each derives its symbolic function in a manner analogous to that of the spoken word. Of course, visual signs, like heard signs, have a non-arbitrary relationship that differentiates them from visual symbols.

How are symbols actually used, whether these be visual or heard symbols? One important use of the symbol is that of eliciting a specific meaning. Eisenson (1957) stresses that most intelligent and normal human beings learn to use language symbols with sufficient proficiency to elicit specific responses. That is, these individuals learn to express specific ideas through symbols according to the needs of various situations. In this sense, a symbol, a short sequence of symbols, or even a long sequence of symbols, may be said to have *cognitive* meaning. That is, it stimulates information—whether true or false—as do statements from textbooks, from mathematics, and from commentators.

In addition, however, symbols may also be used to elicit emotional responses, whether mild or strong, whether sweet or harsh. Such use may be referred to as the *emotive* use of symbols. It is perhaps obvious that in a particular sequence of symbols, both a specific and an emotional meaning may be conveyed, although typically one or the other of these may predominate.

In addition, a third use of symbols is frequently recognized in which the symbol is used to give a request, a command, or an order. This usage of symbols is referred to as the *directive* usage. These three usages, then, the cognitive, the emotive, and the directive, are the three broad applications of symbols that are typically recognized.

In addition, however, certain specialized uses of symbols have been recognized. There may be some question as to the legitimacy of these additional functions, but there can be little question of their existence. The first of these may be called the *ambi-meaning* use of symbols. Here, the evoker *seeks deliberately to put his morpheme sequence together in such fashion as to create a possibility of different interpretations in the mind of his listener.* If such ambi-meaning results accidentally, we have simply poor cognitive use of language, poor directive use of language, or poor emotive use of language. But if such ambi-meaning is the intent of the evoker, then we have a deliberate, specialized function. Under what circumstances would ambi-meaning be the intent of the evoker? In situations in which the evoker is unable or unwilling to commit himself, and in which he may feel an inability or unwillingness of his listener to commit himself, it may be desirable for both evoker and reacter to deal in morpheme sequences of ambiguous reference. More high-level political utterances and academic profundities than we like to admit can be classified as ambi-meaning in nature.

Another classification is the *quasi-meaning*. Phatic communion[1] is one example of this type of interchange. In such usage, highly conventionalized morpheme sequences are presented in situations in which the complete sequence is recognized as having a conventionalized meaning, this conventionalized meaning not necessarily being the true referent either of the individual morphemes or of their order. Fortunately, morphemes are used in this quasi-meaning sense in such stylized fashion that both evoker and reacter usually recognize the intent and situation. If taken literally, such quasi-meaning would frequently be impossible to comprehend. That is, even an observer who is familiar with the lexical meanings of the isolated symbols and the usual effects of sequence on the symbols, would be unable to interpret correctly the reactions to such quasi-meaning communications. For example, a current teenage expression is: "piling up the z's." Like most such expressions, this one will probably have a blessedly short existence. Users of English may have

---

[1] "The term *phatic communion* Bronislaw Malinowski gave to speech which is used to establish the bonds of social communion between individuals. Greetings, pretty compliments, pleasantries, jests, all serve to create a pleasant social atmosphere." (Black and Moore, 1955, pp. 162–3)

difficulty in interpreting this example of quasi-meaning. For those who are curious, the phrase means "sleeping." A heavy-handed adult explanation of this transient literary blight is that it is based on the representation of sleep in cartoons and the funnies by a series of z's.

Finally, the *contra-meaning* of symbols must be recognized. Again, in certain instances, perhaps for humor, perhaps for threat, the evoker will employ a phoneme sequence in a situation in which the exact opposite of the usual signification of the phonemes and their sequence would indicate. Usually, total context plus, in oral speech at least, inflection and facial expression reveal the contra-meaning use of symbols. This is a dangerous technique. If used well, it is effective. If used poorly, its effects can be disastrous. The sleepy hostess who, long after midnight, says, "I'm so sorry that you have to go," is sometimes an example of this phenomenon.

If one tries to generalize and to pull together larger functions of symbols on the basis of the specific uses here indicated, one recognizes, of course, that language is used to communicate. But . . . this is probably not the basic use of language. Perhaps more fundamental is the fact that language enables man to see reality symbolically. To the general semanticist, a disturbing aspect of this function is that symbolic reality may misinterpret objective reality. If such symbolic distortions are not recognized as such, the reaction of humans to their physical environment and to each other will be complicated. To the general semanticist, this is the problem that grows from this usage of language.

As a consequence, users of linguistic forms will derive at least two kinds of satisfaction from the successful employment of these forms. First, there will be what may be termed an objective value. Thus, in the successful use of linguistic forms, the evoker and the reacter may achieve these definite advantages. As Black and Moore (1955, p. 7) state: "(1) Words introduce a refined method of analysis into thinking. (2) They provide a basis of inference, of reaching conclusions not demonstrable to the senses. (3) They make it possible for the mind to conceive the complex rational systems of the world (science, metaphysics, logic, etc. with their many subdivisions)." Perhaps more simply, the objective value of a language enables the user to express his wishes in such [a] way that he may receive them. Such language represents a tremendous extension of the individual's control of his environment.

But, in addition, the successful use of linguistic forms brings subjective values. As will be recalled from the preceding chapter, linguistic forms—as morphemes and language sequences—can acquire secondary reinforcing values. Certain words feel and sound "good." Certain words feel and sound "bad." By verbalizing, then, an experienced user of a language can achieve real subjective satisfactions.

## Communication: A Symbol Function

It is, of course, recognized that communication is a major function of language. Indeed, to the naïve observer of the language process, communication is the sole function of language. Surprisingly enough, however, there is considerable disagreement as to the mode of communication in symbolic function. Whatmough (1956), for example, suggests that in linguistic communication meaning is conveyed from one person to another. This tends to suggest that linguistic symbols, linguistic forms, may be thought of as buckets that somehow or other pick up meaning from the mind of one person, carry this meaning to the mind of another person, and there spill it. There is probably a certain accuracy and cogency in this bucket brigade concept of communication.

Yet it seems likely that the mode of transfer may be accurately viewed in the following sense. Rather than defining the transfer of meaning as being something that occurs from one person to another person, it may be more accurate to regard it, as has Mowrer (1960), as a transfer from one sign to another sign. This distinction emphasizes that if we are to communicate effectively with another individual, that other person must already have—and have neatly related to appropriate linguistic symbols—those meanings with which we shall be dealing. That is, unless the respondent, the reactor, already has meanings related to the symbols used by the evoker, communication stumbles. Examples of this difficulty occur daily in our attempts to communicate with Communist leaders. Words such as "democracy," "freedom," and "elections" seem to have no common significance. Thus, the communicative act may be viewed for the most part as merely changing the signs to which particular meanings are attached, merely shifting or transferring meanings from one sign to another.

## How Symbols Are Learned

The basic learning process by which symbols acquire arbitrary meaning has been discussed in chapter 6. Essentially, what we have is a variety of symbol learning or conditioning. As described previously, if the linguistic form occurs in a situation contiguous to an already established meaning, or experience, the individual ultimately will react to the new symbol as to the old symbol or as to the complete experience.

In the life of the child, this learning experience ordinarily occurs in one of two situations: a formal explanatory situation, or a repeated contextual situation. In the formal explanatory situation, a parent, teacher, peer, or TV ad man seeks to define the meaning of a new or unfamiliar word. In these formal explanatory situations, the word is usually isolated clearly in order that recognition of the symbol will be complete. This isolation may take the form of repeating the word visually or audibly several times, of spelling the word, of saying it with a peculiar voice or inflection, or of printing it with unusually large letters. Thus the linguistic form to be learned is carefully isolated. Concurrently a meaning is related to the symbol. This meaning may be verbal, that is, the new symbol is related to a previously understood verbal sequence. For example, in explaining the word *orange*, the teacher may explain that it is a color, that it is a color something like red and something like yellow. Or, in the demonstration type definition, the teacher would isolate the term *orange* and then point out examples of orange in the child's environment. This formal explanatory situation remains important throughout life. Perhaps it is of greatest importance in infancy and early childhood, but it is a learning experience that most of us continue to experience in later years.

The second major form of learning linguistic forms is the repeated contextual experience. In this circumstance, the listener experiences the new word in a variety of situations. If he is fortunate, these situations will have certain similar elements and certain dissimilar elements. Ultimately, he is able to piece together the similar and separate out the dissimilar and then grasp what the new word means. This is perhaps the more usual way for older children and adults to relate an arbitrary significance to a linguistic form. After hearing a new symbol used in several different contexts, the experienced user of a language will feel some confidence in his meaning.

Both the formal explanatory and the repeated contextual approach usually involve a second phase, that of usage of the symbol. The second phase is most clearly evident in the formal learning situation. The teacher, after completing the explanation, usually suggests that the learner attempt usage of the new form in either a structured or a non-structured situation. In the contextual situation, opportunity for usage usually is not given. Such usage frequently comes spontaneously, and may result in unfortunate experiences. For example, the TV-devoted young daughter of one of the authors referred only to "decorator colors." Any color that she mentioned in a room, in a car, in a landscape, was a "decorator color." Out of her contextual experiences, probably in TV, she had apparently learned the idiom or phrase "decorator color" as one symbol meaning color.

As the above example suggests, an important aspect of usage is the act of *monitoring* and—if necessary—correction. Language learning is not complete until usage has been checked against the standards of the language community. Self-monitoring is the final test of language learning.

## References

Berry, Mildred, and Eisenson, J., *Speech Disorders*. New York: Appleton-Century-Crofts, 1956.

Black, J. W., and Moore, W. E., *Speech*. New York: McGraw-Hill, 1955.

Bloomfield, L., "A Set of Postulates for the Science of Language." *Language*, 1926, II, 153–164.

Eisenson, J., "Aphasia in Adults." In L. E. Travis (Ed.), *Handbook of Speech Pathology*. New York: Appleton-Century-Crofts, 1957. Ch. 12.

Gleason, H. A., *An Introduction to Descriptive Linguistics*. New York: Holt, Rinehart, and Winston, 1955.

Kantner, C. E., and West, R. W., *Phonetics*. New York: Harper, 1941.

Lerea, L., "Assessing Language Development." *Journal of Speech and Hearing Research*, 1958, I, 75–85.

Mead, G. H., *Mind, Self, and Society*. Chicago: University of Chicago Press, 1934.

Morris, C., *Signs, Language, and Behavior*. Englewood Cliffs, New Jersey: Prentice-Hall, 1946.

Mowrer, O. H., *Learning Theory and the Symbolic Processes*. New York: Wiley, 1960.

Stewart, G. R., *Man, an Autobiography*. New York: Random House, 1946.

Van Riper, C., and Irwin, J. V., *Voice and Articulation*. Englewood Cliffs, New Jersey: Prentice-Hall, 1958.

Weiss, A. P., "Conscious Behavior." *Journal of Philosophy, Psychology and Scientific Methods*, 1918, XV, 631–641.

Whatmough, J., *Language*. New York: New American Library, 1956.

## NOMINAL AND VERBAL STYLE

### RULON WELLS

. . . In this and the next two sections I shall confine my discussion to English, and to written English. The advice to shun the nominal style is sometimes put this way: "Don't use nouns where you could use verbs; don't shrink from the use of verbs." This way of putting it takes two things for granted: first, that nominality and verbality are matters of continuous degree, and second, that the continuum is characterized by the proportion of nouns to verbs in a given text. These presumptions, in turn, seem to indicate a "quantization" (quantitative measure) of our variable, by defining it as a ratio—the sort of thing that might be dubbed the Noun-Verb Quotient (NVQ). Before this indication can be precise, however, three points need to be settled.

1. What is a noun? (a) Shall we count pronouns and adjectives as nouns? They share many of the characters that distinguish nouns from verbs. (b) Shall a noun phrase count as a single noun? For example, shall "the foot of the mountain" be reckoned as containing one noun or two?

2. What is a verb? (a) Do nonfinite forms (infinitives, gerunds, participles) count as verbs, as nouns, as both, or as neither? (b) Shall a periphrastic verb like "will do" count as one verb or as two? (c) Shall the verb "to be" count the same as other verbs? (The feeling is sometimes expressed that the copula is not a true verb, since it has a purely logical function. On the other hand, it has person, tense, etc., like other verbs. Thus a discrepancy between its form and its meaning is felt. We might recognize this discrepancy by counting occurrences of forms of "to be" one-half, rather than one; or we might take the view that there is no quantitative way of recognizing the peculiar nature of the copula.)

3. The advice might be formulated a little differently. "Keep the proportion of nouns low and of verbs high." An index that would show whether this advice was being followed would have two parts: a Noun-Word Quotient (NWQ) *and* a Verb-Word Quotient (VWQ). For any

Reprinted from *Style in Language*, ed. Thomas A. Sebeok, by permission of The M.I.T. Press, Cambridge, Massachusetts. Copyright © 1960 by The Massachusetts Institute of Technology.

Rulon Wells is Associate Professor of Linguistics and Philosophy at Yale University.

given text the sum of these two quotients cannot exceed 1.0 and will only equal 1.0 if there are no other parts of speech in the text, but beyond that there is no necessary connection between the two quotients. It would be interesting to determine experimentally whether there is a consistent inverse relation between them.

The problem of quantizing nominality will not be pursued further here. It might well turn out that some of the questions raised are insignificant, for example, that the NVQ of scientific writers differs markedly from that of literary writers, no matter how noun and verb are delimited. But of course these facts could only be determined by experiment, for which reflections such as those of the present paper are a necessary preamble but no substitute.

There is a further consideration of which any treatment, quantitative or otherwise, should take account. Style is understood to be optional like vocabulary, as contrasted with grammar. So far as the writer of English has a choice, what he writes is *his* diction and *his* style; so far as he has none, it is the *English* language. A treatment that respects this optionality will somehow take account of whether, and in how many ways, a sentence with a certain degree of nominality could be replaced by one with a different degree, for example, a highly nominal by a highly verbal sentence. And of course it is understood that mere variation of style is made not to alter the substance or content of what is expressed but only the way of expressing it; underlying the very notion of style is a postulate of *independence of matter from manner*. If a given matter dictates a particular manner, that manner should not be called a style, at least not in the sense that I have been speaking of. But this postulate does not preclude that a certain matter shall favor or "call for" a certain manner—the so-called fitness of manner to matter, or consonance with it.

## Consequences of Nominality

The advice to prefer verbs to nouns makes it sound as though it were a simple substitution, like the choice of familiar words in preference to rare ones, or of short words in preference to long ones. Occasionally this is so, but not in the usual case. In the more nominal phrase "the doctrine of the immortality of the human soul," the particles are different from those in the more verbal phrase "the doctrine that the human soul is immortal"; the one uses prepositions, the other a conjunction. In changing the verb of "He began to study it thoroughly" into the noun of "He began a thorough study of it," we must follow through by a corresponding change of adverb to adjective. The elementary fact of syntax that prepositions and adjectives go with nouns, conjunctions and adverbs with verbs, prevents the contrast of nominality and verbality from being *minimal*.

This fact has two consequences. (1) When nominality is evaluated good or bad, the ground may lie in whole or in part in features entailed by nominality, although distinct from it. (2) And so the nominal-verbal contrast is not a *pure dimension* of style, that is, it is not a variable which can vary without variation in the other basic factors of style.

The aforementioned consequences are necessary ones. Another class must be acknowledged, the probable consequences. From the statistical point of view, necessary consequences appear as those whose probability is 1.0, impossible consequence as those with probability .00, and the less or more probable consequences as those having intermediate probability values.

Even an impressionistic study can estimate some of these probabilities. To facilitate discussion, let us pretend—what is false, but not grossly false—that nominalizing and verbalizing sentences can be paired, so that we can speak of *the* nominal counterpart of such and such a verbal sentence and of *the* verbal counterpart of a given nominal sentence. The intent of this fiction is to concentrate our discussion on differences as near to minimal as is syntactically possible.

A nominal sentence is likely to be longer, in letters and in syllables, than its verbal counterpart. The greater length in the diction of those writers who favor nominal style results from the fact that the noun corresponding to the verb is likely to be longer than the verb—usually because it is derived from the verb stem by suffixes—and the entailed changes (loss of verb endings, replacement of conjunctions by prepositions, etc.) are not likely to compensate. Compare "when we arrive" with "at the time of our arrival"—fourteen letters (including word spaces) replaced by twenty-six, four syllables by eight.

Another likelihood is that the average number of clauses per sentence tends to decrease (the minimum being 1.0), for nominalization replaces conjunctions by prepositions. The sentence "If he does that, he will be sorry" has two clauses; its nominal counterpart "In the event of his doing that, he will be sorry" has only one.

A third likelihood, entailed by the second and also somewhat likely even in the absence of the second condition, is that the number of distinct sentence patterns will decrease. Compound sentences (both with coordinating and with subordinating conjunctions) tend to disappear, so that only simple (subject-predicate) sentences, more or less swollen by parentheses and modifiers, will be left.

## Evaluation of Nominality

Nominality is judged bad by some, good by others.

1. Those who judge nominal style bad judge it so for one or more of the following reasons:

*a.* Nouns are more static, less vivid than verbs. Sometimes this view is defended on deep philosophical grounds. For example, Étienne Gilson (136, p. 199)[1] sees in Aristotle's remark (*De interpretatione* 3.16b19) that "verbs in and by themselves are substantival" a revealing clue to his philosophy; not Aristotle but Thomas Aquinas is the one who gives to "is," to existence *in actu exercito*, its full due. And to the argument that the traditional, semantical definitions of noun and verb are of no avail because what one language considers an action, another may treat as a state, the rejoinder might be made that this is just the point: the contrast of action and state varies with the point of view, and one that does not reduce all actions to states is to be recommended. Something like this seems to be intended by Peter Hartmann, to whom I shall refer in the next section.

*b.* Longer sentences are (on the whole) less vivid and less comprehensible than shorter ones.

*c.* A text whose sentences are all or mostly of one basic pattern will usually be monotonous. Verbal style allows more diversity, and a good style will exploit the genius of its language.

2. Those who judge nominal style good do so implicitly, for the most part; nominal style is practiced more than preached. The implicit reasons in its favor appear to be these:

*a.* It is easier to write. Thus it is natural for those who are more concerned with what they say than with how they say it to choose this style, or to drift into it.

*b.* It helps impersonality. In scientific writing ("scientific" in the

---

[1] On quite different grounds some philosopher mentioned but not named by Aristotle (Physics 1.2.185b28) proposed to replace, for example, "The man is white" by "The man whites," coining a verb for the purpose if need be.

broadest sense, including philosophy, and as contrasted with artistic and literary writing), expressions of personality are frowned upon. Now personality can be avoided in various ways. One is the use of the passive voice. Where the seventeenth and eighteenth centuries would have been anecdotal—"I collected sea anemones at low tide"—the nineteenth and twentieth centuries would cast the reporting subject into the shadow of implicitness: "Sea anemones were collected at low tide." Another way to avoid personality is to avoid finite verbs altogether, by nominalizing.

*c.* Nominality offers another advantage to the scientific writer. The finite verb has not only person but also number and (as does the participle) tense. Of these three dimensions tense is widely felt to be the most fundamental; similarly Aristotle distinguishing the Greek verb from the Greek noun does it on the basis of having or lacking tense (*De interpretatione* 2.16a19, 3.16b6). Now to the extent that a writer can avoid finite verbs and participles (including forms of the verb "to be"), he can avoid commitments as to tense. Indeed, it is partly because of this fact that the pairing of nominalizing and verbalizing sentences is a fiction. "At the time of our arrival" has not one verbal counterpart but two, "when we arrived" and "when we arrive."

*d.* The very fact that nominality is contrary to conversational style has its value. It sets off the writing as esoteric, specialized, technical. Nominal style in English can be used to play the role (although much less conspicuously and effectively) that Latin played until several hundred years ago.

Certain neutral remarks can be made about these judgments. Those who approve nominal style and those who disapprove it are not in utter disagreement. Its advocates do not claim that it is graceful or elegant, and its critics do not deny that it achieves impersonality and the rest. But after the mutual concessions, a residue of disagreement remains. It is admitted by all that verbal style is harder to write than nominal style; is it *worth* the trouble? This would raise the broader question whether good style is being urged for its own sake (i.e., as an end), or as a means to some other end, or on both grounds. Advocates of nominal style usually defend it as a means to an end; its attackers might argue that it does not achieve its end, and that for the very same end verbal style is more effective. In that case, verbal style would be preferable to nominal both as an end and as a means. . . .

## RHETORICAL QUALITIES OF WORDS

RICHARD E. HUGHES
P. ALBERT DUHAMEL

A writer's choice of words is the most important single factor in determining the effectiveness of his writing. An examination of the manuscript of one of Keats' poems will reveal how carefully he considered each word, writing in first one, then another, before finally deciding which was the one most likely to convey the exact effect he intended. The style of some writers, like Henry James, is characterized by a search for the *mot juste*, the one word which will suggest just the precise shade of expression.

Every word has its own history, and books have been written on the origin and development of words like *nice, taboo, checkmate, bayonet, propaganda, street, by-law,* and countless others. Books have also been written on the distinctive vocabularies of individual writers. But the study of words should be limited by two considerations: one critical, the other creative. It is not only important to study the ways in which certain kinds of words have been used by writers to achieve effects, but also to apply these principles to the improvement of one's own writing.

The classifications according to which words will be studied may be considered as scales stretching between sets of extremes such as abstract and concrete, denotative and connotative, popular and learned. Most words fall somewhere between the extremes; just where is not always easy to determine. Since the various scales are not mutually exclusive, the same word can be measured on several. The location of a particular word on a scale is also subject to change, according to its background or context. After studying a representative sample of a writer's style, it is possible to pick out any tendency he may have to use words which fall on a particular segment of these scales.

### Usage and the Dictionary

Grammar is concerned with clarity; rhetoric, with effectiveness. To be effective a word must be correct, but every correct word is not

From Richard E. Hughes and P. Albert Duhamel, *Rhetoric: Principles and Usage.* © 1962. Reprinted by permission of Prentice-Hall, Inc., Englewood Cliffs, N.J.

Richard E. Hughes is chairman, Department of English, and P. Albert Duhamel is Director of the Honors Program, at Boston College.

necessarily an effective word. To be aware of all the possibilities from which he can choose the most forceful word, or to understand why an author uses one word instead of another, the student of style must be a dedicated student of dictionaries. He must realize what dictionaries cannot tell him as well as absorb what they can.

Dictionaries are not depositories of "true meanings." Words are arbitrary signs, and there is no necessary connection, except possibly in the case of onomatopoeic words, between the sound of a word and what that word signifies. What the word signifies depends on how it is used by educated speakers of the language.

Just as the stock-quotation pages of a newspaper list but do not dictate the values of stocks, so dictionaries list but do not legislate the meanings of words. The stock-pages can only summarize how a stock has behaved in the market in the past; they cannot predict what it will do in the future. The dictionary can only record how a word has been used in the past; it cannot predict its use in the future. Dictionaries like *Webster's New International* record all the most important meanings of all the words in the language. Other dictionaries, such as dictionaries of synonyms, slang, or American usage, are more specialized. The *Oxford English Dictionary* not only gives the definition of some 424,825 words but it also illustrates how the words were used at various stages in their history by quoting from contemporary documents. It is an essential reference work for anyone who really wants to know just how effective a word was in a particular context and how its past meanings might give it a peculiar appropriateness in his own writing.

No writer could possibly expect to use, nor any reader to recognize, more than a fraction of the million or so words which are estimated to constitute the vocabulary of the English language. Among the major English writers Robert Browning is frequently considered to have commanded the most extensive vocabulary—some 35,000 words in all. The average college student has been credited with the ability to recognize some 60,000 words, and to use some 20,000 in his own writing. These figures indicate how small a part of the total English vocabulary even the average educated user of the language can bring into play.

Dictionaries strive to record all the words used by all speakers and writers but the process of dictionary making is so involved and requires so much care that a new edition cannot be published every year. Language, on the other hand, is a constantly changing, growing organism, with new words being added and established words altering their meanings. Between the 1934 edition of *Webster's International Dictionary* and the 1961 edition, the English language was enriched by thousands of new words like *brainwash, countdown, lead-time, over-kill*. Older words, like *rocket, jet,* and *computer* underwent extensive changes in denotation and connotation.

The construction of a definition for a word may be compared to searching for the least common denominator of a group of numbers. Some words, like *cirro-cumulus*, require only one definition, for all the citations recording their usage will be found reducible to one least common denominator of meaning. Other words, like *get*, may require dozens of definitions, for they are used in so many different ways that it is impossible to reduce all of the citations to a few common denominators of meaning. The *Oxford English Dictionary* overcomes some of these limitations by illustrating the more generalized definitions of a word and by illustrating its actual use in the works of different writers. But to overcome the limitations of the dictionary, the student must train himself to observe how words are being used in current literature and current speech.

The norm or standard used by sensitive speakers and writers is the usage of educated people on their best linguistic behavior. Standards of word usage can be compared to standards in social manners. Everyone may be said to have two sets of manners: informal and formal. The informal manners are called into play at home, among friends, in relaxed or familiar circumstances. More formal manners are reserved for those ceremonial occasions which require more rigorous standards of conduct. The writer should choose a standard in keeping with his purpose, his subject matter, and his expected readers.

The conservatives encourage the perpetuation of established usage by demanding near-formal behavior on all occasions. The liberals encourage growth and change by encouraging informal behavior on all but the most demanding of occasions. The only solution for the writer is to bear in mind that he is writing to be effective, not to make an issue of a particular word or expression. Whenever a writer uses a learned word to impress or a vulgar word to shock, he is not furthering his purpose.

The problem of defining standards of usage is particularly important in English because the English language is rich in synonyms for almost every word. Many of these synonyms are sufficiently similar that they might serve to convey the same idea with some clarity. All of the following words, as well as many others not cited here, could be used to convey the idea of a female person: *lady, madam, matron, mistress, dowager, girl, woman, wife, miss, mademoiselle, femme, frail, dame, skirt, sister, tomato, chick, squaw, goody, gammer, vixen.* Now no two of these words have exactly the same implications. A woman could not be both *miss* and *wife*; *girl* and *dowager* are far apart in age and behavior. But in some informal contexts the word *girl* could be applied to the same person who would be called a dowager in a more formal context to convey warmth of feeling, pathos, or heavy-handed irony. A standard dictionary would distinguish between *goody* and *gammer* but only the *Oxford English Dictionary* could give a writer a real feeling for the differences in their connotations. *Skirt, dame, chick, femme,* would all be labeled as colloquial or slang in the dictionary, but only current experience with the language would reveal which was still in use, which might be used to make a point in informal circumstances, and which was inadmissible even in an informal context.

## Precise Language and Mass Language

The mid-twentieth century is a period which favors informality in dress and manners of living. This, coupled with the development of the mass media of communication, has encouraged the development of a language which sacrifices precision to ease of composition and communication. Advertisers in these media have also preferred the "soft sell," the indirect, casual approach, instead of blatant, direct merchandising. Informal English can be understood by more people than formal English. Formal English, like formal manners, requires more education and more information than are possessed by mass audiences.

The result has been the development of what may be called "mass language." Mass language is language which presents the reader with a response he is expected to make without giving him adequate reasons for having this response. A word like "wonderful" is used to describe a hat, a car, a day, any kind of experience—anything—and the reader is expected to supply a more exact implication.

Mass language abounds in clichés, jargon, pretentious diction, euphemisms, and worn out metaphors, all of which have one thing in common: imprecision. They are all approximations, compromises, or substitutions for more precise terms.

The use of mass language in daily speech is not as severe a detriment to clarity or effectiveness as it is in writing, for, in speaking, gestures, intonations, pauses, and other circumstances can combine to make some of the vague, overworked words more effective. But a writer who uses a mass word instead of a more precise word invites his audience to bend that word to fit into its own categories and preconceptions, to force his ideas into old patterns of thought. The writer who is determined to be effective must use every opportunity, every word, to influence and direct his audience.

Mass language also has an effect on the writer himself, for it serves to block the development of any originality of thought or of style. Effective writing must not only be clear writing, it must also have color and emphasis. The overworked cliché is neither colorful nor emphatic.

A simple example of mass language is the way in which the word *get* is used to describe almost any action which can be performed in the course of a day. In a brief conversation it is possible to hear someone talk of "getting up" in the morning, donning a "get-up," "getting up" a party, "getting" an idea, "getting" a donation, "getting" somewhere, "getting" the culprit, "getting" ready, and "getting" off. For each of these expressions, there is a more precise word: *arising, dressing, arranging a party, perceiving, receiving, arriving, apprehending the culprit, preparing,* and *departing.*

Adjectives also acquire great popularity and then fade quickly away, emptied of all meaning. The adjective *awful* once had a very particular and important meaning, "to fill a person with awe." But after it had been applied to every kind of object and experience, from a garish hat to stubbing one's toe, it has become almost meaningless. *Tremendous* and *massive* are currently being overworked so that, in a very short time, they too will convey little. *Anxious* is currently appearing where *eager, desirous, in a hurry,* and *worried* would be more accurate; *furnish,* in similar fashion, serves for *supply, provide, donate,* or *contribute.*

The list of words being exhausted in mass language could be extended almost indefinitely. Examples are as close as the editorial page of any newspaper. A single editorial yielded the following examples of a passion for clichés: "heap of trouble," "drown in red ink," "jobs for the many," "tolerable proportions," "irresistible demands," "modestly called," "occasion no astonishment," "pervades our existence," "conjure up bugaboos," "ingenious way," "make life easier," "normally perceptive." To make sure that the first newspaper examined was not an unusual example, another Sunday paper of the same date supplied the following on its editorial page: "ill service," "candid realization," "not too much to hope," "inevitable delay," "permanent fixture," "manifest an interest," "adopt sanctions," "childish petulance," "brought dangerously close," "engage in activities," "call for a new look," and, quite appropriately, "outworn stereotypes."

## Jargon

In addition to the vague word and the cliché, mass language makes use of jargon. Strictly speaking, jargon is the technical language of a trade or profession. A lawyer frequently uses sentences with many conjunctions such as "nevertheless," "whereas," and "therefore" for he must try to incorporate into his contracts provisions for as many contingencies as he can foresee. A scientist who is not yet certain of the range of significance of his present findings may use expressions such as: "it would seem possible," "it is not unreasonable to suppose," or "it might be considered feasible." But when someone writing for a general audience uses a sentence such as the following he has adopted a pseudo-scientific pose.

> It would seem that it is nothing more nor less than a comparative social condition depending on a relative control over economic goods, the standard of comparison being a group possessing a maximum of such control, called the rich or wealthy.

Although it may be difficult to perceive at first, all that is hidden behind this pretentious phrasing, the conditional mood, the gratuitous "more nor less," is a definition of poverty. Jargon, therefore, can be defined as the use of pretentious words, phrases, circumlocutions, which are inappropriate in the contexts wherein they are used.

Jargon is the language spoken by the man who says "in the matter of" when he means "about"; "a long period of time" when he means "a long time"; "in the capacity of" when he means "as"; "resembling in nature" when he means "like"; and "in some instances" when he means "sometimes." The jargonist is fascinated by the unnecessary polysyllable and always prefers words like "activate" to simpler words like "form" or "establish." He is always referring to "areas of study," "problems in terms of which," "variant factors," "in this regard," "in countless cases" and using other phrases which leave the reader or hearer with a vague feeling that there must be more complexities about the subject than he can perceive. Finally, the jargonist cannot resist the possibilities of sentences which begin, "It is, perhaps, not an unjustifiable assumption to . . ." But the inappropriate use of jargon may have an effect opposite to that intended: the creation of a suspicion in the minds of an alert audience that a better-informed writer would use language more accurately and responsibly.

One of the by-products of the use of jargon is a style with a high proportion of structural words (prepositions, conjunctions, articles, auxiliary verbs and phrases) to content words (nouns, adjectives, verbs, and adverbs). Such a style lacks vigor and directness. The use of pretentious words, round about expressions, and unnecessary phrases forces the writer to use more structural words to introduce these refinements, so that the effect of the whole is rather obscure.

The following paragraphs are taken from a *Time* magazine account of Pat Brown's attempt to win the governorship of California. Although its circulation is large enough for it to qualify as one of the mass media of communication, it is notable for its attempts to avoid mass language. In the following excerpt the writer loses no opportunity to picture Pat Brown as he wants his reader to see him. Every word is specific and the reader is not obliged to supply his own content for vague terms.

> California's Attorney General "Pat" Brown marched across the lobby of San Diego's U.S. Grant Hotel, his stocky body (5 ft. 10 in., 200 lbs.) rolling like a sea captain's, his brown hair carefully slicked with Vaseline Hair Tonic, his ample jowl set with fierce, self-conscious determination. Suddenly he stopped, whirled, brought the men behind him to a skidding halt. "Where is everybody?" cried Pat Brown. "Anybody missing? Are we ready to go?" An aide soothed him: "Don't worry, Pat. Everybody's here." Brown looked carefully around just to make sure. "Well," he explained, "I want to get out there while people are still going to work." He spun, led the way out the door, clambered into a Plymouth station wagon. Edmund Gerald Brown, 53, Democratic candidate for Governor of California, odds-on favorite in what may be the most important contest of Election Year 1958, was on his way to a 6:15 A.M. appointment with destiny. He did not intend to be late.
>
> Destiny was waiting last week on the San Diego waterfront, where Pat Brown "officially" opened his campaign against William Fife Knowland, 50, retired as Republican leader of the U.S. Senate to run for Governor of California.[1]

The same information, translated into mass language, would read something like this.

> California's Attorney General, "Pat" Brown launched his campaign to win the Governorship of the State of California early one morning last week. Accompanied by several members of his personal staff he went out to meet the early-shift dock workers and shake their hands.

[1] Courtesy *Time*; copyright Time, Inc., 1958.

The *Time* account is precise, filled with details, slanted to give one impression, true, but detailed and effective. Every verb and every modifier achieves some part of the author's total purpose. The mass-language account conveys the gist of the information but it does not do so with color or emphasis.

## Euphemism

Another failure to use words effectively is known as euphemism—the substitution of a word with pleasant implications for a word with unpleasant suggestions. The obvious euphemisms of the Victorian period, *limb* for *leg* and a *love child* for *bastard*, have become very rare. However *passed away* is still used as an euphemism for *die*, and the newspapers prefer *criminal assault* to *rape*. Euphemisms are commonly used to make jobs seem more important or socially more acceptable. Bill collectors are now known as *adjusters*, janitors as *sanitary engineers*, and undertakers as *morticians*. Students graduating from college are never looking for jobs; they are all looking for *positions*.

Euphemisms are logically indefensible, but socially unavoidable. They are illogical because, as Juliet says, "a rose by any other name would smell as sweet." It is the thing which is good or bad, not its name. What is unpleasant to contemplate is not the word *die*, but the fact of death. Changing the word but keeping the message intact is like using a code, but who is being taken in? *Love child* or *illegitimate child* carry the same social stigma as *bastard*. It is the idea of illegitimacy which society has found censurable, not the sound used to express it.

But euphemisms are a form of taboo, and, like the taboos of any society, they form part of the social code of manners of society. In some societies these take the form of dietary restrictions, in others they may be forbidden places, persons, or names. Contemporary society insists upon the observation of fewer taboos than primitive societies, and today's writer need not use as many euphemisms as the Victorian. Knowing what euphemisms form an active and integral part of the social manners of a society is an aspect of that general sensitivity to language usage which must be part of the equipment of every effective writer.

A subtle form of euphemism is known as "elegant variation." According to the rules of elegant variation a paper on Shakespeare for instance, may name its subject only once. After that, he must be referred to as "Ben Jonson's contemporary," "the Bard of Avon," "the author of

*Romeo and Juliet,"* and "the creator of Hamlet." Although monotonous repetition is to be avoided, its distracting or obscure alternatives may defeat their purpose.

## Worn-out Metaphor

One final source of mass language worth mentioning is the worn-out metaphor. Among the more common are: "ring the changes on," "take up the cudgels for," "toe the line," "run roughshod over," "stand shoulder to shoulder," "play into the hands of," "no axe to grind," "grist for the mill," and "fishing in troubled waters." If figurative language is to be used, it must be original.

In a brilliant essay on "Politics and the English Language," George Orwell suggested six rules which would help a writer avoid mass language!

1. Never use a metaphor, simile, or other figure which you are used to seeing in print.
2. Never use a long word where a short one will do.
3. If it is possible to cut a word out, always cut it out.
4. Never use a passive phrase where you can use an active.
5. Never use a foreign phrase, a scientific word or a jargon word if you can think of an everyday English equivalent.
6. Break any of these rules sooner than say anything outright barbarous.[2]

These are sound rules not only for effective writing but also for effective thinking. Mass language is too widely and firmly entrenched to be got rid of overnight. But a start can be made by avoiding the tendency to think in terms of ready made phrases, pretentious sounding words, clichés, worn-out metaphors or euphemisms which are in wide use in the mass media of communication. Part of the task of revision of any piece of writing should be to make sure that every such obstacle to effectiveness has been removed.

## Concrete and Abstract Words

Concrete words refer to specific things which can be pointed to, or experienced, or felt. Abstract words are signs or symbols for relations,

[2] George Orwell, "Politics and the English Language," from *Shooting an Elephant and Other Essays* (New York: Harcourt, Brace, & World, Inc., 1960).

ideas, concepts, which are not directly sensible. The word *abstract* comes from the combination of the Latin *trahere*, meaning *to draw*, and the preposition *abs* meaning *out of*. An abstract word is, therefore, a label used to identify certain general qualities which have been drawn out of several particulars. Everyday language is a mixture of the abstract and the concrete: "our car," "our home," "our books," "our neighbors," "right," "truth," "democracy," and "fair play."

Although both types of words are essential to communication, the abstract can pose more problems than the concrete. Disagreements over concrete words can be resolved by referring them to the objects themselves. Even the most unusual concrete word, from *adytism* to *zymurgy*, can be so clarified. The word *fair*, as it is commonly applied to denote a just or unbiased act, is a much more common word and yet much harder to define because it stands for an abstraction. Although there is usually a core of established meaning to every abstract word, there is usually an indefinable periphery of implication.

Semanticists discourage the use of abstract words. Consider the following sentence from the *National Review*.

> The stark political realities of Western retreat are the direct product of decades of cultivation of characterological weakness on the bases of a sedulous propagation of the philosophical error which goes under the name of relativism: the doctrine that no truth in reality exists; that whatever a culture believes is as good as what any other culture believes (cannibalism or human sacrifice are not wrong, only "culturally relative" modes of human action); that therefore the West has nothing of which to be proud, nothing for which to fight, nothing worth dying for.

The reader encountering such a sentence has to supply some kind of concrete meaning for "political realities," and "Western retreat." Then he must decide just what is meant by "direct product" and "characterological weakness." "Decades of cultivation" is also puzzling because it is not clear just what and how many decades are intended, or what is meant by "cultivation" in this abstracted sense. By the time he arrives at "relativism" he is grateful for the definition which the writer provides, but whatever the sentence gains in clarity from that point on by a greater use of more concrete words, it loses through the use of interrupting clauses.

It is always a good idea to define any abstract word which is going to be crucial to any discussion and to illustrate it as clearly as possible. The following sentence actually contains a larger percentage of abstract words than the one above, but it is not as difficult to understand. John Locke demonstrates that it is possible to use abstract words without forcing the reader to supply his own clarification. He sometimes uses words and clauses in pairs, one throwing light on the other. Thus "choose" helps make the abstract use of "authorize" a little clearer, and the clause "to destroy that which every one designs to secure by entering into society," helps make the succeeding clause, "that for which people submitted themselves to legislators of their own making" a little more concrete. Also he sometimes adds a few words of clarification as in the phrase, "as guards and fences to the properties of all members of the society."

> The reason why men enter into society, is the preservation of their property; and the end why they choose and authorize a legislative, is, that there may be laws made, and rules set, as guards and fences to the properties of all the members of the society: to limit the power, and moderate the dominion, of every part and member of the society: for since it can never be supposed to be the will of the society, that the legislative should have a power to destroy that which every one designs to secure by entering into society, that for which the people submitted themselves to legislators of their own making; whenever the legislative endeavor to take away and destroy the property of the people, or to reduce them to slavery under arbitrary power, they put themselves into a state of war with the people, who are thereupon absolved from any further obedience, and are left to the common refuge, which God hath provided for all men, against force and violence. Whensoever therefore the legislative shall transgress this fundamental rule of society; and either by ambition, fear, folly or corruption, endeavor to grasp themselves, or put into the hands of any other, an absolute power over the lives, liberties, and estates of the people, by this breach of trust they forfeit the power the people had put into their hands for quite contrary ends, and it devolves to the people, who have a right to resume their original liberty, and, by the establishment of a new legislative (such as they shall think fit), provide for their own safety and security, which is the end for which they are in society.[3]

If the writer's purpose requires the discussion of an abstract subject he must use the necessary terms, but since it is also part of his purpose to persuade his readers to his point of view, he must do what he can to make that point clear and easily understood. Contemporary readers have come to expect much less demanding fare than unrelieved abstract discussions. In 1946 Dr. Rudolf Flesch published a book entitled *The Art of Plain Talk* which contained a Readability Formula. According to this formula

[3] John Locke, *Treatise on Civil Government.*

the greater the number of short sentences, concrete words, and personal references, the easier a book is to read and the more likely it is to be read. Devotees of this formula can go to the extreme of writing everything in a style usually associated with a first-grade reading primer. Ease of reading is not synonymous with quality of expression, but the writer who is working with abstractions can increase his chances of reaching a wider audience by illustrating some of the abstractions with concrete applications and supplying synonyms or parallel expressions. If some of his sentences tend to be long, he should be sure to make the interrelations of the parts particularly clear.

## Popular and Learned Words

Frequently confused with the scale which distinguishes between concrete and abstract words is the scale which distinguishes between popular and learned words. The English language has a large number of pairs of synonyms, one of which is popular and frequently heard in daily speech; the other, referred to as the "learned word," is only occasionally heard but more frequently read. In *Words and Their Ways in English Speech*, Greenough and Kittredge named some pairs:

> *The same, identical; speech, oration; fire, conflagration; choose, select; brave, valorous; swallowing, deglutition; striking, percussion; building, edifice; shady, umbrageous; puckery, astringent; learned, erudite; secret, cryptic; destroy, annihilate; stiff, rigid; flabby, flaccid; queer, eccentric; behead, decapitate; round, circular; thin, emaciated; fat, corpulent; truthful, veracious; try, endeavor; bit, modicum; piece, fragment; sharp, acute; crazy, maniacal; king, sovereign; book, volume; lying, mendacious; beggar, mendicant; teacher, instructor; play, drama; air, atmosphere; paint, pigment.*[4]

The popular word in each of these pairs tends to be monosyllabic and direct (*round, thin, fat*, and *bit*). The corresponding learned word tends to be polysyllabic and more vague in its implications (*circular, emaciated, corpulent, modicum*). The popular word is usually of Anglo-Saxon origin (*brave, king*, and *book*), the learned word is usually a word borrowed from Latin (*valorous, sovereign*, and *volume*). A style which is based mainly upon popular words tends to be more direct and straight-

[4] J. B. Greenough and G. L. Kittredge, *Words and Their Ways in English Speech* (New York, 1902), p. 20.

forward; one which contains a high percentage of learned words tends to be more sonorous, involved, and demanding of the reader.

There is always a tendency to equate popular words with concrete words, and learned words with abstract words, but the two scales involved are based on completely different criteria. The concrete-abstract scale is based upon the referents of words, the popular-learned scale is based upon the level of usage. The same word can be both concrete and popular as *behead*; or concrete and learned as *decapitate* or *deglutition*. The same word can be popular and abstract as *brave*, *fair*, *just*; learned and abstract as *valorous* and *veracious*.

The older borrowings from Latin, French, and Italian retain little of their original color. More recent borrowings from Arabic, Russian, Hindu, or the South Seas languages—words like *harem*, *intelligentsia*, *pariah*, *taboo*—still retain some of the flavor of their original contexts. The writer who is aware of these retained overtones of meaning can use the evocative power of these words very effectively, not only to add color in narration and description, but to lend vigor to any passage.

The writer who finds himself with a choice between words in a learned-popular pair must be guided first by a desire to be clear and precise in his communication. Then he can take into consideration the tone he wants to give to his composition as a whole, and how the circumstances of his writing, his audience or the occasion, can be allowed to influence his choice of a learned over a popular word. Although these word-pairs are synonyms, there are shades of difference between them—*annihilate*, to take but one example, does not mean exactly the same as *destroy*. Then there are some words in these pairs which are obviously pedantic: *deglutition*, *conflagration*, *mendicant*, or *umbrageous* should not be used in place of *swallowing*, *fire*, *beggar*, or *shady*. An audience would rightly suspect that they had been used for the impression they might make. A notorious government directive once instructed office workers to "terminate the illumination" when all that was intended was that the last one to leave make sure he "put out the lights." Painfully unusual words call attention to themselves when their proper purpose should be to call attention to the idea. The reader who is driven to a dictionary to discover the precise meaning of a learned word which is out of place in the midst of an otherwise undistinguished piece of informal prose will not return to his reading impressed with the writer's erudition. He will return irritated, impatient with the pretenses of the writer and having forgotten the trend of the argument.

There are times when there is no proper substitute for words like *antinomies, recidivist, irredentist, analeptic, ambages, cerements, passe-menterie, supererogation, cramoisy,* and *autochthonous.* As such times, the writer should not hesitate to use them, provided he is sure of their exact meaning and their appropriateness both to context and to audience. As the use of learned words in proper context does not constitute jargon, so the use of popular words in proper context is not to be confused with vulgate. Vulgate is the substandard dialect of English with a very limited vocabulary which is used by uneducated people. It disregards rules of syntax, links singular nouns with plural verbs, pronouns to incorrect antecedents, and almost completely reverses the rules governing the copula. Vulgate can be readily detected by its use of expressions like *O.K., jerk, ain't, guy, caf,* and *exam.* Vulgate is admissible in narrative writing only to characterize persons who would normally speak that way, but it must be avoided in all other kinds of writing.

## Connotation and Denotation

Words can also be ranged on a scale which distinguishes denotation from connotation (*see also* Chapter 4). Except for structural words like articles, conjunctions, prepositions, and verbal auxiliaries, all words have a connotation as well as a denotation. English is remarkably rich in groups of words all having similar denotations but very different connotations.

The denotation of a word, it will be recalled, is what the word specifically points to, its core of meaning. The connotation of a word is what the word suggests, a less easily definable aura which can expand and contract with time and the experience of its readers.

The chemists use formulae like $H_2O$, mathematicians symbols like Pi, botanists terms like *Acer Rubrum*, and zoologists labels like *Felis Leo* which are intended to point clearly, simply, directly to specific things and to be as free as possible from all overtones and suggestions. Next in line on the denotative-connotative scale, moving from the pole of pure denotation towards pure connotation, are everyday words for everyday things. Words like *chair, water, house, car, book,* and *desk* also point to very specific things and are without much connotation for most people. Indeed, the more specific the referent of a word, the more likely the word will be more denotative; the vaguer the referent, the more likely the word to tend towards the connotative end of the scale. Adjectives like *archaic* and *venerable* have a core of meaning, *aged* or *antique*, but they also have a lot of suggestive power. Words like these occupy almost the very center of the scale and the context in which they are used may tip them in one direction or the other. Next, there is a group of words which, though not without specific referents, seem to be used more for their flavor than for what they expressly point to. Words like *troika, samovar, hansom, crenellated, hashish* can evoke more than they state. Finally we come to words which have been created for their connotative powers, words like *scrumptious,* or *feathery* which have been used so frequently in advertising contexts that their residual function is almost purely connotative.

In any group of synonyms some of the words will be more connotative than others. All of the following words have a core meaning which means approximately *to criticize: admonish, chide, scold, rebuke, reprimand.* Yet their connotations are very different. *Rebuke* is almost all denotation; it means to criticize sharply. *Chide* is perhaps at the other end of the scale for it suggests light and almost indulgent correction. *Scold* and *admonish* are somewhere near the middle of the scale for both indicate criticism but the first implies irritation and the second, exhortation. *Accuse, charge, incriminate* and *indict* all denote the same idea of calling someone guilty of an action, but all imply different degrees of severity and modes of procedure. *Hesitate, falter, procrastinate,* and *dawdle* are another group of words with a common meaning but different overtones of suggestion.

Words acquire their connotations from social and personal sources. The personal experiences of living and learning are the source of the connotations attributed to a word. For the boy who grew up on a midwestern farm, a *plug* may be an old faithful farm horse; for the city-bred, it may be a broken-down old horse; for the race track tout, it may be any poor bet. The first time we hear or read a word, the connotation is slight. The oftener a word is used, the greater the number of connotations it acquires. Words heard in a favorable context acquire favorable connotations; those associated with unfavorable contexts become themselves unfavorable. The words *Communism* and *Fascism*, when used today, always elicit an unfavorable connotation among hearers who would be hard-pressed to give them a definition which would be adequate to set them off from one another. When these two terms first began to come into general use in the earlier years of this century they were learned terms, with precise denotations. Creators of propaganda succeeded in giving them unfavorable connotations by repeated use in association with unfavorable ideas. The word *propaganda* was itself, once, a neutral word meaning the dissemination of ideas and information. It still means the same today but it connotes dissemination of information with biassed intent.

The difference in effect of a style which uses mainly denotative words from that of a style which uses mainly connotative words can be illustrated by placing side by side two poems on the same general subject. The first group of lines is taken from Robert Herrick's seventeenth century poem entitled "The Hock Cart." This was the last cart-load of the harvest to be taken to the barn. Herrick's poem describes the harvest in terms which are specific, mainly denotative, frequently concrete and popular.

> Some bless the cart; some kiss the sheaves;
> Some prank them up with oaken leaves:
> Some cross the fill-horse, some with great
> Devotion, stroke the home-borne wheat:
> While other rusticks, less attent
> To prayers, than merriment,
> Run after with their breeches rent.
> Well on, brave boys, to your Lord's hearth,
> Glitt'ring with fire; where, for your mirth,
> Ye shall see first the large and chief
> Foundation of your feast, fat beef:
> With upper stories, mutton, veal
> And bacon (which makes full the meal)
> With sev'ral dishes standing by,
> As here a custard, there a pie,
> And here all tempting frumenty.

John Keats' "To Autumn" also celebrates the joys of harvest, but in an almost unrelieved series of connotative terms. Every line suggests rather than specifies a picture.

> Season of mists and mellow fruitfulness,
>   Close bosom-friend of the maturing sun;
> Conspiring with him how to load and bless
>   With fruit the vines that round the thatch-eves run;
> To bend with apples the moss'd cottage-trees,
>   And fill all fruit with ripeness to the core;
>     To swell the gourd, and plump the hazel shells
>   With a sweet kernel; to set budding more,
> And still more, later flowers for the bees,
> Until they think warm days will never cease,
> For summer has o'er brimm'd their clammy cells.

To say that one poem uses more connotative words, or fewer, than another, is not to say that one poem is better than another. The use of a different kind of words has a decided effect upon the kind of poem and reflects a difference in the poet's intentions.

This difference of effect resulting from the kind of word choice can also be illustrated in two prose passages which do occur not very far apart in Edmund Burke's *Conciliation Speech*. In both instances Burke was defending the same proposition: that Parliament should conciliate the colonies. In the first passage, his reason was the growing importance of colonial trade. Here he felt sure of his facts and addressed himself to his readers in denotative terms. He lets the statistics speak for themselves; the speech is direct; the words without emotional implications.

> Excuse me, Sir, if turning from such thoughts I resume this comparative view once more. You have seen it on a large scale; look at it on a small one. I will point out to your attention a particular instance of it in the single province of Pennsylvania. In the year 1704, that province called for £11,459 in value of your commodities, native and foreign. This was the whole. What did it demand in 1772? Why nearly fifty times as much; for in that year the export to Pennsylvania was £507,909, nearly equal to the export to all the colonies together in the first period.

In the following passage Burke's reason for demanding a conciliatory attitude towards the colonies is their growing resourcefulness in extending their fishing industry. Here Burke does not rely on statistics or the denotative word, though these were available. Instead he addresses himself to his readers' imaginations and emotions with stirring, connotative evocations of the adventuresomeness of the Americans.

> As to the wealth which the colonies have drawn from the sea by their fisheries, you had all that matter fully opened at your bar. You surely thought these acquisitions of value, for they seemed to excite your envy; and yet the spirit by which that enterprising employment has been exercised, ought rather, in my opinion to have raised your esteem and admiration. And pray, Sir, what in the world is equal to it? Pass by the other parts, and look at the manner in which the people of New England have of late carried on the whale fishery. Whilst we follow them among the tumbling mountains of ice, and behold them penetrating into the deepest frozen recesses of Hudson's Bay and Davis's Straits, whilst we are looking for them beneath the arctic circle, we hear that they have pierced into the opposite region

of polar cold, that they are at the antipodes, and engaged under the frozen serpent of the south. Falkland Island, which seemed too remote and romantic an object for the grasp of national ambition, is but a stage and resting-place in the progress of their victorious industry. Nor is the equinoctial heat more discouraging to them, than the accumulated winter of both the poles. We know that whilst some of them draw the line and strike the harpoon on the coast of Africa, others run the longitude, and pursue their gigantic game along the coast of Brazil. No sea but what is vexed by their fisheries. No climate that is not witness to their toils. Neither the perseverance of Holland, nor the activity of France, nor the dexterous and firm sagacity of English enterprise, ever carried this most perilous mode of hard industry to the extent to which it has been pushed by this recent people; a people who are still, as it were, but in the gristle, and not yet hardened into the bone of manhood.

## Literal and Figurative Use of Words

The most traditional means of studying the way in which word choice can influence style is to group words not on the basis of what they stand for but on the basis of how they are used. Since earliest times rhetoricians have distinguished between the use of words in their literal sense and words in their figurative sense.

Every word has a literal sense which is its direct, matter-of-fact meaning. Some words have never been used in a figurative sense but this is not to say that they cannot be so used; all words may have a figurative sense, which is a secondary, derived meaning, requiring that the literal meaning be understood only in a transferred or altered sense. The literal meaning of the adjective *wooden* is "something made of wood." It is in this primary, matter-of-fact sense that it must be understood in such expressions as "the wooden door," "the wooden box," "the wooden desk." But it may also be used in such expressions as, "his manners were wooden," "his gait was wooden," or even "his talk was wooden." Since, obviously, no one of these actions is made of wood, the primary meaning of *wooden* cannot apply. Instead it must be understood in an altered or modified sense. Those parts of the meaning of the word, *wooden*, such as *stiff*, *rigid*, *brittle*, which might conceivably be applied to manners, gait, or talk, must be transferred from the context where they are directly applicable to another context where they are only partially applicable. To say that a person's manners were "wooden," is to say that they were stiff in the way in which wood is stiff. The reason for using *wooden* instead of stiff is that *stiff* is an abstract word, whereas *wooden* instantly develops a clear mental picture.

In *Othello*, Shakespeare has Iago say:

> Our bodies are our gardens, to the which our wills are gardeners; so that if we plant nettles or sow lettuce, set hyssop and weed up thyme, supply it with one gender of herbs or distract it with many —either to have it sterile with idleness or manured with industry —why, the power and corrigible authority of this lies in our wills.

Here Iago is using several words in a transferred sense, but the most obvious are "garden" and "gardeners." The literal meanings of these two ordinary words are obvious, but the direct meaning has been altered, changed, and generalized so that a "garden" is no longer just a place to grow vegetables, but a human body; and the "gardener" is not a mere tiller of the soil, but the very self.

In order to be able to transfer a word from its literal context to its figurative meaning the analogy either expressed or implied in every figure of speech must be perceived. Since an analogy is a comparison between two things which are not completely alike, every analogy is by definition a limited comparison; it cannot be carried out to the last detail. Everyday speech is filled with figurative expressions implying an analogy of which most users of the language are only dimly aware. A person is "scared as a rabbit"; another "timid as a lamb"; another's face is "pale as a sheet." The analogy implicit in all these figures of speech can be expanded and clearly expressed as a proportion. To be scared as a rabbit means that one's behavior is to the ideal of courage as a rabbit's behavior is to that ideal, and so on.

Writing which limits itself to the use of words in their literal sense is denotative, clear, direct, and precise. Writing which makes extensive use of words in their figurative senses tends to be connotative, suggestive, and colorful. New and fresh figures of speech add vigor and emphasis to language by leading the mind to see analogies and relationships which it had never noticed before. Worn, trite figures of speech, such as those which have been used as examples, do not add vigor to expression. On the contrary, they may detract from it like any other hackneyed expression or dead metaphor.

Sam Johnson once characterized the style of Jonathan Swift with the statement, "The rogue never hazards a metaphor." Every use of figurative expression is a calculated risk, taken by the writer in the hope that by saying something differently he will say it more forcefully. Swift took few chances, as can be illustrated from almost any passage taken at random from his works. In a passage of description, such as the following, its absence is especially significant.

> The master horse ordered a sorrel nag, one of his servants, to untie the largest of these animals, and take him into the yard. The beast and I were brought close together, and our countenances diligently compared, both by master and servant, who thereupon repeated several times the word *Yahoo*. My horror and astonishment are not to be described when I observed in this abhominable animal a perfect human figure: the face of it indeed was flat and broad, the nose depressed, the lips large, and the mouth wide. But these differences are common to all savage nations, where the lineaments of the countenance are distorted by the natives suffering their infants to lie grovelling on the earth, or by carrying them on their backs, nuzzling with their face against the mother's shoulders. The forefeet of the Yahoo differed from my hands in nothing else but the length of the nails, the coarseness and brownness of the palms, and the hairiness of the backs. There was the same resemblance between our feet, with the same differences, which I knew very well, though the horses did not, because of my shoes and stockings; the same in every part of our bodies, except as to hairiness and color, which I have already described.

The result is a style which has always been admired as an example of clarity, and of writing which appeals much more strongly to the reason than the imagination.

The following paragraph, taken from an extended description of a fleet's defending itself against air attack in the harbor of Alexandria during World War II, illustrates the way in which figures of speech can convey something of the color and fierceness of sight and sound.

> And deafening as was the roaring which now filled our ears it was possible to isolate many of the separate sounds which orchestrated the bombardment. The crackle of shards which fell back like a hailstorm upon the corrugated roofs of the waterside cafes: the scratchy mechanical voices of ships' signallers repeating, in voices of ventriloquists' dummies, semi-intelligible phrases which sounded like "Three o'clock red, Three o'clock red." Strangely too, there was music somewhere at the heart of the hubbub, jagged quartertones which stabbed; then, too, the foundering roar of buildings falling. Patches of light which disappeared and left an aperture of darkness at which a dirty flame might come and lap like a thirsty animal. Nearer at hand (the water smacked the echo out) we could hear the rich harvest of spent cannon-shells pouring upon the decks from the Chicago Pianos: an

almost continuous splashing of golden metal tumbling from the breeches of the skypointed guns.[5]

This short paragraph contains numerous figures of speech: two similes in "like a hailstorm," and "like a thirsty animal," six metaphors in "orchestrated the bombardment," "voices of ventriloquists' dummies," "quartertones which stabbed," "harvest of spent cannonballs," "Chicago Pianos," "splashing of golden metal"; some alliteration as in "scratchy mechanical voices of ships' signallers," some assonance as in "foundering roar," and onomatopoeia in "crackle of shards."

The most common figure of speech is the simile, an expressed comparison between two things unlike in most respects but alike in the respect in which they are compared. Everyday speech contains many similes. Persons are said "to grin like a Cheshire cat," "run like a deer," and "work like a horse." These are tired comparisons but it is obvious that the original comparison was an illuminating juxtaposition. The following poem is built up through a series of similes.

### A PALINODE

As withereth the primrose by the river,
As fadeth summer's sun from gliding fountains,
As vanisheth the light-blown bubble ever,
As melteth snow upon the mossy mountains:
So melts, so vanisheth, so fades, so withers
The rose, the shine, the bubble, and the snow
Of praise, pomp, glory, joy—which short life gathers—
Fair praise, vain pomp, sweet glory, brittle joy.
The withered primrose by the morning river,
The faded summer's sun from weeping fountains,
The light-blown bubble vanished forever,
The molten snow upon the naked mountains,
   Are emblems that the treasures we uplay
   Soon wither, vanish, fade, and melt away.

EDMUND BOLTON 1600

Similes keep touch with reality; their very explicitness emphasizes that they are only comparisons. The metaphor, though seemingly only slightly different from the simile in definition, is very different in total effect. A metaphor is commonly defined as an implied comparison between two things unlike in most respects but alike in the respect in

---

[5] Lawrence Durrell, *Clea* (New York: E. P. Dutton & Co., Inc., 1960).

which they are compared. On the surface it seems as if the only difference between the simile and the metaphor is that the comparison is expressed in the first and only implied in the second. Actually the difference is much greater because a metaphor does not state that something is *like* something else, it says that it *is* something else. Herbert Read wrote that "meaning is an arrow that reaches its mark when least encumbered by feathers." The force of the metaphor depends upon the identification of meaning with the flight of an arrow.

The first three quatrains of the following sonnet contain metaphors defining a man's age in terms of the time of year, the time of day, and the expiration of a fire. The metaphors are most compactly expressed in the last line of each quatrain; the first three lines of each set supply details to make them more clear and meaningful.

### SONNET LXXIII

That time of year thou mayst in me behold
When yellow leaves, or none, or few, do hang
Upon those boughs which shake against the cold,
Bare ruin'd choirs where late the sweet birds sang.
In me thou see'st the twilight of such day
As after sunset fadeth in the West,
Which by-and-by black night doth take away,
Death's second self, that seals up all in rest.
In me thou see'st the glowing of such fire
That on the ashes of his youth doth lie,
As the deathbed whereon it must expire,
Consum'd with that which it was nourish'd by.
   This thou perceiv'st, which makes thy love more strong,
   To love that well which thou must leave ere long.

WILLLIAM SHAKESPEARE

*Catachresis* is a species of metaphor wherein the comparison involves the violent rapprochement of two ideas. When Macbeth says, "I have supp'd full with horrors," he has identified two ideas, eating and horrors, which do not go together easily. The result is a forceful image which shocks the attention.

*Metonymy*, in the strict sense, is the use of a word for something closely associated with it. Thus one may address "the chair," in a debate, the "Head of a government" in a document, and "the heart" of a judge. Here *head*, *chair*, and *heart* are used for the persons with whom they are commonly associated. Thus a military command may be referred to as *top brass.* Shakespeare wrote, "Bell, book, and candle shall not drive me back," meaning that he would not be deterred even by excommunication, for bell, book, and candle are the common signs of the ceremony of excommunication.

*Synecdoche* is the use of a word which literally denotes a part to stand for the whole. An army can be described as "marching feet"; a navy as so many "sails" or "keels"; a work force as composed of so many "hands." In current slang a car is frequently referred to as "a set of wheels," and an airplane as "wings."

*Personification,* sometimes known as *Prosopopoeia,* is the attribution of human qualities to animals, abstractions, or inanimate objects. The Vice in medieval morality plays was sometimes a personification of the evils which tempt man to sin. Aesop's fables are a series of prosopopoeias attributing human qualities to foxes, birds, and all sorts of other animals. Closely linked to personification is the figure of *hypotyposis* which is a lively description and counterfeit presentation as in the following of the Confederate soldier.

> Let me picture to you the footsore Confederate soldier, as, buttoning up in his faded gray jacket the parole which was to bear testimony to his children of his fidelity and faith, he turned his face southward from Appomattox in April, 1865. Think of him as, ragged, half-starved, heavy-hearted, enfeebled by want and wounds, having fought to exhaustion, he surrenders his gun, wrings the hands of his comrades in silence, and lifting his tear-stained and pallid face for the last time to the graves that dot the old Virginia hills, pulls his gray cap over his brow and begins the slow and painful journey.[6]

The emotional possibilities of such a figure are too obvious to require comment.

*Hyperbole* is a deliberate exaggeration which could not possibly be meant literally. Thus one speaks of "millions of people in the downtown stores before Christmas." Mark Antony cried out, "Let Rome in Tiber melt and the wide arch of the rang'd empire fall," in his exaggerated protestation of the depth of his love for Cleopatra.

*Antihimeria* is the technical term for the substitution of one part of speech for another, an adjective for a noun, an adverb for a verb. Shakespeare wrote: "dizzy with more clamors Neptune's ear." Here the adjective *dizzy* has been made into a verb resulting in a more vivid and

---

[6] H. W. Grady, *The New South* (Columbus, Ohio: Charles E. Merrill Books, Inc., 1904).

suggestive description of an action than could have been possible with any of the verbs already available.

*Hypallage* is the application of a word to something to which it could not properly be applied. In *Midsummer Night's Dream*, Bottom reports that: "The eye of man hath not heard, the ear of man hath not seen, man's hand is not able to taste, his tongue to conceive, nor his heart to report what my dream was." The verb linked to each noun is an impossible action for the subject to perform in the literal sense: the eye cannot hear, the ear see, the hand taste, the tongue conceive, or the heart report. The effect of attributing these actions to these senses is to suggest that Bottom's experiences transcended the possibilities of all the senses. This same phenomenon is known to the psychologist as *synaesthesia*, the attribution of perception to one sense of something normally perceived by another.

Figures of speech are not essentially artificial or contrived. No writer sets out intentionally to use hypallage or antihimeria but he sometimes finds that the rush of ideas or emotions has suggested unorthodox combinations of words or images. A close study of the style of a writer will usually reveal an affinity for some figures in preference to others. A recent investigation of Shakespeare's style reached the following conclusions.[7]

> He effects sudden and vivid concentrations of meaning by a poetically superb and daring use of antihimeria (nouns as verbs), catachresis (verbs and adjectives employed in a transferred sense), hypallage (the transferred epithet), the compound epithet, metaphor, metonymy, syllepsis of the sense, negative and private terms. He secures swiftness of movement, compactness, and emphasis through anastrophe (inverted word order), parenthesis, zeugma (one verb serving two or more subjects), brachylogia and asyndeton (omission of conjunctions).

## Schemes of Words

In addition to figures of speech involving the use of words in their non-literal sense, rhetoric has always been concerned with the impact of words in patterns called "schemes." Schemes are the arrangement of words, in either their literal or figurative senses, to generate patterns of

[7] Sister Miriam Joseph, *Shakespeare's Use of the Arts of Language* (New York: Columbia University Press, 1947), pp. 288–89.

sound or rhythms. The schemes are numerous, some quite common, and some very rare in modern writing.

The most common scheme is *alliteration,* which consists of using several words in close proximity beginning with the same letter. A simple, clear illustration is the laconic message sent by an airplane pilot: "Sighted sub; sank same." *Assonance* is similar to alliteration but is built around the repetition of similar sounds in medial or final positions. Thus the first stanza of Poe's poem "The Bells" repeats the "i" sound.

> Hear the sledges with the bells—
>    Silver Bells!
> What a world of merriment their melody foretells!
>    How they tinkle, tinkle, tinkle,
>       In the icy air of night!
>    While the stars that oversprinkle
>    All the heavens, seem to twinkle
>       With a crystalline delight;
>       Keeping time, time, time,
>       In a sort of Runic rhyme,
> To the tintinnabulation that so musically wells
>    From the bells, bells, bells, bells,
>       Bells, Bells, bells—
> From the jingling and the tinkling of the bells.

*Antithesis* may be considered as a scheme of words since it consists of setting contraries in opposition as in the following example:

> Drown desperate sorrow in Edward's grave,
> And plant you joys in living Edward's throne.

The Renaissance, which admired a style which used schemes of words, looked upon John Lyly's novel, *Euphues,* as a model of effective expression. The following sentence, taken from that work, illustrates the way in which antitheses could be combined with alliteration to produce a highly patterned style which would be considered very artificial by contemporary readers.

When parents have more care how to leave their children wealthy than wise,
    and are more desirous to have them maintain the name
                                        than the nature of
                                          gentleman;
when they put gold into the hands of youth
where they should put a rod under their girdle;

when instead of awe they make them past grace

and leave them rich executors of goods
and poor executors of godliness,

then it is no marvel that the son, being left rich by his father's will,

becomes reckless by his own will.

*Anaphora* is the scheme wherein several clauses, sentences, or phrases begin with the same word. In the third part of *Henry the Sixth* Shakespeare gives the king the following lines:

> When this is known, then to divide the times—
> So many hours must I tend my flock,
> So many hours must I take my rest,
> So many hours must I contemplate,
> So many hours must I sport myself,
> So many days my ewes have been with young,
> So many weeks ere the poor fools will wean,
> So many months ere I shall shear the fleece.

*Epistrophe* is the reverse of anaphora and is distinguished by a pattern wherein several clauses end with the same word. *Symploce* is a combination of anaphora and epistrophe so that two or more clauses begin and end with the same words. Figures of speech and schemes of words can lend color and vigor to writing, but, when they reach the obviously contrived effect of symploce, it is important to make sure that the tail has not begun to wag the dog, that they are not being used just to demonstrate a versatility with words.

## Summary

The true test of a poetic mind is the ability to invent new metaphors. Aristotle said in his *Poetics* (xxii) that it is one thing that cannot be learned from others. What can be learned, however, is the way in which some words or figures of speech are better adapted than others to help a writer achieve a particular purpose. Not everyone can be a poet and coin metaphors, but all the other resources of the English word store are available.

Once a writer becomes aware of these resources he will also come to realize that he must discipline himself if he is to be effective. In his essay on *Familiar Style*, William Hazlitt warned against the dangers of becoming a "hieroglyphical writer." These are the writers who are "besotted with words," with a great passion for the schemes of sounds and the figure of personification. They use the diction of emotion and images of poetry, but words and images are isolated and unrelated to any groundwork of feeling which would be their only reason for being. They are jargonists for "Objects are not linked to feelings, words to things, but images revolve in splendid mockery, words represent themselves in their strange rhapsodies. Words affect them in the same way by the mere sound, that is, by their possible, not by their actual application to the subject in hand."

Unless the choice of words is controlled by a firm habit of testing each to make sure that it is the best available for the context and purpose, then the dangers of becoming a "hieroglyphical writer," to use Hazlitt's phrase, are ever present. Whether they are known as "hieroglyphical writers" or jargonists, they are the writers who will never be effective for "They will flounder about between fustian in expression and bathos in sentiment. They tantalize the fancy, but never reach the head nor touch the heart."

# 5 Delivery

Delivery is yet another important means of persuasion. The speaker's physical appearance before an audience is most influential. An audience may judge a speaker's worth and his control over the materials of his speech from his appearance and his voice. Thus delivery helps to establish credibility and forcefulness. It often helps to determine a speaker's *ethos*.

To communicate with an audience, seeking to influence them in a predetermined direction, can be a most terrifying experience for a speaker. There is always the possibility of failing to influence through some physical or vocal incapacity. But there is also the greater possibility that a speaker can create, through his physical presentation, a setting which makes the audience more receptive to his ideas. He may do so by combining the thought, language, and action of his speech into a coordinated communication which not only reveals a well-prepared speech script but also represents his own inner experience precisely as intended.

It is quite natural to wish to ensure oneself against the uncertainties of public speaking, and it is surely not unusual to seek some precise, sure way of regulating one's external impression. From the beginning of the development of a conscious art of public speaking there has been a firm recognition of the need to discover ways of developing effective delivery. But there has also been a suspicion accompanying this recognition that the use of effective delivery to gain responses from listeners is not altogether honest. Aristotle, for example, mentioned delivery only briefly and then only because he believed that the unsophistication of audiences made it necessary. Ideas, he believed, should stand on their own merit, rather than be dependent upon vocal and bodily activity. On the other hand, some theorists, such as Cicero, have considered it of great value. Quintilian, the great Roman schoolmaster, in the first selection of this section defends this point of view. Although written in the first century A.D., his discussion is still quite pertinent and sound.

Theories of delivery in the history of rhetorical theory fall into three main categories: the imitative, the mechanical, and the "think-the-thought." The imitative theorists believed that a speaker could develop good delivery by imitating the examples of other speakers. This method of copying often failed to recognize the individuality of the speaker and the uniqueness of his speech situation. Although most rhetoricians would agree that a speaker can profit by the example of other speakers, there are few who would advocate only the direct and often servile imitation of the "great" speakers of the day. The mechanist school had and still has many adherents, since man feels safest when he can compare his own performance with a set of rules. From empirical studies of speakers, proponents of the mechanist school set up rules for correct expression of thought and emotion. Since the mechanical theory leaves little room for adaptation at the moment of delivery, it often leads to an inflexible form of communication. Speakers of this school also tend to pay more attention to the manner of their speaking than to *what* they are saying. The "think-the-thought" school emphasizes the thought of the speech itself, leaving response to the thought to govern the method of delivery. One of the chief exponents of this school was James A. Winans, who believed that the speaker should be *vitally* aware of what he was saying as he said it, responding to his own ideas while he was discussing them with his audience. In "Conversing with an Audience," Winans provides one of the classic representations of this school. Thus the public speech becomes a part of a *dialogue* in which the speaker shares his ideas with his audience.

"Developing Effective Visible Action" by Andrew Weaver and Ordean Ness and "Reducing Tensions" by Otis Walter and Robert Scott deal with two of the problems of beginning speakers. The first discusses the general principles of effective bodily action, and the second the causes of stage fright and its cures.

Paul Heinberg, in an experimental study "Relationships of Content and Delivery to General Effectiveness," demonstrates the continued concern of rhetoricians with delivery. His conclusions emphasize the importance of delivery in ensuring effective communication.

## INSTITUTES OF ORATORY

### QUINTILIAN

Delivery is by most writers called action; but it appears to derive the one name from the voice, and the other from the gesture; for Cicero calls action sometimes the language, as it were, and sometimes the eloquence of the body. Yet he makes two constituent parts of action, which are the

---

From Quintilian, *Institutes of Oratory*, Book XI, Chapter III, trans. John S. Watson (London: Henry G. Bohn, 1856).

same as those of delivery, voice and motion. We, therefore, make use of either term indiscriminately.

As for the thing itself, it has a wonderful power and efficacy in oratory; for it is not of so much importance what sort of thoughts we conceive within ourselves, as it is in what manner we express them; since those whom we address are moved only as they hear. Accordingly, there is no proof, that proceeds in any way from a pleader, of such strength that it may not lose its effect, unless it be supported by a tone of affirmation in the speaker. All attempts at exciting the feelings must prove ineffectual, unless they be enlivened by the voice of the speaker, by his look, and by the action of almost his whole body. . . . Indeed, as words have much power of themselves, as the voice adds a particular force to thought, and as gesture and motion are not without meaning, some great excellence must be the result when all these sources of power are combined. . . . How much power gesture has in a speaker, is sufficiently evident from the consideration that it can signify most things even without the aid of words. Not only a movement of the hand, but even a nod, may express our meaning; and such gestures are to the dumb instead of speech. Dancing, too, unaccompanied by the voice, often conveys a meaning, and touches the feelings; the state of a person's mind is seen in his looks and walk; and in the inferior animals, which are destitute of speech, anger, joy, fondness, are discoverable from the glances of their eyes, and other indications from the movements of the body. Nor is it surprising that such signs, which must at any rate depend on motion, make such impression on the mind, when even painting, a voiceless production, and always keeping the same form, penetrates into our innermost feelings, and with such force that it seems at times to surpass the power of words. On the contrary, if our gesture and looks are at variance with our speech; if we utter anything mournful with an air of cheerfulness, or assert anything with an air of denial, not only impressiveness is wanting to our words, but even credibility.

Gracefulness also lies in gesture and motion; and hence Demosthenes used to study action while looking into a large mirror. . . . In action, as in the whole body, the head holds the chief place, as contributing to produce both the gracefulness which I have just mentioned, and expressiveness. What contributes to gracefulness, is, first of all, that the head be held in a proper and natural position; for, by casting down the head, humility is signified; by throwing it back, haughtiness; by leaning it on one side, languor; by keeping it rigid and unmoved, a certain degree of rudeness. It must receive, in the next place, appropriate motions from the nature of the subject on which we speak, that it may agree with the gesture, and act in conformity with the hands and oscillations of the body. . . . But the chief part of the head is the face. With the face we show ourselves suppliant, menacing, soothing, sad, cheerful, proud, humble; on the face men hang as it were, and fix their gaze and entire attention on it; even before we begin to speak, by the face we express love and hate; from the face we understand numbers of things, and its expression is often equivalent to all the words that we could use. . . . But what is most expressive in the face is the eye, through which the mind chiefly manifests itself; insomuch that the eyes, even while they remain motionless, can sparkle with joy, or contract a gloomy look under sadness. To the eyes, also, nature has given tears, which are the interpreters of our feelings, and which burst forth in grief, or trickle gently down in joy. But when the eyes are in motion, they assume an appearance of eagerness, or disregard, or pride, or sternness, or mildness, or threatening; all of which feelings will be manifested in the eyes of an orator, according as his subject shall require. But rigid and distended, languid or torpid, wanton or rolling, they ought never to be; nor should they ever seem to swim or look watery with pleasure, or glance sideways, or appear as it were amorous, or as if they were asking or promising something. As to keeping them shut or compressed in speaking, who would do so but a person utterly ignorant or silly? . . . Much effect is also produced by the eye-brows; for they in some degree form the look of the eyes, and exercise a command over the forehead, which, by their influence, is contracted, raised, or lowered. . . .

As to the hands, without the aid of which all delivery would be deficient and weak, it can scarcely be told of what a variety of motions they are susceptible, since they almost equal in expression the powers of language itself; for other parts of the body assist the speaker, but these, I may almost say, speak themselves. With our hands we ask, promise, call persons to us and send them away, threaten, supplicate, intimate dislike or fear; with our hands we signify joy, grief, doubt, acknowledgment, penitence, and indicate measure, quantity, number, and time. Have not our hands the power of inciting, of restraining, of beseeching, of testifying approbation, admiration, and shame? Do they not, in pointing out places and persons, discharge the duty of adverbs and pronouns? So that amidst the great diversity of tongues pervading all nations and people, the language of the hands appears to be a language common to all men.

The gestures of which I have hitherto spoken naturally proceed from us with our words; but there are others that signify things by imitation; as when, for example, we intimate that a person is sick, by imitating the action of a physician feeling the pulse . . . a species of imitation which ought to be carefully avoided in oratory; for an orator ought to be a very different character from an actor in pantomime, as his gesture should be suited rather to his sense than to his words; a principle which was observed even by the more respectable class of actors. . . . the old masters of delivery have very properly added a direction that the movement of the hand should begin and end with the sense; otherwise the gesture will either precede the sense, or will fall behind it; and propriety is violated in either case. . . .

Such are the excellences, and such the faults, that may be shown in delivery; and the orator, after these have been set before him, has many other things to consider.

In the first place, he has to reflect in what character he himself appears and to whom, and in whose presence, he is going to speak; for it is more allowable to say or do some things than others in addressing certain persons, or before certain audiences; and the same peculiarities in tone, gesture, and walk, are not equally becoming before a sovereign, before the senate, before the people, and before magistrates, or on a private as on a public trial, in a simple presentation as in a formal pleading. Such distinctions, every one who directs his attention to the subject, can conceive for himself.

He has then to consider on what subject he is to speak, and what object he desires to effect. As to the subject, four points are to be regarded; one, with reference to the whole cause, for causes may be either of a mournful or an amusing nature, dangerous or safe, important or inconsiderable; so that we should never be so occupied with particular portions of a cause as to forget the general character of it. The second, with respect to the different divisions of a cause, as the exordium, the statement of facts, the arguments, and the peroration. The third, with regard to the thoughts, where everything is varied in conformity with the matter and the addresses to the feelings. The fourth, with reference to the words, in which, though imitation, if we try to make the sound everywhere correspond to the sense, is reprehensible, yet, unless the proper force be given to some words, the sense of the whole would be destroyed.

Delivery ought to exhibit three qualities; it should conciliate, persuade, and move; and to please will be a quality that naturally combines itself with these. Conciliation is produced either by fairness of moral character, which manifests itself, I know not how, even in the tone and in the gesture, or by agreeableness of language. Persuasion depends greatly on assertion, which sometimes has more effect than even proof itself. . . .

One remark must, however, he added, namely, that, as the great object to be regarded in speaking is decorum, different manners often become different speakers; and for such variety there is a secret and inexplicable cause; and though it is truly said that our great triumph is, that what we do should be becoming, yet this, as it cannot be accomplished without art, can still not be wholly communicated by art. . . . Let every speaker, therefore, know himself, and, in order to form his delivery, consult not only the ordinary rules of art, but his own abilities. Yet it is not absolutely impossible that all styles, or at least a great number, may suit the same person.

The conclusion to this head must be similar to that which I have made to others, an admonition that moderation must have the utmost influence in regard to it; for I do not wish any pupil of mine to be an actor, but an orator.

## CONVERSING WITH AN AUDIENCE

### JAMES A. WINANS

Imagine all memory of speech-making to be blotted out; so that there is no person in the world who remembers that he has ever made a speech or heard a speech. Imagine, too, all speeches and all references to speeches in literature, to be blotted out; so that there is left no clue to this art. Is this the end of speech-making? Here comes a man who has seen a great race, or has been in a great battle, or is on fire with enthusiasm for a cause. He begins to talk with a friend he meets on the street; others gather, twenty, fifty, a hundred. Interest grows intense; he lifts his voice that all may hear. But the crowd wishes to hear and see the speaker better. "Get upon this cart!" they cry; and he mounts the cart and goes on with his story or his plea.

From James A. Winans, *Public Speaking*, rev. ed. (New York: The Century Company, 1917).
James A. Winans was Professor of Speech at Dartmouth College.

A private conversation has become a public speech; but under the circumstances imagined it is thought of only as a conversation, as an enlarged conversation. It does not seem abnormal, but quite the natural thing. When does the talker or converser become a speech-maker? When ten persons gather? Fifty? Or is it when he gets on the cart? Is there any real change in the nature or the spirit of the act? Is it not essentially the same throughout, a conversation adapted to the growing number of his hearers as the talker proceeds? There may be a change, of course, if he becomes self-conscious; but assuming that interest in story or argument remains the dominant emotion, there is no essential change in his speaking. It is probable that with the increasing importance of his position and the increasing tension of feeling that comes with numbers, he gradually modifies his tone and his diction, and permits himself to launch into a bolder strain and a wider range of ideas and feelings than in ordinary conversation; but the change is in degree and not in kind. He is conversing with an audience.

Nor is the situation essentially different if, instead of our imagined case, our hero of field or forum is invited to speak before a society, and this time has notice beforehand, has prepared, and speaks in a prepared room, with a chairman introducing him, his hearers arriving at a fixed time and sitting down in regular array. There are differences to be sure; but these differences do not change the nature of the act of speech.

I wish you to see that public speaking is a perfectly normal act, which calls for no strange, artificial methods, but only for an extension and development of that most familiar act, conversation. If you grasp this idea you will be saved from much wasted effort.

*Public and private speech compared.* Let us examine the more important differences which will occur to the reader of this chapter. First, it may be said, a public speaker talks more loudly than one in conversation. Well, a public speaker, just as a private speaker, should speak so as to be heard without strain. If you have occasion to speak to a person at the other end of a long table, you raise your voice. If you wish to speak across a noisy stream, you may have to shout. This would not be ordinary speaking to be sure, but it is still conversation and not at all abnormal. The difference is altogether a vocal one. You speak loud enough to be heard.

Again, one is told, the public speaker does all the talking; in conversation there is a give and take. These statements are misleading. There are many conversations in which one party does all or nearly all the talking. Because an old man talks continuously to a young man who listens respectfully, we do not say the old man is making a speech. Our imaginary speaker talked continuously before he got on the cart, with but little response from his hearers. Nor is it true that the public speaker does all the talking. The audience applauds and thereby says, "We approve." It may hiss and thereby say, "We disapprove." Questions may be asked and encouragement shouted. But all these expressions are only audible signs of what is going on in any audience whether quiet or not. His auditors are thinking answers to the speaker's questions, or asking him questions, or assenting, or making objections; and the experienced speaker has learned to read less demonstrative, but no less certain signs of the thoughts and moods of his hearers. He can tell by attitude and facial expression whether the other party to this conversation is interested or bored, approves or disapproves, understands or is puzzled, and he amplifies a point or touches it lightly in accordance with what he sees. The story is told of how Rufus Choate reiterated the arguments and pleas of one of his jury addresses for three hours after eleven men were won, until he saw the stern face of the twelfth juror relax in sympathy. Many a passage of good oratorical prose can be turned into a dialogue by writing out the questions and objections that lie plainly between the lines. . . . The young speaker can do nothing better for himself than to fix firmly in mind that public speaking is a dialogue and to emphasize constantly the part of the audience, anticipating and watching for its response.

A third difference is said to be that the public speaker prepares, while the converser speaks as things occur to him. It is true that a public speaker should prepare when there is opportunity; but he is none the less a public speaker because he is too indolent, or too busy, or is called upon too suddenly. Nor is a man less a converser because he prepares for a private conversation.

Suppose a student is chairman of a committee formed for resistance to the abolition of cherished holidays. This student has an appointment with the President of the University for the purpose of presenting the views of the student body. He talks with his committee. One says, "This is a good argument to use." Another, "That is not the way to put it; this is the way to reach the President." After discussing the arguments, the chairman remembers that the President has promised him but ten minutes. He must cut out some arguments and find brief ways of presenting others; and by the time of his appointment he knows just about what he intends to say and how he will say it. We will suppose that the President says very little, simply listens attentively with but an occasional question. We are assuming a wise student; hence he does not take a loafing attitude or talk slang. He talks as directly and pointedly and in as good language as he can and stops on time. Has he made a speech or conversed? Conversed, of course; but he has sifted his ideas, adapted them to his hearer, and has not presumed upon his hearer's time. He has followed a method excellent for a public speaker.

Suppose further, that at the end of the conversation the President says, "Mr. Smith, I wish you would come to the faculty meeting to-morrow and say there what you have here." At faculty meeting our chairman has fifty or a hundred hearers. He has to raise his voice a bit, he stands up, perhaps no questions are asked; but if he has the good sense and self-control to talk to the faculty in the same spirit and largely in the same manner as when he spoke to the President alone, he will probably make an effective speech.

If, on the other hand, he adopts a tone and manner strange to himself, but which he may consider as belonging to speech-making, he may easily be ridiculous.

It is a matter of adaptation. If we are told that public speaking demands more dignity of manner or of language, the answer is already plain: All depends upon circumstances. Our student, though discussing the same subject, talks to a fellow student in a more free and easy way than to the President and he talks to the faculty in a manner different from that in which he addresses a meeting of the student body. In a similar way can be met other arguments made to prove that public speaking and private conversation are essentially different acts, and that therefore the former calls for essentially different methods.

On the other hand, I do not maintain that public and private speech are *ordinarily* just alike. We usually have no difficulty in distinguishing conversation from speech-making. Conventional differences, such as that the public speaker usually stands before a considerable group to talk while the converser usually does not, make a distinction. Ordinarily, too, the public speaker does speak more loudly, does talk more continuously, does make more preparation, and especially he does have to deal with more minds. These and other differences may be important. They may make public speaking *seem* quite different from private speaking; but since there is practically nothing true of public speaking that may not be true at times of conversation and nothing true of conversation that may not be true of public speaking, we can hardly hold the differences essential. They are not essential to the problem of delivery, and particularly to the narrow phase of delivery we are about to consider, the delivery of sentences with correct emphasis, pause, pitch and inflection. Still, despite the essential identity of public and private speaking, it is misleading to say that one speaks to an audience just as to one person.

A good deal of space has been given to this discussion, because this conception is fundamental to all our work, and experience justifies the elaboration. Perhaps there are few that would maintain that public speaking is something far removed from other speaking; but there are many who vaguely feel that there is a vast difference. As a consequence, they begin to speak in a strange tone, they adopt a manner stiff and pompous, they talk over the heads of their audience, vociferating loudly; or perhaps, they take a dull monotonous tone, lacking the lively communicative inflections of conversation. They may adopt a pompous diction in an abortive attempt to imitate Webster at his worst; or, what is the strongest evidence of their perverted conception, they endeavor to speak by a marvelous system of rules, which tell them when their voices should go up, when down, what words to emphasize, when to use guttural tones, when aspirate, and where to pause.

*Certain common misconceptions removed.* Before proceeding to our positive teaching on delivery it will be best to guard against certain misunderstandings which often arise. *First*, public-speaking, to be conversational in quality, need not sound like conversation, certainly not like ordinary conversation. Conventional differences may make it sound very different. However, conversation has many different sounds. Much depends upon the hearer, the situation, the subject and the speaker.

The same man in discussing the weather, politics, literature, religion, may have several different manners. He may be listless while speaking of your hobby, but while talking of his own impassioned. The diction of the commonest man tends to become elevated when he speaks of elevated subjects, even in private conversation. We should note, also, the possibility of getting a distorted conception of the style of a speaker like Webster because most of us read only isolated passages, and the lofty strain of an impassioned peroration may be very different from the body of the speech. Each part is fitted to its place. Nearly all have read Webster's apostrophe to the flag at the conclusion of the Reply to Hayne; few have read the four-hour address. Most school children have met with Webster's terrible description of the tortures of the murderer's mind, so far from ordinary discourse; but very few indeed have read the whole of that masterly address to the jury in the trial of the murderer of Captain Joseph White. Read all and you will understand the assertion of one of Webster's contemporaries that Webster talked to the jury as if he were a thirteenth juror who had just stepped out in front in order to address them better. Again we must remember that the conversational style of Webster,—of whom Carlyle wrote, "No man was ever so great as Daniel Webster looked," and who made the British laborer exclaim, "By Jove, there goes a king,"—that the conversation of such a man would not sound like that of more commonplace people. An acquaintance has told me that he was amazed by Roscoe Conkling's ability to pour out impromptu a lofty diction in the Senate or on the stump, until he knew Conkling personally and found that he never let down in his vocabulary. The grand style was his natural language.

*Secondly*, do not suppose when you are urged to be conversational in public speech that you are expected to be less careful, or dignified, or strong, or eloquent, than you would be otherwise. There is nothing in this advice to restrain us from the exercise of our highest powers. Perhaps there is no better way to make the point than to quote what has been said of Wendell Phillips, the great anti-slavery orator. George William Curtis said of him, "It was simple colloquy—a gentleman conversing." Yet that there was no lack of power is evidenced by the storms he stirred up. A Richmond newspaper, which detested his doctrine of abolition, said of him, "He is an infernal machine set to music!" Thomas Wentworth Higginson said of Phillips:

> The key-note of the oratory of Wendell Phillips lay in this: that it was essentially conversational—the conversational raised to its highest power. Perhaps no orator ever spoke with so little apparent effort, or began so entirely on the plane of his average hearers. It was as if he simply repeated, in a little louder tone, what he had just been saying to some familiar friend at his elbow. . . . The colloquialism was never relaxed, but it was familiarity without loss of dignity. Then as the argument went on, the voice grew deeper, the action more animated, and the sentences came in a long sonorous swell, still easy and graceful, but powerful as the soft stretching of a tiger's paw.

To take an example from present day speakers, Maud Ballington Booth has said that in speaking "she never was conscious of dropping a sense of conversation"; yet she is a speaker of rare power. One of the greatest feats I have ever known was when Mrs. Booth held for two hours and a quarter the close attention of an audience at Cornell University, an audience surfeited with lectures. True, her story of work in the prisons was fascinating; but a touch of the forced, unnatural manner affected by some speakers would have sent us to boredom in half the time, nor could she have held us had there not been in her delivery real power.

Please understand clearly that to have conversational quality in your public speech does not require a low tone, or a careless manner, or undignified English. So far as our present problem is concerned, use what manner seems good to you. Give your thoughts fitting garb; to plain thoughts plain expression, to heightened thoughts heightened expression. What I am now urging is, that, whatever else you do, you should make your speech genuine communication. Do not look upon public speaking as a performance, but as a genuine dealing with men.

*Thirdly*, and quite in line with the preceding, *do not understand that I am advocating* what is called sometimes "the conversational style." I advocate no style. The word suggests too strongly that all should speak in one manner, while we should stand for individuality. I urge only that our public speaking should be conversational in its elements, and that each should develop and improve his own best conversation. It is not conversational style but *conversational quality* that we want in our platform delivery. Do not understand that this is some new thing; or that there are various kinds of good speaking and that speaking which has conversational quality is one of them. As we are using the term there is no good speaking that is not conversational; and there never has been in any age whether grand or simple.

It is true that Phillips is called the exemplar of the "conversational style," and that it is frequently said that since his time American public speaking has been reformed until, as Goldwin Smith says in his *Reminiscences*, you will go far to hear an old-time "spread-eagle" speaker. Not only is the pomposity of former days passing; but the old formality also, and perhaps too much of the real dignity of earlier times, have disappeared along with the heavier private manners and speech of our fathers. Properly understood as referring to the speaking of to-day as compared with that of fifty or a hundred years ago, the term *conversational style* is unobjectionable. But that is not what we are considering here. It will be best to avoid the term.

A *fourth* common misconception remains to be dealt with: Since the first important thing for the beginner to do is to stand up and talk with his audience, some are quick to say, "Just be natural." This advice is plausible but hardly helpful. What does this phrase "Be natural," constantly used to signify all that is good, mean? The savage is nearer to nature than the civilized man; yet he is hardly a model. The child is more natural than the adult. As Henry Ward Beecher says, if nature were the ideal we should remain infants. It is natural to be bad as well as to be good. It is natural for some to stammer, for others to strut, for others to be afraid of audiences. Indeed, is it not natural for some to be affected?

At least affectation comes without effort. It is natural for many on the platform to be unnatural. The advocates of "Be natural," as an all sufficient guide are quite as likely as any to strut and bellow.

It is manifest that we are juggling with various meanings of the word natural. It may mean (1) in a state of nature, untrained; (2) unaffected, sincere, not artificial, or exaggerated; or (3) in accordance with nature's laws, normal. The word as generally used is too loose for our purpose. If it is good to be natural in the first sense, then all education must be wrong. We wish to develop nature and remove defects in speaking, as in all else. Too often the plea of naturalness is made as a defense for faults. If your mannerisms are objectionable to your hearers or decrease your effectiveness, they should be remedied if possible, whether "natural" or acquired. Most of that which we call natural is merely acquired habit.

Taking the second meaning of natural, we shall find that the plausible advice, "Be natural," is difficult of application by the beginner, and that it is indeed "natural to be unnatural." Most beginners feel embarrassment. Even old speakers suffer and rarely face an audience on an occasion of importance without a strong feeling of tension. At best the simple advice, "Be natural," is of but negative value, meaning for us, Don't consciously assume strange tones and manners. It will be best to avoid the phrase altogether, unless we define it each time we use it. We shall be helped more in escaping embarrassment and attaining genuine naturalness, when we look further and find out how to be natural. The phrase may seem odd to you, but we need sometimes to learn how to be natural. We need now to learn how to act in accordance with nature and to develop habits that will hold us to the normal under the stress of the platform. Let us look more closely into the nature of conversational speech, in order to learn what we have to develop and adapt to public delivery.

*Conversational delivery analyzed.* Let us turn to a common experience. Why is it that a small boy in school reads "See—the—horse—on—the—hill" without a trace of meaning in his tone, and yet five minutes later on the playgrounds shouts the same words to his playmates with perfect expression? And why is it that if the teacher insists that Johnnie read over his sentence and get its meaning before reading it aloud, he will read with far better expression? And why, if the teacher then asks him to stand facing his class and read or tell the story to them, does he read with really good expression? The reason for his first improvement is apparent: in his first reading all his mind is given to recognizing words as words. They are without content for him; they bring no meaning, no picture to his mind. His expressionless voice is a true index of his impressionless mind; or rather, to be strict, his high strained tone expresses truly the anxious strain of his attention to the symbols before him. When he grasps the meaning, expression comes into his voice. He not only understands, but if he has a marked success, he has more than bare understanding: the objects and incidents of which he reads are present to his imagination. The horse is to him a real and significant object at the instant he speaks the words. He has approached the conditions of his playground conversation. He is "thinking on his feet"; he *creates, or re-creates, the thought at the moment of delivery.*

But our small boy is still more successful in his reading when he is made to feel that he is reading or telling his story to his classmates. To throw the statement into a phrase we shall make much use of, Johnnie succeeds when he reads or speaks with a *sense of communication.* On the playground he has the most perfect expression of all, when with no thought of how he says things, he uses perfect tone, emphasis, and inflection. Still the advice, "Forget your delivery," will be of little aid to the embarrassed beginner. We can forget only by turning our attention to something else. Forget embarrassment then by holding your mind to your subject-matter and your business with your audience. Hold firmly to the conception that you are there to interest them, not in your speaking, but in your ideas; to convince or persuade them. Look for their response. Stand behind your speech, and embarrassment will disappear. As soon as you can carry out these injunctions, whatever your faults, you will be a speaker.

*What to do.* To summarize, then, your delivery will have the desired conversational quality when you retain upon the platform these elements of the mental state of live conversation:

1. *Full realization of the content of your words as you utter them,*[1] and

2. *A lively sense of communication.*

When the first element is lacking we may characterize the delivery as *absent-minded;* when the second is lacking we may describe the delivery as *soliloquizing, not communicative,* or *indirect.*

---

[1] It may be said that the first element is included in the second; but it is doubtful if this is true in all cases. At any rate, both elements need stress. In practice much attention must be given the first; and a great deal of what follows is intended to show how to develop full realization of content. This depends primarily upon mastery of subject-matter; but beyond this is needed the well established habit of "thinking on one's feet."

*These directions needed*. Put so simply these directions may strike some as needless. They may ask, "Do not all sensible speakers think as they speak, and do they not realize that they speak to communicate?" Many years of observation convince me that these natural questions must be answered in the negative. The faults of absent-minded speaking and soliloquizing speaking are very common. Of course, there is usually some consciousness of the meaning, but not always. Mind you, no half grasp will do. Nor is it enough to grasp the bare meaning; the emotional content also must be realized.

To fail of contact, to be indirect, is very common indeed. Young speakers too often look upon public speaking as an exhibition; and older speakers frequently fall into a perfunctory manner, especially those who speak frequently and in a routine way. Moreover, many of those who do in a measure fulfil the conversational conditions, suffer from a wrong start. The man who begins his career as a speaker because he "has something to say which he wishes very much to say," and continues for the same reason until his habits are fixed, and who has no false notions of speaking, may come naturally to a genuine delivery. But if a speaker begins with the notion that he speaks to make an exhibition of his delivery, or that delivery is an external, mechanical thing to be manipulated according to rule, or in imitation of a model, he will probably develop a conventional tone and other bad habits that will resist the force of even a strongly felt message and an eager audience. Unfortunately, most of us have made a wrong beginning with our reading and speaking, and have the habit of perfunctory delivery. We began to read with all our attention on pronunciation, and to "speak pieces" we did not understand, in order to make admiring aunts and jealous neighbors say: "How splendid! I heard every word!" when our delivery was really an abomination,—neither song nor speech.

*The conversational elements in reading*. Perhaps it is more common to read than to speak absent-mindedly and indirectly. The minister, for example, reading hymn or scripture lesson, with his mind on his sermon, or on who has come to church, may proceed with but the vaguest consciousness of the meaning of what he reads and with no feeling that he is reading to answering minds. He may pronounce the words in a sonorous ministerial tone. And his congregation? How rarely do they really listen! If indifferent, they think of business or fashions; if devout, they piously feel it is all good and true and are affected by the sound regardless of sense, like the old lady who always wept when she heard "that blessed word, *Mesopotamia!*" In many churches there is a feeling that nothing really counts but the sermon, and there is a notable shifting and coming to attention when sermon time comes. In those churches where the reading is of chief importance, the members of the congregation get the meaning, so far as they do, by following the service in their individual books. And all this is but the natural result of the perfunctory reading that prevails. When a preacher takes the pains to study out the significance of what he reads, throws off the ministerial tune, and reads as one who has thought to convey, the congregation looks up with surprised interest and thinks, "Why, really, what a remarkable chapter that is!"

What I have elaborated in regard to the reading of preachers is true generally of the reading of other speakers. Whenever a speaker in court or on the platform begins to read a quotation, the audience is likely to suspend listening until the speaker explains the meaning of what he has read.

*The conversational element in speaking from manuscript.* The speaker with manuscript in hand is peculiarly tempted to repeat empty words, because it is so easy for him to do so. Nothing is easier than to recognize and pronounce words without any recognition of their contents. Yet speaking from manuscript need not be empty and monotonous. It may be lively and communicative, if the speaker exerts himself to think and keep in touch with his hearers.

*When speaking from memory.* The reading speaker is not popular, but by no means all readers carry manuscript to the platform. The speaker who memorizes should succeed better than the speaker with manuscript; for he can better keep in touch with his audience. As compared with the extemporaneous speaker, he is freed from the harassing necessity of choosing ideas and words from the many offering themselves, and from the necessity of determining order. He can, therefore, give all his mind to presenting his thought to his audience. Probably, much as we admire the ability to speak extempore and necessary as it is to the well-equipped speaker, most of the great speeches have been delivered memoriter. But too often one who delivers a memorized speech really only reads, and reads badly, giving all his mind to recalling the words. Sometimes he is reading from a manuscript before his "mind's eye"; or his "consciousness is empty of all but the sound and feel of the words."[2] This tendency to keep mere words uppermost, we

---

[2] "The difference between speaking sense and nonsense is this: in the latter case, consciousness is empty of all but the sound and feel of the words; in the former, the words are the expression of a conscious situation, the discharge of an aggregate idea." *Private letter from Professor E. B. Titchener, quoted by permission.*

must earnestly fight against. The method by which one memorizes is important and will be treated later; but the gist of the matter is: hold yourself to the thought first, last and all the time, and avoid the parrot-like repetition of words.

Some hold that a speech committed to memory cannot be delivered with spontaneity; but observation proves that this is not true. It has been said concerning the practice of George William Curtis, one of the best speakers of the last generation: "He practised that perfect memorization which has the virtues of extemporization without its faults." Higginson tells this story of Wendell Phillips:

> I remember that after his Phi Beta Kappa oration, in which he had so carried away a conservative and critical audience that they found themselves applauding tyrannicide before they knew it, I said to him, 'This could not have been written out beforehand,' and he said, 'It is already in type at the *Advertiser* office.' I could not have believed it.

It is all a matter of re-creating the thought, and it is a poor thought that cannot be thought more than once. A man in earnest, let us say a senior canvassing for a class memorial fund, or a candidate for office, will converse spontaneously enough though he has prepared even his words and has repeated them in a dozen different conversations. The chronic story teller often finds his adventures growing in thrills as the years go by, if only he can find new listeners.

Whitefield, one of the greatest of preachers, declared that he was at his best the fortieth time he delivered a sermon. The lecturers of the Lyceum and Chautauqua platforms may repeat their addresses hundreds of times, and yet deliver them with freshness. Again, when weary or indifferent, the best of them, for example, Mr. Bryan, may give you as little sense of personal contact as a phonograph. The book agent who keeps his mind alert and is keen about his business will not remind you, as some poorer solicitors do, that his talk was handed him by his company.

*When speaking extemporaneously.* So indirect and monotonous is much of the speaking by the memorizing method, that it is widely condemned. The extemporaneous method is most popular of all. It has faults and virtues which may be discussed later; but here it is in order to point out that not even this method is free from the faults under consideration. We must all know by observation that it is quite as possible to make a speech without well controlled thinking, as it is to converse without "knowing what we are talking about." The extemporizer's mind is more likely to be active; but under the stress of choosing and rejecting, he may fall into confusion. Any experienced speaker knows how possible it is to talk on without knowing at the end of a period what he has been saying. Extraneous thoughts come,—an engagement forgotten, the train to be caught, disturbances in the audience,—yet the speaker talks on, probably forming grammatical sentences, but rambling and "marking time." Again, the effort of thinking out a point not thoroughly mastered before, or consideration of a point now first presenting itself, may throw him into a reflective frame of mind; his thought loses the objective character needed. As a result he breaks contact with his audience and soliloquizes.

The extemporaneous speaker, therefore, needs quite as much as others, a firmly fixed habit of always holding his mind firmly to the matter in hand and of speaking directly to his audience. To fix this habit requires for most persons time and practice. The beginner has to develop his powers, as does the athlete,—powers which serve well enough for ordinary purposes, but not for extra strain. Until this habit is fixed and he has found himself as a speaker, the student should avoid all methods that tend to draw him away from the fundamentals.

*With special reference to directness.* More speakers fail in the second conversational element than in the first. It is highly important that we understand the distinction between communicative and non-communicative, or direct and indirect, speaking,—a distinction more easy to feel than to put into words. We hear a speaker, perhaps we follow his thought, yet we do not feel he has business with us. If he asks questions, we do not feel provoked to reply even mentally. We are not participators, but idle spectators. There is no challenge to our attention. With another speaker we feel contact. It has been said[3] of Count Okuma, the Japanese statesman: "It is easy to understand the delight with which he is always heard upon the platform. He is master of the art of being intimate with his audience—which is the secret . . . of the highest quality of public speaking."

We may follow a speaker who lacks directness of delivery, from sheer interest in the subject-matter, or from a sense of duty; but our attention is not due to delivery. Such attention is wearying and can hardly be expected from the average audience. The thought may be worthy, the language fitting, the delivery may be otherwise good,—voice

[3] Hamilton Wright Mabie in the *Outlook*, June 14, 1913, p. 331.

clear and pleasing and the modulation true; and yet lacking the communicative element, the speaking does not reach or grip. It may be the speaker is thinking intently, but as he lacks touch with his audience, his speech is only soliloquy. We say of another speaker, "He talks over our heads"; and this points to more than the character of thought or vocabulary. The speaker may literally talk and look over our heads; or, though his eyes are turned toward us, he may be practically unconscious of our presence. Some advance from soliloquy to monologue and talk at us, or thunder at us.

But true speech is a dialogue; better even than talking *to* us is talking *with* us. It is conversation with an audience. The audience is conceived of by the speaker as responding, asking questions, approving and disapproving. He dwells on an idea till he is sure of the response. He never follows his own train of thought to the ignoring of the thoughts of his hearers. This conception brings into the speaker's voice the tone we call *direct* or *communicative*.

We should make sure, in our efforts to be direct, that this tone springs from mental attitude, from a felt contact with our hearers; for it, no more than other tones, should be assumed as a trick of delivery. The attempt to put on directness is likely to result in an over-familiar, confidential, or wheedling tone which is most objectionable.

It takes courage and self-control to speak straight to an audience. This is not because of embarrassment merely, but because of the necessity of commanding and directing the thoughts of many. There are times when the speaker feels that it is his will against the combined wills of his hearers. The point was well put by a former student who, from being a rather weak speaker in college, developed a direct and effective style while preaching to western cowboys: "I tell you, when your congregation may jump out of a window or dance in the aisle if you lose control, you have to *grip* them!" If the speaker weakens and retires within himself, he quickly loses control and a restless inattention ensues almost as distressing as these "wild and woolly" extremes. Said President Stryker of Hamilton College, at his best an orator of great power, "It is four-fifths will power."

We should emphasize in connection with directness, the *effect of the eye*, which is quite as important as the voice in maintaining contact. The speaker should look at his hearers squarely. No dodging will do; no looking just over their heads, or down the aisle, or at a friendly post. The speaker who meets the eyes of his hearers will rarely see their eyes turn away from him and he will rarely lose contact. But the temptation is often strong upon the young speaker to turn away; not merely because of nervousness, but also because the necessity of thinking tempts him to drop his eyes to the floor, or raise them to the ceiling. But the time for meditation has passed; his facts, arguments and conclusions should be clearly arranged in his mind. His thinking now should be of that objective sort that is best stimulated by contact with his audience. Of course a speaker who has no opportunity to prepare, may be pardoned if he fails to observe this rule, and those who speak from notes cannot; but the loss of force is easily noted.

While a speaker should avoid a constantly shifting gaze, he should neglect no part of his audience. The part directly in front should receive most attention. Many speakers develop a bad habit of addressing one side of an audience nearly all the time, with but glances at the other. The neglected side soon grows restless. Do not let an habitual posture cause you to neglect any part of your audience. Make all feel that you are talking with them. "I wonder," said a freshman, "why Prexy preaches all his sermons at me." "Why," replied his friend who sat on the other side of the chapel, "I thought Prex. aimed them all at me!" It must not be inferred from the above that a speaker should stride forward with a fierce gaze and an "I-am-going-to-make-you-listen" air. It must be strength with ease, and self-confidence with respect for others,—"a gentleman conversing."

*Restraint and half-directness.* Many beginners speak in a half-direct way. They are not entirely lacking in the sense of communication; but they do not come out of themselves and vigorously take command of their hearers' attention. Sometimes they defend themselves against criticism by declaring that they do not like noisy, demonstrative speaking, thus showing that they mistake the critic's point. It is true that one may be effective without noisiness. There is a quiet directness which is highly effective; but we should not, as some do, make mere quietness an end in itself. A quiet delivery which fails to hold attention is certainly not desirable. We wish always to have our words listened to and accepted, and usually there is needed a display of frank earnestness. Quiet force is good; but be sure there is force, not indifference. Self-restraint is not the same as self-control; freedom is consistent with dignity.

The beginner, moreover, is rarely able to command the quieter force. He gets on much faster if he throws off restraint. To this end, I urge in particular that he should indulge in great freedom of action (quite regardless of whether he makes good gestures or not); for without free action most never arrive at genuine directness. As a result of dropping restraint, the beginner may speak with needless loudness and exaggerated action; but if he will keep trying to communicate and impress his ideas, he will soon acquire the feeling of direct speech with an audience, and will find that he can preserve this as he tones down to a more composed manner.

We may well note at this point that this quality of communicativeness is not merely a matter of delivery. Much depends upon composition, upon how the ideas are put into words, and very much upon the character of the ideas themselves. This last will grow clearer before we reach the final chapter.

*Conversational delivery not necessarily good.* There is a strong tendency to assume at this point that when a speaker has succeeded in reproducing conversational mental conditions upon the platform, then his delivery will be perfect, or "good enough"; and likewise a tendency, when asked to explain conversational public speaking, to ascribe to it all the virtues a speaker may possess. But it is obvious that if one's conversation has defects, his enlarged conversation may have these defects enlarged. Faulty pronunciation, indistinct enunciation, nasal or provincial twang, throaty tones, lack of range or of agility of voice, are but examples of faults that may be transferred to the platform. A rational study of technique may be beneficial after the first success is won. A rational study of technique requires that the student shall never look upon technical matters as of first importance, though they are often very important indeed. It is due in part to over-emphasis of technique that the elocutionist often falls under the condemnation of sensible folk. One reason for insisting that the class of faults mentioned in this paragraph should be attended to after rather than before conversational conditions are secured, is that we are prone to feel that the part of a subject which we take up first is the most fundamental. It would seem that many never get beyond the conception that public speaking is entirely a matter of the manipulation of voice and gesture.

We were speaking in the last paragraph of faults of delivery. There are of course many other reasons why a speaker whose delivery is thoroughly conversational, may yet be a poor speaker. He may have a weak vocabulary, or careless habits of thought and composition; he may lack information and ideas, or understanding of audiences; he may be deficient in imagination, earnestness and strength; he may have an unpleasant personality.

It should be pointed out, however, that *many of these faults tend to disappear when public speaking is thought of as a larger conversation.* For example, one earnestly reaching out for the understanding of one's audience, will make more effort to be distinct than in ordinary conversation; and often effort is all that is needed. Nervousness may cause a speaker to use his voice badly; but it is clear that he is less liable to this fault when he looks upon public speech as a larger conversation, calling for a normal use of his voice, than if he assumes strange tones. If our young speaker talks too rapidly,—and no fault is more common with beginners,—a direct attempt on his part to slow down often results in increase rather than decrease of rate. But if a speaker holds himself to a full realization of the content of his words, he will pause much of necessity; and if he is earnestly striving to talk with his audience, he will soon realize that an audience cannot be carried so rapidly as one listener. Deliberation will be the natural result. Again, if a speaker comes into intimate contact with his hearers, he is more likely to observe what manner of persons they are and adapt his message to their understanding, beliefs and feelings.

*How the student should begin.* We shall proceed to more definite suggestions; but we have already enough for a practical beginning. The first thing the beginner has to do is to gain the power to stand up and talk with an audience. Many will not find this easy, some because of embarrassment and some because of bad habits already established. In any case the effort should be to accentuate the mental conditions of conversation. In the measure in which the student succeeds in doing this he will succeed in expressing his ideas with true emphasis, inflection, etc. (The doctrine of this chapter goes much further than delivery in this narrow sense, but we shall limit ourselves to this here.) If at first he does not succeed, he must keep on trying. The chief remedy for failure to express is more thinking, a firmer, more complete grasp of the ideas and more effort to talk with his hearers. He must not let mere words fill his mind. Words he must have, but they must remain subordinate to the thought. He must establish the habit of speaking no phrase until its meaning is distinct in his mind. And, as will become clear in the following chapters, the thinking indicated in this chapter is not a mere dry, cold process, but is to be taken broadly as including imagination and feeling. To carry out these suggestions, the student should at once prepare simple speeches and deliver them to whatever audiences are available.

*Much practice needed.* Mental habits need forming and reforming. Long practice may be needed, too, before the expression, though correct, will be adequate. We often wish to express a wider range of thoughts and feelings on the platform than in conversation. This fact makes necessary the development of the power of expression. To this end we need not practise on a "set" of tones, such as "low aspirate orotund" and "high, pure, aspirate, fast"; but we may wisely practise expressing a large variety of ideas and sentiments, using both our own productions and those of others which we have assimilated. In such practice we should always seek the right expression by means of a firm grasp of content and the effort to communicate directly to auditors, real or imaginary. (An imagined audience is very patient and helpful for practice purposes.) As a result, we shall find the response of voice to mind growing more prompt, certain and satisfying. And since, on the other hand, the effort to express develops that which we seek to express, we shall find in such practice that harmonious development of thought, feeling and voice which is the truest vocal training.

*The place of voice training.* To this may be added the physical training of breathing and other exercises for strengthening, purifying and freeing the voice. Any exercises for bettering the response of voice and muscle to the action of the mind may be welcomed; provided always that we never confuse ourselves with the notion that somehow these means *are* public speaking, that we do not think of such means at all when speaking, and never try to substitute them for thinking. Exercises should be employed strictly as exercises; and it is best that they should be kept back until the beginner has gained the power to maintain conversational conditions upon the platform, through actual practice in addressing the class or some other audience.

*Do not be mechanical.* If you have understood the foregoing, you will see that there is no place in our scheme for the mechanical stressing of words, pausing and the like. If you have made a practice of consciously fixing emphasis, pause and inflection, abandon the practice. It is unnecessary and it will hinder you in acquiring the right mental attitude. If there is any time for that practice at all, it is not at this stage. It is unnecessary for reasons already stated. The voice reflects the mind with remarkable fidelity. "Expression," says Cicero, "is always perfect." A clear thought is clear in expression, and a hazy thought is hazy in expression. Our voices respond promptly and instinctively to our changing thoughts, feelings and moods, and to the varying situations in which we find ourselves. As a rule we take no thought of emphasis, pause, inflection and tone; yet the expression comes true. When we do take thought of it, it is most often not to express ourselves better, but to conceal indifference, eagerness, dislike, fear, or other mood. Wrong emphasis is due to failure at the moment to discriminate values; wrong pausing is due to failure to distinguish the units of thought; the wrong tone is prompted by the wrong feeling. The remedy is complete thinking and sincere feeling. The voice ordinarily responds without conscious direction because this is one of the earliest reactions fixed in the nervous system. Why should not this response be as true in public as in private speech, provided we can maintain upon the platform conversational mental conditions?

Mechanical methods of expression have been reduced to rules, which I refer to only because many readers of these pages may have had experience with them. For example, a rule states that a conditional clause should end with a rising inflection. In speaking the sentence, "If I go down town, I will do your errand," the voice should rise at *town*. We may admit that this is usually true, yet insist that the rule is both unnecessary and a positive evil. Both points are vigorously put by Nathan Shepard:[4]

> Another of the rules of the elocutionist is: 'Pause before and after the emphatic word, and put a circumflex upon it.'
> Where did you get this rule? From conversation. Finding that we do this naturally, let us do it mechanically. We do it by instinct in private talking, let us do it by rule in public speaking. Finding that while eating, every time your elbow bends your mouth flies open, therefore this rule: When your elbow bends, open your mouth. . . . If you deprive the speaker of his pauses and emphasis and inflections, what is left for his brains?

The last sentence touches the greatest evil in all mechanical methods: They check thinking. If we fix the precise manner in which a sentence shall be delivered and then, as is usually done, drill this delivery till there is no danger that the vocal organs will perform otherwise than in the manner prescribed, what indeed is there left for the speaker's brains? This easy substitute for thinking is usually relied upon; and this is the more true because the student of mechanical training rarely conceives of speaking as other than a matter of making his voice and hands go right. He manipulates his voice as an organist manipulates his instrument, and when he changes his tones for this or that emotion, you almost see him pushing and pulling the stops. But instrumental music is an artificial matter, while the response of voice and gesture to thought and feeling is a matter of the deepest instincts of our nature, and

---

[4] *Before an Audience*, p. 69.

mechanical methods, which are a necessity to the musician, are a positive hindrance to the speaker. Besides, the rules are only half true; they conventionalize speech; and they are cumbersome and needless. The agents of expression will respond to right mental action; let us therefore attend to the thinking. If at first the unfamiliar conditions of the platform may interfere, the remedy is not an arbitrary substitute for thought, but *more thinking and truer feeling.*

One particularly bad form of the mechanical method is that which marks on the speaker's manuscript the pauses, inflections, tones, gestures and emphatic words. Following out such a scheme takes the mind off the meaning of the words, puts attention upon a mechanism, interferes with the sense of communication, and in general has all the faults of mechanical method in the most definite form.

*Do not imitate.* Mechanical methods do call for some study on the part of the student; but the method of learning delivery by imitation of another lacks even this redeeming feature. It relieves from all necessity for thinking, and trains to absent-minded delivery. Moreover, when a student has delivered one speech by imitation, he is helpless when he attempts another. But worst of all is the suppression of his own individuality.

Fight against it as we may, there is nothing better for any one of us than his own individuality, developed and improved. David cannot fight in Saul's armor, nor is the ass a success in the lion's skin. It is the fate of the imitator to copy the mannerism and miss the spirit. The result is caricature. What Schopenhauer says of style in writing can be applied to delivery: "Style is the physiognomy of the mind, and a safer index to character than the face. To imitate another man's style is like wearing a mask, which, be it never so fine, is not long in arousing disgust and abhorrence, because it is lifeless; so that even the ugliest face is better." In the words of Wackernagel, "Style is no lifeless mask laid upon the substance of thought; it is the living play of countenance, produced by the expressive soul within." These brilliant statements of Buffon's thought, "Style is the man himself," are more true of delivery than of composition; because delivery is a more instinctive and intimate expression of personality than printed words.

In condemning conscious imitation as a method of learning to speak in public, I do not overlook the fact that we learn to talk in the first place largely by unconscious imitation and that imitation is a large factor in education. It may be admitted that in treating some special minor faults, imitation may be valuable as a last resort. It is the easiest of all methods for the teacher, and may be justified sometimes when quick formal results are necessary. There are some who are slow in responding to other methods. But all this does not alter the fact that imitation is the poorest of methods and disappointing in the long run; for it does not ordinarily set the student on a course of normal development. And for those mentally able to "run alone," it is well-nigh disgraceful. No man with proper self-respect will be content to follow, as his principal method, imitation, even of the best; and, in the nature of things, the imitator must usually imitate the mediocre.

I recognize the fact that students have learned to speak well by all sorts of methods and by no method. But as there are ways and ways, I have tried to show you the way which after eighteen years of experience as a teacher, I believe promises the least waste of effort and the surest arrival. Nevertheless, the way is not an easy one; *Think* is its "open-sesame"; and while we teachers can lead you to the platform we cannot make you think.

## DEVELOPING EFFECTIVE VISIBLE ACTION

ANDREW T. WEAVER
ORDEAN G. NESS

In discussing the nature of public speaking, we pointed out that a speaker uses both verbal and non-verbal symbols to "express" his ideas; that he sets up both sound waves and light waves as he speaks; that usually he stimulates both the ear and the eye of the listener or observer. In this chapter and the next, we are going to see *how* the speaker's body sets up the light waves and sound waves which stimulate his listener's eyes and ears, and *how* these actions can be improved to make communication between speaker and listener more meaningful and effective.

The visible code probably was primitive man's most effective way of making his wants and wishes known to those about him. Therefore, it

From Andrew T. Weaver and Ordean G. Ness, *An Introduction to Public Speaking* (New York: The Odyssey Press, Inc., 1961). Reprinted by permission of The Odyssey Press.

Andrew T. Weaver was Professor Emeritus of Speech, University of Wisconsin. Ordean G. Ness is Professor of Speech, University of Wisconsin.

seems logical to begin an attempt to improve speech with its most fundamental part, the visible symbols. We shall discuss such elements as posture, movement, gesture, and facial expression.

Right from the start, however, it must be understood that a firm differentiation between "body" and "voice" in speech is simply impossible. Voice is just as physical as are visible bodily actions. Bodily action furnishes not only the visible symbols of speech but the vocal symbols as well. Satisfactory voice control, involving as it does the coordinated operation of a large number of relatively small muscles, can be acquired only after general muscular control has been established. In normal speech, voice and visible action operate in an integrated fashion. The ideal public speaker was described by someone who said of Barton Booth, the famous English actor (1681–1733): "The blind might have seen him in his voice and the deaf have heard him in his visage." The separation we are making in these chapters is arbitrary, to permit us to point up the principles of effectiveness in each.

## Principles of Effectiveness

There are four general principles of effectiveness in the use of visible speech: (1) *animation*, (2) *strength*, (3) *coordination*, and (4) *variety*. These are but variant aspects of the single inviolable law of visible action: *Everything the speaker does should assist him in stirring up those meanings and only those meanings that will help him accomplish his purpose.* There is very little possibility of a speaker's visible action being neutral; every posture he assumes and every motion he makes are almost certain either to increase or to decrease his effectiveness. He cannot dodge the issue of visible action; if he tries to get along without it, the most obvious and significant aspect of his visible behavior will be his deficiency in this most fundamental part of the speech code.

One factor which makes the visible code so important is *empathy*. As we have seen, when we watch a speaker, we enter into some of the physical activities which his visible actions stimulate us to copy. For the most part, our imitative actions will be slight and more or less unconscious. We may frown, smile, sit up in our chair, slump down, and thus follow every movement of the speaker. If what we do as we observe him is a part of the reaction he wants to elicit from us, his visible code is operating successfully in stirring up meanings within our minds; if not, he is failing.

## Animation

No healthy, living muscle is ever completely relaxed; some degree of contraction is always present. This minimum contraction is called muscular tone. Each so-called "muscle" actually consists of a large number of individual fibers. Some of these fibers are always contracted; the number contracted determines the muscle's tone at any particular moment.

One of the most significant differences among people is in muscular tone. The high-strung, nervous, excitable person presents a picture of high muscle tone. The lethargic, easy-going, slow-moving person shows low tone. One of the characteristics of emotional behavior is a general heightening of tone all over the body, to facilitate quick and vigorous action.

The speaker should show sufficient general muscular tone to appear alert and ready for action. The audience unconsciously interprets this tone as meaning that the speaker is free from hampering inhibitions, in good health, and interested in communicating with them. In speech, the active individual has a very great advantage over the inert individual. We find it difficult enough to stir up meanings in the minds of others when we are using all of our speech resources. It is impossible for us to do our best if we are immobile. Many speakers seem to use their bodies merely as mechanisms for uttering language; those who observe them *see* little that helps in understanding what is being said. The low muscle tone of the performer is empathically reflected in the observer. On the other hand, too much muscular tension should be avoided. A nervous, high-strung speaker who is in a perpetual whirl of motion cannot help causing considerable restlessness in his audience. The result may be either distraction, embarrassment, or even amusement.

## Strength

Sufficient muscular animation will help to give a speaker the dynamic quality necessary for effective communication. Alertness and animation, however, may be superficial. Strength, on the other hand, is present when the speaker vigorously desires to communicate. Obviously the degree of strength which he may use in his physical actions should vary from situation to situation, from purpose to purpose, and from audience to audience. When a person speaks to a large group, he will have to enlarge and strengthen his visible symbols, as compared with his practice in ordinary conversation. A speaker trying to arouse action on the part of his listeners may exhibit greater strength than he would if his purpose were strictly informative.

### Coordination

Before we can effectively use the basic patterns of visible speech, we have to be sure that we have established proper coordination among our various muscle systems. If a speaker's action is to be pleasant to contemplate, it must be graceful, smooth, and economical, rather than awkward, jerky, and wasteful. Not only must each physical action appear to be coordinated and smooth within itself; it must also be synchronized with the other elements in speaking. The visible code must be closely integrated with the audible. Movement of any sort does not exist for the sake of the movement itself, but for the contribution it will make to the speaker's total communicative purpose.

### Variety

Speaking is, in a very real sense, living. So variety, "the spice of life," is a very important ingredient of speech. Constant repetition of any stimulus, no matter how effective it may be at first, will eventually wear it out, or fatigue the audience. We have seen the important function of variety in maintaining attention; we shall be stressing it as an essential characteristic of voice and language style. Here we suggest that it must be used in the visible code. A speaker who does not vary his posture, who repeats the same movements throughout his speaking, who "saws the air" with the identical gestures again and again, or whose face is a perpetual frown (or smile), eventually will wear down his audience; his visible code will diminish in effectiveness.

## The Elements of the Visible Code

### Posture

Many of the most fundamental impacts of a speaker upon the mental processes of those to whom he speaks come from his posture. Some speakers, by the unfortunate physical attitudes they assume, negate everything else they put into the visible and vocal codes. Not only does bad posture have unhappy consequences in the reactions of others, but it may make it difficult if not impossible for the speaker himself to maintain a clear and vigorous line of thought and to utilize all his physical resources. For example, if a speaker drapes himself over a desk in such a way as to tie up his hands and arms, he may find that he cannot use them effectively when he needs them, and he may also find that he is not sufficiently alert to follow his own line of reasoning clearly and forcefully.

*Common errors in posture.* One of the typical mistakes in posture is too much relaxation of the muscles that hold the body erect; the bearing of the speaker suggests an indifferent attitude toward himself, his subject, and most important of all, his audience. The other extreme is equally to be avoided; the speaker who maintains a rigid, immobile *physical* attitude is likely to suggest inflexible *mental* attitudes. His tensions reduce his capacity for easy and forceful movements and contribute to his own feeling of awkwardness.

*Characteristics of effective posture.* Keep in mind that your listeners will take note of your posture, not only when you are standing in front of them, but also when you rise to speak, when you walk toward the platform and become the center of attention, and when you leave the rostrum. A satisfactory posture is one in which you can control all of your muscles with a minimum of effort. It is one which permits the greatest amount of freedom to move or gesture. Posture should suggest self-respect, confidence, and a proper attitude toward the audience. To stand with feet wide apart suggests mental instability. To keep the feet too close together may make the audience feel that they, too, are likely to lose their balance. To stand with one foot behind the other and with the weight settled back away from the audience is likely to stir up meanings that will not help you.

Inexperienced speakers are often bothered about what to do with their hands. For some reason or other, we are never so conscious of these appendages as when we stand in front of an audience. *Do not worry about them.* They don't look like hams to your listener; they only feel that way to you. Let your arms hang relaxed at your sides. In this position they are easily available for any gesture you may need. But placing a hand occasionally in the pocket, or resting it on the speaker's stand, or behind the back, is by no means wrong or bad. It may be just the "right touch," in certain circumstances. An effective speaker finds many good uses for his hands, as we shall see later. The general position of your hands should be such that it will promote these uses. You should realize, however, that when you place your hands behind you or in your pockets for any great length of time, your audience may find it impossible to do likewise, and, consequently, the empathic effect can be unfortunate.

In many public-speaking situations you will use a lectern or stand. It is a convenience to you, a place where you can unobtrusively place your outline or notes. It is not, as so many speakers seem to feel, a "rock of Gibraltar" to which you must cling. There is no doubt that an inexperienced speaker may find some comfort in being able to stand near or behind a lectern, especially during the first moments of his speech. But you should never let the stand become a barrier between you and your audience.

There are, therefore, no rigid rules for effective posture. Just remember that your speaking posture should indicate (1) a desire to communicate with your audience, (2) a reasonable degree of confidence in yourself, and (3) mental and physical stability.

### Movement

Movement means shifts in the speaker's position or location. All of us realize that a moving object catches our eye, especially if it is moving in a field of relatively motionless objects. So, one of the principal functions of physical movement in speaking is to get and hold attention.

When we read printed material, we find that we are aided in understanding how the author is developing his ideas and how he progresses from one major idea to another by certain devices of punctuation, particularly the indentation scheme in paragraphing. A speaker can use movement similarly in marking his transitions from one point to the next so that the audience may follow the development of his thought patterns. The skillful use of movement by a speaker can add significance to the spoken word.

*Common faults in movement.* Perhaps the most common fault observed among speakers is irrelevant movement. The speaker may be nervous and, therefore, unable to control his muscles and use them purposefully. He wanders about the platform, giving the impression of taking time out as he does so. Such movement creates a picture of lack of poise and balance; the speaker's movement is saying, "I am ill at ease." The other extreme, unnatural immobility, is just as bad; the speaker freezes to the spot and seems unable to move away from it. In a quite different way, he is saying to the audience what the other speaker has said by too much movement.

*Principles of effective movement.* The paramount principle here is that all movement must be motivated, i.e., *it must spring from a specific intent to communicate meaning.* Movement isn't something added on to speaking; it is a vital and integral part of it. When you have finished discussing your first major idea and you take a step to one side before starting your next, you should not be saying to yourself, "I will move here because I need to introduce some movement into my delivery." Rather you should move because you want to point up the fact that you have completed one phase of your thinking and that you are about to start on another. Unmotivated movement is usually distracting—*meaningful in the wrong way.*

The amount of movement needed depends upon various factors in the speech situation. A fatigued audience, sleepy or uncomfortable, may react favorably to more movement than will a refreshed audience, wide awake and sensitive to more delicate types of stimulation. A large audience usually likes more movement than does a small one, perhaps because they are more likely to find distractions around them. Audiences made up of people who live active lives and who work with their hands enjoy more movement on the part of speakers than do sedentary, mental workers. Audiences of young children require more physical movement than do more mature audiences. About the only safe rule to follow is: Study the situation, learn about the habits and tastes of your audience, and adapt your action to the requirements of the particular situation.

### Gesture

While movement involves changes in location, gesture consists of visible signs made with the hands, arms, head, face, and eyes. Since gesture is more definitely conventionalized than posture and movement, there are special principles to guide the speaker in its use.

*Common faults in gesture.* Awkward gestures call attention to themselves. Why? Because they lose their symbolic character in the general feeling of strain and even shock that they produce empathically. Gestures should be graceful, not to evoke the comment that they *are* graceful, but because when they are not so, they draw attention to themselves and away from the ideas and feelings they should symbolize. Gestures must seem to be part of total bodily action. The hand must not be used as an isolated agent; it is part of the arm and the arm is a part of the whole body. While the action of the part should be dominant, it should not seem to be separate. Jerky, abrupt gestures are awkward and consequently likely to draw attention to themselves.

Generally, gestures of the hand and arm should begin near the midline of the body and move away from it, rather than toward it. The eyes of the audience tend to focus on the speaker's face and on the vertical midline of his figure and any hand action that interferes with a full and continuous view of the face or cuts this line is likely to call attention to itself and thus be distracting.

The speaker's eyes are among his most effective agents of gesture. It is an almost fatal mistake not to *make and maintain eye-contact* with the audience. When a speaker looks out of the window or just over the heads of his audience, he is misusing one of the best means at his disposal for controlling their behavior. It may be a little difficult to look people squarely in the eyes as you talk with them, but the effort to do so is thoroughly worth while.

*Principles of effectiveness.* We have already suggested some of the principles of effectiveness in gesture. There are three additional fundamentals that need to be considered: (1) *timing*, (2) *reserve*, and (3) *habitualization*.

(1) *Timing.* Just as gesture develops before language in the child's speech, so gesture should precede the utterance of words in adult speech. A reversal of the normal order produces a comic effect. Suppose when someone asks you, "Where is the house?" you look straight at your questioner and answer, "Right over there." Then, after you have finished speaking the words, you turn and point to the house. The proper sequence of events is: (1) turn the body, (2) point to the house, and (3) then utter the words. Gesture and vocalization normally overlap, of course, but the gesture begins first.

(2) *Reserve.* In speaking to the players, Hamlet put the principle of reserve about as well as it can be stated: ". . . for in the very torrent, tempest, and, as I may say, whirlwind of your passion, you must acquire and beget a temperance that may give it smoothness." *Temperance* is a synonym for what we call *reserve.* We never like to watch a speaker who seems to be exerting himself to the uttermost; we want to feel that if he had something still more important to say, he would have adequate available resources. Therefore, you should avoid all-out action, in favor of moderation.

Reserve does not imply weakness. Strong, well-defined action, which stems from real motivation, should characterize every element of the visible code. What we have said about reserve is also related to variety in the use of gestures. Just as any single gesture must be kept under control, so you must avoid the over-use of any one gesture or movement.

(3) *Habitualization*. No part of the speech code ever can function with greatest effectiveness so long as it is produced consciously and voluntarily. So it is with gesture; when we have to stop what we are saying to think up and execute a gesture, it is almost certain that the gesture will not serve effectively as a symbol. We must acquire a set of unconscious habits that will take care of themselves during speaking. The objective is to train our muscles to the point where we safely can trust them to their own inner feedback controls while we concentrate on what we are saying, the reactions we are getting, and the purposes we are trying to accomplish.

*Kinds of gestures*. There are probably as many kinds of gesture as there are speakers, subjects, and situations. However, it may be helpful to make a rather general classification. It would seem that there are three identifiable types: (1) *descriptive gestures*, (2) *suggestive gestures*, and (3) *emphatic gestures*.

(1) *Descriptive gestures*. Descriptive gestures are literal, denotative, and objective. They are used to produce clear mental pictures of size, shape, position, and physical relationships. When we say, "The pitcher stands there, the first baseman there, and the catcher here," we should use descriptive gestures. When we say, "The tube was about *so* long and *so* big around," we should use descriptive gestures.

(2) *Suggestive gestures*. Suggestive gestures are figurative, connotative and subjective. Such gestures give us mental concepts of entities that cannot be seen with the physical eye; they are symbols of feelings and attitudes. A shrug of the shoulder indicating indifference, a shake of the head that says "No," a wave of the hand that stands for rejection—these are suggestive gestures.

(3) *Emphatic gestures*. The emphatic gesture is ordinarily not substituted for words as is the suggestive gesture; it is used to reinforce words. When we say, "It's no use for you to tell *me* that. I will *not* believe it!" or,"Never! *Never! NEVER!*" we may shake our head, stamp our foot, slap our hands together, or pound the desk to emphasize what we are saying; these actions are emphatic gestures.

## Directness

Good public speaking is as much like good conversation as circumstances permit. Of course, the circumstances in which one is speaking in public often make it desirable that the variation from ordinary conversation be considerable. It is impossible to speak properly to twelve thousand people using the same sort of vocalization, the same visible action, or the same language, as would be adequate in presenting similar meanings to one or two people in conversation. But, as a general principle, the most effective public speakers employ the conversational manner of delivery.

There are amazing differences between the speaking techniques of the mediocre and the skilled conversationalist. The positive quality of dynamic conversation results to a considerable extent from the speaker's lively, intelligent use of the visible code. He is physically alert and active, he reinforces his ideas with movement and facial expression, he describes with gesture, and—perhaps most important—he makes direct contact with his listeners.

*Directness* is the essential quality of effective public speaking. In Professor Winans' phrase, directness means speaking with a "lively sense of communication." It means really *saying something to somebody*, and not simply *delivering a speech in the presence of somebody*. A very amusing little cartoon which appeared in a daily newspaper recently showed a pompous looking speaker, standing before an audience saying, "Ladies and gentlemen, before I begin my speech, I want to say something." It is not difficult to imagine what his speech was going to be like!

From the physical point of view, you will achieve directness by establishing *eye contact* with individuals in your audience. Looking in the direction of the audience will not do it; you actually must *see* them. Think of good conversationalists you have met; when they are talking to you, they look you in the eye. The eye, more than any other member of the body, reveals what you are thinking. When you *make contact with* your listeners in this way, you show them that you mean what you say, that you want them to grasp what you say, that you want to see their reaction to what you say. Let your eye contact be made with individuals in all sections of the audience. *But* let it rest for a moment on each person you select so that you make real contact. The speaker whose eyes flit rapidly here and there creates a feeling of restiveness just as surely as does the speaker who gazes out the window or over the heads of his audience.

You must keep in mind that successful communication is a reciprocal process. You will succeed only if you can set up a circular response between yourself and your audience. The feedback you get from your listeners serves as your best index of how well you are communicating.

Good eye contact will make feedback possible. When you practice physical directness, you will discover that you can achieve with little effort the flexibility and animation characterizing good vocalization. You will find yourself adapting your behavior to your listeners' responses in all the factors of speech. You will realize the satisfaction that comes from true communication.

## REDUCING TENSIONS

OTIS M. WALTER
ROBERT L. SCOTT

Stage fright is universal and desirable. Few speakers report facing audiences with perfect calm; over ninety-five per cent of beginning speakers report that stage fright makes them feel uncomfortable—and your authors strongly suspect that the other five per cent might have felt just a little nervous. Although you may feel that your reactions to tension are worse than anyone else's, remember that your classmates feel the same about themselves. Although our symptoms may vary somewhat, few of us will shake visibly before an audience as Cicero's contemporaries reported that he did. Stage fright is a natural response to a situation perceived to be potentially trying. The symptoms we experience as speakers are akin to those which our far-removed ancestor felt that morning so long ago when he came face to face with a saber-toothed tiger at the entrance to his cave. His tension readied him to run or fight. Although we should neither run nor fight, we also need the vigor and power that the reaction can impart. Far from being the disadvantage that the beginning speaker often feels it to be, stage fright can be a distinct advantage to the speaker. Physically it helps provide energy for faster, more intense, and more varied activity. It can even speed the thinking process and, at the very least, should make the speaker more alert and sensitive than he would "normally" be. A partial list of some of the

Reprinted with permission of The Macmillan Company from *Thinking and Speaking* by Otis M. Walter and Robert L. Scott. © The Macmillan Company 1962. Revised from material in *Today's Speech* (September 1954).

Otis M. Walter is Professor of Speech at the University of Pittsburgh. Robert L. Scott is Professor of Speech at the University of Minnesota.

changes that take place in the body indicate that the organism may obtain more energy under tension:

1. More blood sugar, which furnishes energy, is made available.
2. Insulin, which increases the permeability of body cells to blood sugar is secreted, so that more food can get inside the cells.
3. Thyroxin, which speeds the burning of sugar inside the cells, is secreted.
4. Blood pressure is increased.
5. The rate of respiration is increased.
6. Nerve conductivity is slightly increased.
7. Poisons are more readily removed from the system, thus reducing toxicity and fatigue.
8. More oxygen is made available to the blood so that more fuel can be oxidized.

Thus stage fright adds more fuel to the furnace, opens the draft so that the fires can burn better, and carries away the smoke faster. Because of these reactions, many experienced speakers report that they can think more rapidly in front of an audience than they can in the less stimulating comfort of their armchairs. Although we certainly do not recommend it as a universal practice, especially to beginners, some experienced speakers report that they barely outline those parts of their speeches which they wish to be most powerful, preferring to restrain their impulses toward final composition until they are standing before the audience where tension will energize their thinking and produce a better product than could be created without the presence of stage fright! More to be pitied than the young speaker with stage fright is he who is not excited by the prospect of giving a speech. This rare person will lack the energy, the swiftness of thought, and the potential physical power of the more normal, tense speaker. So the second step in reducing stage fright is to recognize that it is potentially beneficial to the speaker, and that it needs only to be brought under control.

If tension is universal and desirable, why talk about reducing it? Perhaps the question and its answer are too obvious to mention, so we shall do no more than that. The beginning speaker may find excessive tension can interfere with his communicative processes. At any rate, he may wish to be somewhat less uncomfortable than he has felt in his initial experiences. With knowledge and experience he can expect to become more at ease, more confident in his ability to meet the challenges of speaking. But he will, and should, retain the tendency to become tense in anticipating speaking and in standing before an audience. We will, therefore, help the student control, rather than abolish, stage fright.

## The Nature of Stage Fright

Despite its name, stage fright is not limited to the stage. It is a rather common reaction that goes under the name of "anxiety neurosis." Both the anxiety patient and the speaker who suffers severe stage fright seem to experience the same physiological reaction of increased heartbeat, increased blood pressure, and increased metabolism. Both experience tension and dread. In both, the dread is not justified by the immediate situation that produces it; the beginning speaker, for example, is faced with a classroom of students who are also beginners, who are more or less friendly, who are pulling for him, and who may be even suffering with him. The fear he experiences springs not from such a sympathetic situation where mistakes are tolerated and even expected, but as with the anxiety patient, from his previous experiences with people and from his conditioning. Thus the reaction of stage fright is a neurotic reaction characterized by an unjustified fear. To reduce this fear we must understand some aspects of the anxiety neurosis and how it may be reduced when it occurs in "normal" people.

## Causes of Stage Fright

Anxiety and stage fright occur whenever the self is "divided" so that what a person *is doing*, what he *wants to do*, and what he thinks he *should do* are different things. We are frequently faced with situations that divide us. Perhaps everyone is momentarily "divided" when the alarm clock sounds. The student who wants to make good grades but who must work his way through college may be divided about how much time to spend on studies and how much on work. Such kinds of divisions of the self are common and unavoidable. Such conflicting desires can be one of the principal causes of human misery, for an unintelligent adaptation to such desires seems to be the source of much unhappiness and of much neurotic behavior. Many Caspar Milquetoasts who cannot face other people with confidence have made maladaptive responses to conflicts. So has the soldier who returns from war but who cannot settle down and work for his goals. The man who must drink himself into somnolence to ease his tension is one who is reacting poorly to a conflict. When the conflicting desires tear too strongly, some react as does the catatonic patient, sitting on the floor of the psychopathic ward, oblivious and unmoved by the world about him. His world has torn him so powerfully that he will no longer take notice of it. The speech situation is not so dramatic for the speaker with strong stage fright, but that situation is of the same sort. The speaker is trying to persuade his class, or trying to get a good grade, or at least trying not to make a spectacle of himself. But at the same time he wishes he were not speaking and that he could leave the platform as quickly as possible. He *must* speak, but he doesn't *want* to. He is divided, and responds with neurotic anxiety which he calls "stage fright."

With the healthy person, on the other hand, what he wants to do, what he should do, and what he is doing are the same; since he is not divided, he plunges wholeheartedly into his activities, enjoys them more, and produces more than the person who is at war with himself. He faces situations that might divide him, but he responds to them in such a way that they cannot cause a serious division in his desires or his efforts. The healthy speaker will use his energy to communicate his ideas, and not to restrain himself or build up nervous tension. The problem for the anxiety patient and the stage frightened speaker is to find ways of getting back together, of making themselves whole, of cementing their desires together. For normal people, it is not difficult, and always worth the trouble.

## Treatment of Stage Fright

To understand the principle involved in making a divided person a whole person, we might look at the famous medieval donkey who starved to death between two stacks of hay; he couldn't decide which one to eat first because they were equally large, equally succulent, and equally distant. But in order to prevent starvation, all he needed to do was to move toward either stack of hay and eat it. What was required was that he strengthen the desire to eat one stack of hay, and nullify or weaken the desire to eat the other stack. It is this process of reinforcing some desires while nullifying and weakening others that is the basic method for treating conflicts and divisions in normal people.[1] There are many

[1] Conflicts that produce deep-seated neuroses or seriously maladjusted behavior should be treated by a skilled psychologist or psychiatrist, since facility in diagnosing these difficulties and skill in treating them requires long preparation and broad experience. Our advice is not for such kinds of divisions, but only for those normal people who can improve their reactions to situations that divide them, particularly in speaking situations.

ways in which a speaker can locate and reduce those things that divide him so that when he *must* speak, he will *want to*. Let us consider the ways he may increase his desire to speak and weaken his reluctance and fear of speaking.

### Combating Unfortunate Previous Experiences

Often a student has had an unfortunate experience that has predisposed him to react to all audience situations with stage fright. The fifth grader who, during Parent's Night, was supposed to recite a poem but who forgot his lines in the middle of the poem and thus felt that he had disgraced himself before his teachers, his classmates and his parents, will feel reluctant to speak, perhaps for many years, before an audience. Or the young actor who accidentally tripped, during the performance of the class play, and fell against the canvas scenery and tore a hole in it may feel uneasy for a long time whenever he faces an audience. The student who has had such an experience should immediately take the following steps to reduce the negative effects of it.

1. He should recall the experience fully. The process of recalling may be temporarily painful to him, but to "forget" or repress the experience is apt to cause harm. Such experiences cannot be "forgotten" and the mere act of recalling them may greatly reduce their influence upon the speaker.

2. He should discuss the situation with his instructor who will want to know if any of the students have had such an experience. The act of talking the problem over with another will help him get perspective on the problem, as well as further reduce any effects that repression of the memory may have had on him.

3. Above all, the student should work as hard as possible to give good speeches so that he may feel the reassuring power of success. After he realizes that he has given several good speeches, his feelings of confidence will return, nullifying the effects of his past failure. By the application of his intelligence to the techniques of speaking, he may rapidly substitute a feeling of success for his old feelings.

### Choice of Subject

The speaker's choice of a significant subject can help increase his desire to speak. If he has chosen a subject that he knows is not a significant one, and that he suspects the audience will recognize as superficial, his reluctance to speak and the possibility of having stage fright will be increased. When, on the other hand, he knows that he has found a topic that is worth both his time and that of his audience, when he knows the subject can stimulate both him and his audience, he will have reduced one of the factors that divide him and produce stage fright. Thus the choice of subject is one determinant of his confidence that is under his control.

### Preparation

When a speaker knows that his speech is poorly prepared, unclear, uninteresting, or lacking in profundity, he is almost sure to have stage fright because he will not have the same desire to speak as will a well prepared person. Thorough preparation, on the other hand, can contribute to the speaker's feelings of security and thereby increase his desire to speak. The speaker who knows that he has thought through the problems inherent in his subject, who knows the subject better than anyone else in the room, who knows he has a clear speech that is supported with vivid and sound supporting material, and who has practiced the speech so that he knows he can deliver it well, will *want* to speak. But when he fails to prepare carefully, and knows he is not telling the audience anything they do not know as well as he does, when he is aware the materials in his speech are unclear and dull, and when he is uncertain about his ability to deliver the speech, he cannot avoid feeling threatened. Thus preparation can reduce the conflicts of the speaker and increase his ability to plunge into the speech wholeheartedly. The speaker who is not prepared cannot feel confident, and hardly deserves to.

### Forming Proper Habits of Delivery[2]

A person often reacts with anxiety or fear to those situations in which a complex series of uncustomary acts is required. New situations are really multi-conflict situations. Remember the first time you drove an automobile? It was necessary for you to operate the steering wheel, accelerator, brake, and possibly the gear shift and clutch pedals in coordination with what you saw through the windshield. Since you had

[2] For this idea, the writers are indebted to Professor Clarence T. Simon for his article "Complexity and Breakdown in Speech Situations," *Journal of Speech and Hearing Disorders,* 10 (1941), pp. 199–203.

no ready reactions for doing this, you were not quite sure of what to do. As a result of this complex series of acts, you probably experienced a case of anxiety similar to stage fright. The situation was complex and required all your mental attention. You may even have asked whoever was with you not to disturb you by talking while you performed some particularly "difficult" new reaction in turning or backing. But notice what happened as you became more practiced. You could slow down, speed up, drive around corners easily and at the same time carry on a conversation, smoke a cigarette, and listen to the radio! The situation, although seemingly more complex, no longer could arouse anxiety because you had habituated a number of responses that could meet the situations with which you were confronted.

Thus a complex series of acts was, psychologically at least, simplified by making these acts habitual. Habits, of course, tend to be independent of one's attention. The phenomenon of reducing complex acts to habits in order to make them relatively independent of one's attention is applied in many fields. The good football player must have habituated hundreds of coordinated acts in order to play with ease and to be free to focus on the activities of his teammates and opponents. Basic training in the armed services is an attempt to fix certain habitual reactions so that the combatant will respond automatically and, to a greater extent, without fear. One may be nervous at his first formal banquet lest he pick up the wrong spoon and eat the wrong item with it at the wrong time. Practice, however, insures confidence on such occasions by making the necessary skill habitual.

Public speaking is, for the beginner, a complex situation. The beginner must walk to the platform with dignity, stand at ease, remember to look at his audience, respond to his ideas and reflect this response in his voice and body. He will not yet have formed habits to direct his voice and body automatically. For him, this situation is complex and he therefore responds with fear and anxiety. Whenever anxiety or fear has risen from this perception of complexity, the only possible way of dealing with it is to practice enough so that all the complex techniques of speech will become habitual. The student must habituate his posture, reflection of a communicative attitude, and responsiveness of his voice and body by practice prior to the final delivery of the speech. Unless he has fixed these techniques, he cannot help but respond with considerable anxiety.

Taking a speech course will tend to reduce the amount of stage fright a person has. One reason for this reduction is obvious. During the experience of speaking frequently before audiences, the speaker has already begun to make habits of certain techniques and may now spend his mental attention responding to his ideas. But if the student wishes to achieve confidence and poise quickly, he must work actively to make the techniques of speaking automatic so that he may use his attention for more important things.

### Recognizing the Intrinsic Significance of One's Ideas

Many beginning speakers undoubtedly volunteer to give their speeches because they want to "get it over with." Some may wish to speak to complete the requirement of the course, or so that they can gain more experience in public speaking and come closer to learning how to give a good speech. Such factors will, of course, increase one's desire to speak. These factors, however, are *extrinsic* to the ideas and materials of the speech itself. They may make a contribution to the wholeheartedness of the speaker, but they are not the most helpful ways of increasing the speaker's desire to speak. To be sure, one may use such extrinsic factors if they seem to help, but the most mature and most desirable way of increasing one's desire to speak is to grasp the intrinsic significance of one's ideas.

Why do good speakers want to speak? It is because they are alive with an idea that they believe is important. It is because they feel that they know something that the audience ought to know. It is because they have clarified a problem, or found answers to important questions, or have an idea that demands that they communicate it to others. Therefore, the best way to increase one's desire to speak is to recognize the intrinsic significance and merit of one's ideas. When a man has caught the fire of an idea, his desire to plunge into the speech wholeheartedly will be at its maximum. But often beginning speakers do not really grasp the significance of their ideas. Their delivery reflects a lack of understanding of the consequences of what they say. Their speaking is lifeless, timorous, dull, and lacking in power. They do not grasp the significance of their ideas because they assume that it is easy to understand an idea and its consequences. It is not. Who understood the consequences of the ideas of Galileo? Perhaps not even Galileo himself. Or who understood the consequences of the ideas of Newton in 1700 or of Einstein in 1910? To understand the significance of one's ideas requires effort. But the student can increase his understanding of the intrinsic merit and importance of his ideas, and in so doing, increase his desire to speak and build his confidence. We shall suggest a method by which he may do this, and in following this method, the speaker may uncover additional ideas and materials that he will find useful in the speech itself.

The student should ask himself the following questions about his ideas:

1. In what ways are these ideas important today?

2. How do these ideas relate to the material needs of my audience? To their psychological needs? To their philosophical or spiritual needs?

3. In what ways might my ideas influence the attitudes and behavior of the audience?

4. Are there times in the past when these ideas might have performed a useful service?

5. If these ideas are accepted, how will they change the future?

6. Am I, by experience, interest, or study, especially qualified to discuss these ideas?

7. Is this the only time I may have to express these ideas to these people?

8. Is this occasion a particularly opportune time to express these ideas? Focusing one's attention on answers to these questions will help the speaker develop the kind of attitudes that will make him want to speak. If he is aware of the intrinsic significance of his ideas, his desire to speak will increase, and he will have a deeper understanding of the importance and value of his speech. Moreover, he will begin to develop the kind of attitude toward himself, his ideas, and his audience that itself is persuasive. His delivery, when he reflects these ideas, will tend to have the directness, variety, vitality, intensity, and poise that comes through dedicating one's self to ideas. He will, thus, have developed through a deeper understanding of the speech in relation to himself, his audience, and the occasion many positive attributes of good delivery.

Needless to say, the speaker who cannot answer at least some of these questions in such a way as to provide helpful ideas that increase his desire to speak has chosen his subject poorly or has not caught the significance of what he is doing. But if he has chosen a worthy subject, he must not fail to grasp its importance. To miss the power that can be derived from a significant idea is to miss one of the speaker's sources of strength. The power of a great idea is the source of strength that gave confidence—and much more—to men like Socrates, Jesus, Lincoln, Churchill, and others. Great ideas have inspired people and nations to confidence and whole-hearted effort during times of danger and deprivation. Those possessed by a great idea do not fear. Those completely possessed by such an idea are undaunted by hunger, pain, persecution, torture, or the threat of death. If the perception of a great truth can do so much to alleviate such tortures, it is not too much to expect that when a speaker begins to grasp the significance of an idea it will reduce his weak-in-the-knees feeling on the occasion of a short speech in a beginning class!

Thus the real challenge to the speaker is not stage fright, but rather a challenge to stretch his mind around ideas. It is a challenge to recognize, appreciate, understand, and dedicate himself to ideas. The challenge calls one to set his mind on significant and worthwhile ideas. It calls one to bury self-centered thoughts and fix attention outside one's self on the highest thoughts a man can think. When he answers the challenge to stretch his mind around great ideas, he not only gains confidence and sets foundation for good delivery, but he becomes a speaker deserving of the attention of the audience. Such a man is not only a more effective human being; he is likewise a more worthwhile one.

## RELATIONSHIPS OF CONTENT AND DELIVERY TO GENERAL EFFECTIVENESS

### PAUL HEINBERG

Rhetoricians have deliberated for centuries about the relative importance of content and delivery in determining the effectiveness of speeches, but so far the amount of scientific research bearing upon this issue has been negligible. This study is one attempt to discover the nature of these relationships. Specifically, the purpose is to ascertain the

Paul Heinberg, "Relationships of Content and Delivery to General Effectiveness," *Speech Monographs* (June 1963), pp. 105–107. Reprinted by permission of the Speech Association of America and of the author.

The author is an Assistant Professor of Speech at the University of Iowa.

relative weightings of content and delivery in determining the general effectiveness of speeches of self-introduction and speeches to persuade.

## Procedure

Fifty-three students in public speaking courses at the State University of Iowa and at Oklahoma State University gave a speech of self-introduction at the beginning of the course and a speech to persuade (on an idea, not a product) at the end of the semester. Each speech was recorded on tape, and the first two minutes of utterance following the

**TABLE I.  Reliabilities of Judges' Ratings**

| Factor Rated | Self-Introductory Speeches | | Persuasive Speeches | |
|---|---|---|---|---|
| | Reliability of Average In-dividual Rater | Reliability of Mean of 8 Raters | Reliability of Average In-dividual Rater | Reliability of Mean of 8 Raters |
| Content | .39 | .83 | .40 | .85 |
| Delivery | .62 | .93 | .56 | .91 |
| General effectiveness | .55 | .91 | .60 | .92 |

identification of the subject were preserved. So that content could be judged apart from delivery, these two-minute samples were transcribed. By listening to the recordings, eight judges rated delivery, and eight others evaluated general effectiveness. A third group of eight rated the manuscripts for content.[1] All three groups used a seven-point scale, but content judges, unlike the others, were required to place at least one manuscript in each of the extreme groups. These critics, who placed each sample into one of the seven piles, also differed from their colleagues in that they were requested to go through each pile after sorting to insure themselves of its homogeneity. All judges were enjoined to consider the scale units as equidistant. They did not receive any definitions of content, delivery, or general effectiveness.

Reliabilities of the judges' ratings, as shown in Table I, were

[1] All judges had at least fifty hours of graduate credit and at least one year of experience as instructors in public speaking at the college level. The University of Iowa Research Foundation paid the judges for their services and thus provided the project with valuable support.

estimated by Ebel's Analysis of Variance technique.[2] All means are highly reliable.[3]

The assumption of linearity seemed tenable on the basis of an inspection of the distribution of points about the lines of best fit, which were computed[4] for each scattergram. These lines are as follows:

*Self-Introductory Speeches*[5]

$$D = 0.9C + 0.2 \quad (S.E.E. = 0.8)$$
$$C = 0.6G + 1.7 \quad (S.E.E. = 0.4)$$
$$D = 0.8G + 0.6 \quad (S.E.E. = 0.6)$$

*Persuasive Speeches*

$$D = 0.6C + 2.1 \quad (S.E.E. = 0.8)$$
$$C = 0.9G + 1.0 \quad (S.E.E. = 0.6)$$
$$D = \quad G + 0.1 \quad (S.E.E. = 0.4)$$

## Results

The equations[6] expressing the regressions of general effectiveness mean ratings on the content and delivery mean ratings for each group of speeches are as follows:

Self-introductory speeches
$$G = .63C + .56D - .82 \quad (S.E.E. = .44)$$
Persuasive speeches
$$G = .42C + .74D - .50 \quad (S.E.E. = .37)$$

To estimate the relative importance of content and delivery in predicting general effectiveness, beta values were employed because the variance of the mean ratings for content was less than the variance of the mean ratings for the other measures. Transformed into percentages these weightings mean that (*a*) 38% of the effectiveness of self-introductory

[2] J. P. Guilford, *Psychometric Methods* (New York: McGraw-Hill Book Co., Inc., 1954), 395–397.

[3] One probable cause for the lower reliability for content ratings is the requirement unique to this set of judges that they use the extremes of the seven-point scale. Another is that the content means were more homogenous than the means of the other criteria.

[4] Quinn McNemar, *Psychological Statistics* (New York: John Wiley and Sons, Inc., 1949), pp. 103–107.

[5] G, General effectiveness; C, Content; D, Delivery; S.E.E., Standard Error of Estimate.

[6] Helen Walker and Joseph Lev, *Statistical Inference* (New York: Henry Holt and Co., 1953), pp. 318–326.

speeches is attributable to content and 62% to delivery and that (*b*) 24% of the effectiveness of persuasive speeches is associated with content and 76% with delivery. Hence, delivery is far more influential than is content in determining the general effectiveness of these two types of speeches.

Intercorrelations among content, delivery, and general effectiveness tend to bear out the analysis obtained through computing regressions in that the delivery-general effectiveness *r*'s are higher than those between content and general effectiveness (see Table II).

**TABLE II.    Intercorrelations of Content, Delivery, and General Effectiveness for Self-Introductory and Persuasive Speeches**

|  | $r_{CD}$ | $r_{CG}$ | $r_{DG}$ |
|---|---|---|---|
| Self-introductory speeches | .648 | .808 | .851 |
| Persuasive speeches | .595 | .772 | .887 |

## Discussion

The present study of the relative degrees of influence of content and delivery deals with very short segments of speeches and pertains only to self-introductions and to attempts to sell ideas. Moreover, any extension of the results beyond the present experiment rests upon the assumption that *content*, *delivery*, and *general effectiveness* have the same meanings elsewhere as they did for the three groups of trained judges. *General effectiveness*, it should be particularly noted, is what college speech teachers think makes a good speech, and how well such an opinion correlates with a practical criterion, such as the amount of information retained or the extent of attitude change, is beyond the scope of this study.

Perhaps the greatest contribution of the present investigation is the formulation of a method which other experimenters may use in testing the content-delivery relationship with changes in the variables. Specifically, a better understanding of the general relation of content and delivery to effectiveness necessitates studies using a variety of (1) audiences, (2) speakers, (3) types of speeches, (4) topics, and (5) media. Studies also are needed to validate *general effectiveness* as a concept of the speech expert—how does his rating correlate with retention, attitude change or some other measure of obtained effect? An examination of further findings, besides perhaps revealing a lawfulness in the relative influence of content and delivery, also may lead to a basis for classifying speeches which is empirically justified rather than logically postulated. Significant thought-provoking questions pertaining to the present study, however, do not belong entirely to the future. If delivery is three times as influential as content in persuasive speaking, what are the implications for curriculum building and classroom teaching? Should more time be given to delivery and less to content? Does this finding make persuasion more of a mechanical skill than an intellectual art? And does this unexpected ascendancy of delivery as a constituent of effectiveness reflect adversely upon the attitudes of our present society? If a panel of trained, highly educated judges assigns such a small role to content, what hope is there that people generally are responsive to fact and reasoning? Perhaps departments of speech should redefine *general effectiveness* and give greater emphasis than they have heretofore to analytic listening so that content will become an increasingly influential constituent of effectiveness.

## Summary

Twenty-four trained college speech teachers evaluated fifty-three transcriptions of (*a*) student speeches of self-introduction and (*b*) student persuasive talks. According to regressions of general effectiveness on content and delivery ratings, delivery is almost twice as important as content in determining the general effectiveness of self-introductions and is almost three times as influential as content in determining the effectiveness of attempts to "sell" an idea.

# 6 Ethics of a Speaker in a Democracy

No student beginning his study of public speaking can avoid facing the problem of his ethical responsibilities. As a speaker, he must ask himself what right he has to advocate a particular form of action; whether it is ethical for him to try to change the beliefs, feelings, and conduct of others; how he can be sure that he is "right" and his audience "wrong" in their opinions. As a member of an audience, he must ask himself whether a speaker is sincere, honest, and acting with good will toward his listeners. These questions have been the subject of inquiry throughout the history of man. Plato envisioned a "right rhetoric" designed to promote the good. Aristotle felt that the real function of the speaker was to make the truth prevail.

The speaker of today must also assume this responsibility. He must be aware of the techniques of "hidden persuasion" and recognize the existence of speakers who assume no responsibility for what they say to obtain their objectives. The speaker who uses whatever means he can to sell a product he does not believe in, who makes promises he has no intentions of keeping, who refuses to assume a moral responsibility for every word he utters is as unworthy of our attention today as he has ever been. The following news report illustrates such a misuse of responsibility.

San Francisco, July 15—Senator Peter H. Dominick of Colorado said today that he was only spoofing when he read to the Republican convention last night an alleged quotation from the *New York Times* of 1765.

The Senator was asked about a reference because there was no *New York Times* in 1765. The present newspaper was founded in 1851. Several earlier versions had existed briefly, starting in 1813. "I know that," Mr. Dominick said. "There were no daily newspapers in 1765." The mention last night left some delegates and television watchers with the impression that the Senator was reading a passage from a newspaper article published in 1765.

He was speaking in opposition to the proposed platform amendment to condemn extremists.

"The *New York Times* worried editorially about the extremism of Patrick Henry in 1765," Mr. Dominick said. Then he read what purported to be a quotation from that day criticizing Henry.

Presumably the passage was supplied to the Senator by Tom Stagg, Jr., a delegate from Shreveport, La. Mr. Stagg was a member of the Platform Committee and had opposed an extremist amendment there on the ground that it might have covered Patrick Henry in his day.

Mr. Dominick declined to identify the source of the alleged quoted passage today. He said he was doing further research to be certain where it originated.[1]

The study of public speaking should make you more aware that the excellence of your speech is not always determined by its immediate effect. The quality of your means and ends is also important.

In the art of speaking, as Karl R. Wallace says, ethical standards should be related to both the means and the methods of preparing and delivering your speech. Although Wallace addresses "teachers of communication," the questions he raises must be answered by every speaker. The speaker should prepare himself with full understanding that his responsibilities include working to attain good ends through good means, for only then can he truly help to promote a society based on mutual understanding and respect. As Henry Nelson Wieman and Otis M. Walter say in their attempt to show the relationship between ethics and rhetoric, "*. . . ethical rhetoric has the promise of creating those kinds of communication which can help save the human being from disintegration, nourish him in his growth toward uniquely human goals, and eventually transform him into the best that he can become.*"

[1] From *The New York Times*, July 16, 1964.  © 1964 by The New York Times Company.  Reprinted by permission.

## AN ETHICAL BASIS OF COMMUNICATION

### KARL R. WALLACE

On a recent plane trip a friend of mine sat beside a citizen of Wisconsin. Inevitably the conversation came around to the junior Senator from that state. Part of the dialogue went like this:

Karl R. Wallace, "An Ethical Basis of Communication," *The Speech Teacher* (January 1955), pp. 1–9. Reprinted by permission of the Speech Association of America and of the author.

The author is Head of the Department of Speech and Theater Arts at the University of Illinois.

FRIEND: What do you think of Mr. McCarthy?

CITIZEN: Well, I happen to know him personally, and I just don't like him at all. And I don't like his investigating methods, either—his badgering people and twisting their words around and acting like he owned the whole Committee.

FRIEND: It's too bad you Wisconsin people don't have a chance of turning him out of office.

CITIZEN: What'd we want to do that for? He's doing a darn good job of blasting out those Communists. There ought to be more of it.

FRIEND: If there were an election tomorrow, would you vote for McCarthy?

CITIZEN: Yes, I would.

The conversation points up the age-old problem of judging the right and wrong of human conduct. There is a similar difficulty when we come to judge the right and wrong of communication. The problem is essentially this: Does the end warrant our using any means which seem likely to achieve it? Is the public speaker or debater who believes his purpose worthy justified in using any methods and techniques which he thinks would be successful? Is the play director, convinced that his educational objectives are right, free to select any play and employ any methods of interpretation and production which seem likely to be "effective"? Is the speech correctionist, profoundly motivated to help the child with deviant speech behavior, free to adopt any techniques which seem workable?

This is an ethical problem. It is time that teachers of communication confronted it squarely. The signs of warning are about us. One of the more prominent signs is implicit in the widespread growth of research in communication, as may be seen in the serious study of polling techniques designed to measure the effectiveness of persuasive methods, the new interest of political scientists and bureaucrats in methods of propaganda, the progress made by linguists and psychologists in applying scientific methods to the analysis of language behavior. The facts and data thus compiled are of course valuable; nevertheless, it is somewhat disquieting to observe that such research is centered overwhelmingly on processes, operations, mechanisms, and techniques. There seems to be little, if any, prevailing interest in the *character* of the communicator or in the quality of the communicative product. Some parent groups, of course, have shown concern over the character of radio and television programs and over the comic books, but their activities have been largely sporadic and spotty. We are fascinated—often hypnotized—by what happens, how it happens, and why it happens, but we seem to be utterly unexcited by the question: *Ought* it to happen thus? What would be *better*?

There is room to mention here but one other sign of our apathy toward the ethics of communication. We can read it from our own behavior as teachers of speech. As we start out a new class in speech, or as we confront the thoughtful student who wonders if his praiseworthy purpose allows him to give his audience what it wants, we have been known to speak like this: "Remember, in this class we are studying and applying methods and techniques of speaking. Communication is a skill, a tool, and because it is a tool we are not directly concerned with who uses it and what he says, These are matters which the individual speaker must decide for himself. The main business of this course is to help you to become an effective speaker, a successful speaker. After all, the art of speaking is like the art of reasoning, or like mathematics and science, in that morality lies outside them; it is not *of* them; it is not *in* them." This kind of professional position, this disinterested attitude, this kind of easy reasoning, is leading many persons to look anew at the ethics of both the teacher and his student. Communication is in danger of being regarded as merely an art of personal success and prestige and of being forgotten as the indispensable art of social persuasion.

## I

Any professional field which has reached maturity is ever alive to its ethics. Law, medicine, engineering, and journalism have their codes of ethics. The profession of teaching, too, has its code of behavior. The field of speech shows some evidence of recapturing the maturity and stability it once enjoyed, under the name of *rhetoric*, in the educational systems of centuries past. Is it not time for the teacher of the arts of speech to face up to his special commitments? We must confront questions like these: Is there an ethic of communication? Specifically, is there an ethic of *oral* communication, a morality of rhetoric? I believe that there are ethical standards which should control any situation in which speaker and writer endeavor to inform and to influence others. I shall try to indicate where we find these standards and what they are like.

In the first place, ethical standards of communication should place emphasis upon the means used to secure the end, rather than upon achieving the end itself. A political speaker may win the vote, or a competitor in a speech contest may win the prize, but it is far more important that his means and methods, the character of his skill, and, indeed, the quality of his entire product, should conform to standards formulated by competent judges and critics of speech-making. Let us discover why.

If we give much weight to the immediate success of a speech, we encourage temptation. To glorify the end is to invite the use of any means which will work. The end can be used, for example, to sanction distortion and suppression of materials and arguments. We need here only to mention that there are still popular books on speech-making which sometimes offer shocking advice. A recent manual advises the speaker that he may, if necessary, remodel a pet quotation to fill the bill, for, after all, no one will know the difference! Such advice is on a par with the shoddy ethics of the debate coach who exclaims, "If my boys misquote, it's up to their opponents to spot it." The end, moreover, can be readily called upon to justify the misleading manoeuvres, the innuendoes, and the short-cut tricks of the propagandists. The advertiser, in his zeal to sell, is constantly tempted to promise more than he can deliver. In brief, to exalt the end is often to be indifferent about means. As a result, we gradually undermine confidence in communication and, indeed, in all human relations; and with confidence gone, nothing is left but distrust and suspicion.

If we give first prize to the speaker who wins his goal, we not only unnecessarily tempt the honest and sincere man; we undermine the character of the communicator. We associate with "success" such values as popular prestige and personal ambition. We thus give a premium to the man with a compulsive drive, to him who must win at any cost; and we handicap the man who places the welfare of others above his personal gain. We give the advantage to Senator McCarthy; we hand a disadvantage to Secretary Stevens. John Morley, one of the best English critics of public address in the nineteenth century, has clearly described the risk which the popular persuader incurs when he measures his utterance by its immediate effect. To do so may undermine

> a man's moral self-possession. . . . Effect becomes the decisive con-
> sideration instead of truth; a good meeting grows into a final object
> in life; the end of existence is a paradise of loud and prolonged
> cheering; and character is gradually destroyed by the [parasite of]
> vanity.[1]

Finally, the worst evil which follows from an indifference to means is that we make easy the intent of the dishonest, insincere speaker. It is easy to assert high-sounding purposes; it is difficult for the listener to assess

[1] *The Life of Richard Cobden*, 2 vols. (London, 1908), I, 223.

the sincerity of these assertions. In short, as Mahatma Gandhi often told us, "Evil means, even for a good end, produce evil results."

There is a better ethic than that which justifies the means by the end. It is an ethic which respects the means more than the end. It governs both the selection and the presentation of materials. Above all, the ethic measures the quality of the communicative product in terms of the communicator, rather than according to its immediate effect upon the audience. Some 2300 years ago Aristotle suggested the standard:

> [The function of speech-making] is not simply to succeed in persuading, but rather to discover the means of coming as near such success as the circumstances of each particular case allow. In this it resembles all other arts. For example, it is not the function of medicine simply to make a man quite healthy, but to put him as far as may be on the road to health; it is possible to give excellent treatment even to those who can never enjoy sound health.[2]

What does such a standard suggest? It implies, first, that a speaker does the best job he can under the circumstances; and doing his best job means that he has education, training, and competence in the art of communication. In the second place, the comparison of the speaker with the physician and with other arts implies that the standards of communication are determined by those who best know the art, that is, by the teachers and critics of communication. Finally, the passage suggests that since immediate success is not always possible, anyway, the end or purpose of a speech operates principally as a guide or direction. Purpose serves to give organization and shape to the speech, the discussion, or the play; it aids in the choice of means, but it should not dominate the moral values of either the product or the speaker.

It seems clear that the ethical standards of communication should be set by persons who know communication best, and that the standards or code they formulate will express their judgment as to what means are good, what means are bad. If the standards were clearly stated and widely understood, they could be freely used by expert and layman alike to measure the character of any case of communication.

## II

Where does one look for such standards? They are derived from the function of an art. The function of any art takes its ultimate meaning

---

[2] *Rhetoric*, 1355 b 9–14. Trans. W. Rhys Roberts, in *The Works of Aristotle Translated into English under the Editorship of W. D. Ross*, XI (Oxford, 1924).

from what it tries to accomplish in its social setting. What, for example, does a speaker do not only for himself, but also for society, the community?

Although there are many sides to society, its indispensable side is political. Indeed, when society behaves politically it has the technical name, *state*. And the state is simply another name for an association of men. Because it is the largest, most inclusive association we know of, its values and ends are reflected in nearly everything that its citizens do. They are reflected particularly in education and in the arts and sciences. The influence of the political society is stated in this passage from the *Ethics* of Aristotle:

> If . . . there is some end of the things we do, which we desire for its own sake . . . clearly this must be the good and the chief good. . . . If so, we must try, in outline at least, to determine what it is, and of which of the sciences or capacities it is the object. It would seem to belong to the most authoritative art and that which is most truly the master art. And politics appears to be of this nature; for it is this which ordains which of the sciences should be studied in a state, and which each class of citizens should learn and up to what point they should learn them; and we see even the most highly esteemed of capacities to fall under this, e.g., strategy, economics, rhetoric; now, since politics uses the rest of the sciences, and since, again, it legislates as to what we are to do and what we are to abstain from, the end of this science must include those of the others, so that this end must be the good for man.[3]

The passage demands that we recognize two basic facts. First, the political society aims to help its citizens to secure whatever they consider to be the good life. Indeed, the dominant tone of a political group is set by its ethical values. Thus Communism, e.g., has one set of values, democracy a quite different set. Second, the arts and sciences serve the ideals of the political society. Indeed, they share the same ethical values and goals. The art of rhetoric—and all the arts of communication—thus embraces the ethical part of politics. This point Aristotle states flatly in his book on rhetoric, and for this reason in his system of communication he incorporates materials which he borrows directly from the fields of political science and ethical science. For example, in discussing the materials of political oratory, he talks of the good, of

[3] *Nicomachean Ethics*, 1094 a 17–1094 b 7. Trans. W. D. Ross, in *The Works of Aristotle Translated into English under the Editorship of W. D. Ross*, IX (Oxford, 1925).

happiness, of virtue, and of the general welfare. He even advises the political speaker to study ways of political life in different kinds of society. In discussing the speaking of the law courts, he treats of justice and equity. Thus, the instrumental art, rhetoric, shares the controlling ideas of the master art, politics. Hence, communication inevitably must stand for and must reflect the same ethical values as the political society of which it is a part. It is clear, furthermore, that this principle is as true today as it was in Aristotle's time. Although government and politics are much more complex than they were in the days of ancient Greece, the modern political scientist acknowledges that the foundations of the state are laid in ethics.

Is it not becoming clear, therefore, that we look for the ethical basis of communication in the ideals of our own political society? That society, for all its manifest defects, is still a free and democratic society. If we can clearly state the essential values of democracy, we can then suggest an ethic of communication and the ethics of the teacher of speech.

## III

A free and democratic society, first of all, is built on the notion that the individual has dignity and worth. Our society holds that government exists to uphold and preserve the worth and dignity of each and every person. A totalitarian society, on the other hand, holds that the individual lives for the state. In a democracy people are supreme and wield the ultimate power. In totalitarianism the state is almighty and is the final source of all power. The difference is crucial; it is as sharply different as black and white, as tyranny and freedom. The phrase, "dignity and worth of the individual," leads to a state of mind best described by the old-fashioned word, *respect*. Each man respects his fellow man. This fact has led some students of political science to describe a democratic society as a "commonwealth of mutual deference."

Respect for the individual leads us to a second basic belief: a profound faith in equality of opportunity. We believe that a man can best reach his greatest maturity if he has the chance. If we can say with Wordsworth that the child is father of the man, we believe that the child must have the opportunity to become the best possible father of the best possible man. We believe, furthermore, that so far as we are able, every child must be given the *same* chance. Out of such beliefs we have developed the all-important notion of *fairness*. Like the rules of any game, the laws of the political game must be as fair as we can possibly make them.

We hold a third belief that has become one of the great hallmarks of a democratic society. It is the belief in freedom. Difficult as it may be to define freedom, we know well enough that each individual must be given as wide a field to roam in as he wishes. The word also means that if a person in his roaming prevents another man from ranging widely, he must so modify his behavior as to give his fellow a similar opportunity. He can do what he wants to do, so long as he does not hinder another from exercising a like range of choice and of action. So freedom always implies restraint. A person can behave as he wishes in his own home so long as he does not become a nuisance to his neighbors; he can drive his car where and how he wishes so long as he does not endanger others; he can compete as he may desire in business, in sports, in speech contests, so long as he respects the rules.

In a free and democratic society, individuals acting in concert and with deliberation make their own restraints. The restraints are called *legislation* or *laws*. They are policies or guides of conduct. Indeed, they are no different in their origin and effect from the rules of family life or the regulations of a school. Furthermore, individuals through their government set up agencies to which they delegate power for administering the laws, and they create courts charged with the responsibility of enforcing the restraints. Lincoln showed deep wisdom in saying that our political society was of us, by us, and for us. In our democratic society, moreover, we insist that the laws bear equally upon everyone. In effect we say to our legislators and judges: "You must do your best to make laws which will be fair to everybody, and you must enforce the laws in the spirit of fairness and justice."

A free and democratic society rests upon a fourth deep and abiding belief. It is a conviction closely linked to the idea that each individual must have the opportunity of growing and developing to the limits of his ability. The conviction is that every person is capable of understanding the nature of democracy: its goals, its values, its procedures and processes. This belief assumes that persons can acquire the knowledge necessary to form opinions and decisions and to test them by means of discussion and action. As a result of this conviction, a democracy demands that knowledge be made available to all, rather than to the few; it requires that the sources and channels of communication be wide and diverse, rather than limited and one-sided. It cannot tolerate restriction and distortion. Consequently it must cherish and protect certain special freedoms: freedom of speech, freedom of press, and freedom of assembly. Without these freedoms democracy is meaningless: the life of a free society depends upon them.

Is it not evident that each person participates in a political society? that he reflects its values and uses its procedures? In his role as communicator, whether he be playwright or play producer, public reader or public speaker, he must also reveal his political character. What he says and his method of saying it reveal his choices, and the choices a man makes are always an index to his character. Theoretically, of course, a man need not speak at all; or he can choose to speak only to himself, or to refuse to discuss matters of public interest. But if he chooses to speak, he reveals his political soul.

## IV

What, then, are the ethics of the teacher of speech? They are grounded in the public character of public utterance in a free society.

*First*, a communicator in a free society must recognize that during the moments of his utterance he is the sole source of argument and information. His hearers know this fact, and they defer to him. He in turn must defer to them. Accordingly, his speech must reveal that he knows his subject, that he understands the implications and issues relevant to the particular time and occasion, that he is aware of essential and trustworthy opinions and facts, that he is dealing with a many-sided, rather than a one-sided, state of affairs. Although the speaker might find it difficult to know when he has met such standards, he can always direct a test question to himself: Can I answer squarely, without evasion, any relevant question that a hearer might ask? If he can answer *yes* in all honesty, he has met the standard of knowledge. In the learning situation, the teacher of speech has an obligation to teach the art of inquiry and investigation, to inculcate respect for scope and depth of fact and opinion—in a word, to help build the habit of *search*. The teacher has this duty because a free society demands that communication be informative and that knowledge be shared.

How can the teacher help his students develop the habit of searching widely for both fact and opinion? There is no simple answer, of course. Many teachers, both in high school and in college, are well aware of this duty and have developed their own methods of teaching the art of inquiry. But we shall not hurt ourselves if we periodically confront these questions: Am I keeping up with information and opinion on problems that are currently discussed, so that my chances are better, rather than worse, of being a good guide and critic of what my students know or do not know? Am I making sufficient use of discussion methods, in both the classroom and private conference, to stimulate interest and inquiry? Am

I habitually encouraging the classroom audience, upon hearing a student speak, to discuss the adequacy of the speaker's knowledge and the trustworthiness of his materials?

*Second,* the communicator who respects the democratic way of life must select and present fact and opinion *fairly.* One of his great tasks is to help preserve a kind of equality of opportunity among ideas. He must therefore be *accurate* in reporting fact and opinion; he must *respect* accuracy. Moreover, he must not intentionally warp and distort ideas. Nor must he suppress and conceal material which his audience would need in justly evaluating his argument. He must, furthermore, avoid the short-cut methods of the propagandist. He cannot make one word guilty by loosely associating it with another guilty word. He cannot indulge in the tricks of emotion, cannot juggle with reason, at the expense of sound argument. In helping himself meet the standard of justice, a communicator can always quiz himself: In the selection and presentation of my materials, am I giving my audience the *opportunity* of making fair judgments? The speaker who can answer *yes* understands what is involved in the sharing of information and opinion. He knows that he has had a special opportunity to observe, to learn, to evaluate, which most of his hearers may not have had. He knows, accordingly, that one of his jobs as a communicator is to help his hearers compensate for the lack of special opportunity. He realizes that he cannot possibly give them the same chance he has had, but he can give them the best chance that time and occasion will allow. Speaker and hearer, writer and reader, cannot have had the same experience, but they can feel that they have had. In the classroom, accordingly, the teacher of speech must inculcate what I shall call the *habit of justice.* The habit is based on respect for truth and accuracy and respect for fair dealing. Neither can be disassociated from communication in a free society. The teacher of speech must stand for truth and justice in communication because the health and welfare of a free society depend upon the integrity of the communicator.

*Third,* the communicator who believes in the ultimate values of democracy will invariably reveal the sources of his information and opinion. As Al Smith said, a public figure must keep the record straight. A speaker before any audience is by that fact a public person, and he is no exception to the rule. A communicator, moreover, will help his hearers to weigh any special bias, prejudice, and private motivations which are inherent in source materials. He knows that argument and fact are unacceptable if their springs are contaminated. As an investigator preparing for his speech, he has had the opportunity of discovering whether private motives, such as those of self-interest, personal prestige, and personal profit, have merely imparted a special flavor to the source or have made it dangerous to drink. Such information he should share with his hearers. And if he is not already a public character well-known to his audience, he should be willing to reveal frankly his own motivations. The critical question which he poses to himself is this: Have I concealed information about either my source materials or my own motives which, if revealed, would damage my case? The communicator who can answer *no* is in the tradition of public integrity.

In the high school and the college, the teacher of speech must devise methods and techniques which will form the *habit of preferring public to private motivations*. Public communication is responsible communication; it remembers who said what under what circumstances and for what reasons. In this respect it is utterly unlike gossip and rumor which, if not malicious, we may tolerate as idle talk for idle pleasure.

How can the teacher of speech help his young communicators toward habits of fairness, justice, and public accountability? I do not wish to preach here. Let him who is without blemish cast the first stone. Nevertheless, we shall do well occasionally to examine ourselves as objectively as we can and to conduct the inquisition mercilessly. We may ask: In all my relationships with my students, am I as fair as I can be? Do I keep clear the differences between opinion and fact, and do I distinguish between my opinion and somebody else's? When I express an opinion, do I explain its basis, or do I take a short cut and let the opinion rest on my own authority and prestige? Do I respond to questions frankly, without evasion? Am I withholding information, as "not being good for young persons," especially under the circumstances? What kind of censor am I?

Sometimes teachers effectively employ examples of what not to do. For a ready source of illustrations of unfair tactics in public address, the speeches and press releases of Senator McCarthy offer a rich hunting ground. One could start his collection of negative examples by reading Professor Barnet Baskerville's article, "Joe McCarthy: Brief-Case Demagogue," in the September number of *Today's Speech*.[4] Baskerville cites one careful study whose author checked McCarthy's initial charges of Communism in the State Department with the ascertainable facts. The investigator, Professor Hart of Duke University, examining only the

[4] II (September 1954), 8–15.

charges as presented up to the fall of 1951, found that McCarthy's "assertions had been radically at variance with the facts in fifty specific instances."[5] Another examination of two 1952 campaign speeches reveals them as *"a most amazing demonstration of studied inaccuracy."*[6] McCarthy's nationally televised address which attacked Adlai Stevenson (the speech making use of documents from a Massachusetts barn) yields "no less than eighteen 'false statements or distortions' in the text which McCarthy described as having 'complete, unchallengeable documentation.' "[7] Baskerville comments on the Senator's documents, often raised aloft for all to see, "The deceit lies in the significant omissions, and in unwarranted inferences drawn from impressive but often completely irrelevant documents."[8] The article could well be the beginning of a case study in personal and public integrity.

*Fourth*, a communicator in a democratic society will acknowledge and will respect diversity of argument and opinion. His selection of issues, his analysis of the situation, the style of his address will reflect the attitudes which signify admission, concession, and compromise. Nevertheless, his communication will not sacrifice principle to compromise, and he will prefer facing conflict to accepting appeasement. For such a communicator, the test question will ever be this: Can I freely admit the force of opposing evidence and argument and still advocate a position which represents my convictions? The great duty of the teacher of speech is to devise ways and means and to maintain climate which will favor the *habit of respect for dissent*. Can he teach what it means to hold convictions without loss of integrity and at the same time respect the convictions of others? The teacher who can do so is not merely skillful; he is a true representative of the free society.

It is these four "moralities": the duty of search and inquiry, allegiance to accuracy, fairness, and justice in the selection and treatment of ideas and arguments, the willingness to submit private motivations to public scrutiny, and the toleration of dissent—which provide the ethic of communication in a free society.

In view of these moralities, as teachers of speech we can no longer tell even the most elementary student of our discipline that speech skills and techniques, like tools, are divorced from ethical values. We can no

[5] *Ibid.*, II, 5.
[6] *Ibid.*
[7] *Ibid.*, II, 13.
[8] *Ibid.*

longer say that how he uses his art is his own private affair. But we need not be content with an ethic which is external to communication. We need not rely solely upon the familiar, classic positions: "You'd better be good, or your audience may find you out"; or "A good man skilled in speaking will in the long run be more effective than a bad man skilled in speaking." As I have tried to indicate, communication carries its ethics within itself. Public address of any kind is inseparable from the values which permeate a free and democratic community. A speaker is in a deep and true sense a representative of his constitution which defines his way of life, and therefore defines in part the social goals and methods of his rhetoric. His frame of political reference is not that of an aristocracy, an oligarchy, a monarchy, or a tyranny. In a word, there are ethical guides in the very act of communicating; and it seems to me that the guides are the same for all communicators, no matter whether they speak as politicians, statesmen, businessmen, or professional men.


## TOWARD AN ANALYSIS OF ETHICS FOR RHETORIC

HENRY NELSON WIEMAN
OTIS M. WALTER

The rhetorical skills are potent instruments which transmit much of the motive power which decides the destiny of society. An amoral analysis of how communication operates may disregard that destiny and may show more attachment to the handy but arbitrary distinctions between ethics and rhetoric than to the good of humanity. Even though rhetoric may be amoral, people should not be.

If the rhetorician, however, does not wish to be concerned with ethics, moralists *will* be concerned, and some of them who may be ignorant of rhetoric, disdainful of it, or hostile to it may undertake the

Henry Nelson Wieman and Otis M. Walter, "Toward an Analysis of Ethics for Rhetoric," *Quarterly Journal of Speech*, 43 (October 1957), 266–270. Reprinted by permission of the Speech Association of America and of the authors.

Henry Wieman is Professor of Philosophy at Southern Illinois University. Otis M. Walter is Professor of Speech at the University of Pittsburgh.

task of "reform." The purpose of this paper, therefore, is to suggest a standard for the analysis of ethical problems which may become a basis for the ethics of rhetoric.

The unique nature of the human being seems to originate with two complicated and interlocking processes which generate all capacities that we call "human," which turn the biological man into a human being. They are, further, of such nature that they can enable man to transform himself so that he can achieve the highest of which mankind is capable. In these capacities, therefore, should lie the ultimate standard of ethics.

Certain peculiarly human performances such as the creation of literature, art, mathematics, and science have their roots in symbols. The function of the human brain, according to Susanne Langer, is to convert the raw data of sense experience into symbols. The brain, therefore, is not to be conceived of as merely a kind of telephone switchboard, but as a powerful transformer:

> The current of experience that passes through it undergoes a change of character, not through the agency of sense by which the perception entered, but by virtue of a primary use which is made of it [the sense experience] immediately: it is sucked into the stream of symbols which consitute the human mind.
>
> Because our brain is only a fairly good transmitter, but a tremendously powerful transformer, we do things that . . . [the] cat would reject as too impractical, if he were able to conceive of them.[1]

Langer traces the origin of dreams, ritual, magic, and speech to the process of transforming the raw data of sense experience into symbols. But the symbol itself changes the world of man into which it is introduced. Ernst Cassirer also emphasizes the power of symbols "not in the sense of mere figures which refer to some reality . . . but in the sense of *forces each of which produces and posits a world of its own.*"[2] Because the brain transforms the raw data of sense experience into symbols, the human being lives in the world of these symbols which further change his world in a way unknown to animals. Thus the human being will live, fight, and even die for symbols which he believes represent supremely important realities. Writes Professor Karl R. Wallace:

[1] Susanne Langer, *Philosophy in a New Key* (New York, 1948), p. 34.
[2] Ernst Cassirer, *Language and Myth* (New York, 1946), p. 8.

This capacity to symbolize abstractly, to combine abstract symbols into patterns, and to employ symbols in referring to past events and to the possible and probable future—symbolism in this way is, so far as we know, uniquely human. . . .

The symbol is man's peculiar mode of ordering his experience, extending his experience, and refining his behavior. The growth and development of symbolization is almost synonymous with human growth and development; and learning, problem solving, organizing, and evaluating involve high-level symbol behavior.[3]

Clearly, then, the process of symbolism is necessary for the genesis of human personality. The long process of becoming human begins during infancy in part by the acquisition of symbols. Without symbols, of course, there can be no language. Without language much that is peculiarly human is impossible, for there can be no extensive or complicated thinking or problem-solving. Without symbols, in fact, we cannot develop into *human* beings; we can only become animals that are biologically human but psychologically no different from other animals.

Symbolism is also responsible for the continued growth of human personality. Forming concepts, discovering new concepts, and refining older ones are all impossible without symbols. When the process of growth, therefore, is interrupted by interference with the process of symbolism, as in aphasia or senescence, the possibilities for refining, ordering, and expressing experience are severely limited.

Finally, symbolism can transform man creatively and progressively. Without symbols, as we have said, there could be no mathematics, no history, no science, no philosophy or art. Nor could there be any love: that is, the recognizing and appreciating of the needs and interests of other persons and adopting them as our own. Likewise there could be no faith, in the sense of giving one's self in supreme devotion to what one believes to be the guide and goal of life. These human monuments have transformed human life, and symbols can extend this kind of transformation beyond any known limit. In this extension lie our greatest possibilities.

But symbols can be used either destructively or creatively. We seek a guiding principle enabling us to use them creatively. The search will lead us to the second peculiarly human quality, which shares with symbolism

[3] Karl Wallace, "Education and Speech Education Tomorrow," *Quarterly Journal of Speech*, 36 (1950), 179.

the responsibility for the origin of human personality, the nurture of personality in its growth, and finally the capacity to transform it. This quality is the *unique need of human beings for other human beings.* To be sure, animals need other animals for food, for reproduction, and even for companionship—since some die when placed in isolation. But this need of animals for each other is *not* the same as the need of the human being for other human beings, and it must not be confused with mere gregariousness.

George H. Mead makes it plain that man needs other people in order to generate and develop those uniquely human aspects known as "mind":

> Mind arises in the social process only when that process as a whole enters into, or is present in, the experience of any one of the individuals involved in that process. When this occurs, the individual becomes self-conscious and has a mind.[4]

Not only is "mind" developed by association with others, but only by taking the attitude of another person toward himself does man form a concept of "self":

> The human individual experiences himself as such not directly, but only indirectly, from the particular standpoints of other individual members of the same social group, or from the generalized standpoint of the social group as a whole. . . . For he enters his own experience as a self or individual not directly or immediately, not by becoming a subject to himself, but only in so far as he first becomes an object to himself just as other individuals are objects to him, . . . and he becomes an object to himself only by taking the attitudes of other individuals toward himself.[5]

Thus it is *others* that generate our mind and self. We need others, for we need *appreciative understanding.*

Like symbolism, appreciative understanding is essential not only to the generation of human qualities but to the continued growth of the human being. It is *others* that frequently provide the motives for the individual's activity, and make possible shared knowledge and the healthful give-and-take that can be stimulating to further growth and development. Even the development of language requires other people,

---

[4] George H. Mead, *Mind, Self and Society,* ed. Charles W. Morris (Chicago, 1934), p. 134.

[5] *Ibid.,* p. 138.

since we create symbols to communicate with others. We can use language to communicate only when we can mutually understand symbols. To understand symbols, we must know something of what is in the mind of the other person; otherwise we could not grasp the meaning of words or use language. Thus symbolism and appreciative understanding are inseparable, even if distinguishable, processes, and all growth as a result of language requires at least some degree of mutual understanding. Without this interchange, one cannot continue to learn from others and thus increase what one can know, appreciate, and control.

This need for other people also has possibilities of transforming man beyond his present state. On this matter Mead says:

> In the conception of universal neighborliness there is a certain group of attitudes of kindliness and helpfulness in which the response of one calls out in the other . . . the same attitude. Hence the fusion [of interests] . . . which leads to intense emotional experiences. The wider the social process in which this is involved, the greater is the exaltation, the emotional response, which results. . . . This, we feel, is the meaning of life—and one experiences an exalted religious attitude. We get into an attitude in which everyone is at one with each other in so far as all belong to the same community. As long as we can retain that attitude we have for the time being freed ourselves of that sense of control which hangs over us all because of the responsibilities we have to meet . . . but in . . . the religious situation, all seem to be lifted into the attitude of accepting everyone as belonging to the same group. One's interest is the interest of all. There is complete identification of individuals.[6]

The creative transformation of society comes about through the joint operation of symbolism and appreciative understanding. When one, by virtue of his unique individuality, creates some further symbolism, this creation is added to the culture only if that unique individuality is understood by others.

Appreciative understanding of the unique individuality of the other does *not* mean approval of all he thinks, feels, and does. One cannot, however, justly disapprove anything until after one has first achieved an understanding of it. Therefore, appreciative understanding is the necessary prior condition which must be met before disapproval is justified. To be sure, we are caught every day in circumstances which require us to condemn before we achieve any high degree of understanding; but to

[6] *Ibid.*, p. 247.

realize this circumstance is only to realize that human life falls short of perfection. Appreciative understanding is, then, the basis on which any judgment must rest which morally approves or disapproves the conduct of a human being.

Mutual appreciative understanding ends in mutual control. Through this mutuality of concern the purposes of each may be brought to fulfillment even when they are very different. To bring these purposes to fulfillment often requires modification in the purposes and desires of all of us, but it does not require that our purposes or desires be the same. On the contrary, in mutual control, this modification is apt to be most profitable when one finds the purposes, needs, and desires of the other interesting and valuable to his own growth and development.

There are, then, two inseparable processes that are distinctively human: the process of symbolism and that of appreciative understanding. These two processes are constitutive needs of the human being. That is, these processes build the *human* mind and *human* personality, save it from disintegration, sustain it in its growth, and, finally, can transform the human being progressively beyond any known limits.

If this analysis of the unique qualities of the human being and their significance is correct, it follows that an ethical act is one that enables the organism to meet its constitutive need for symbolism and appreciative understanding; an unethical act is one that destroys, prevents, delays, or otherwise limits the possibilities of meeting these needs. The moral law derived from this ethic might be stated thus: *Always act to provide conditions most favorable for appreciative understanding between yourself and all concerned.*

There are some significant relations between this standard and rhetoric. The constitutive needs on which the criterion is based—symbolism and appreciative understanding—are necessary, in a degree, to rhetoric. Persuasion is based on the use of symbols. Furthermore, a persuasive speaker cannot apply the principles of rhetoric unless he can go at least part way toward an appreciative understanding of his audience. Audience adaptation, in fact, demands that one begin by taking the attitude of what Mead calls "the other" toward his own arguments. Speakers do not necessarily go as far toward appreciative understanding as may be necessary ethically, but they must at least start on this road. Thus the constitutive needs must be met in some degree for there to be any persuasion at all.

An especially close relation between our ethical criterion and rhetoric is suggested by the doctrine of *ethos*. *Ethos* may be defined as those aspects of the speaker himself that affect his belief-making power.

In order to develop desirable *ethos*, the speaker must satisfy our two primal needs to the greatest possible extent. If, for example, he lacks skill in symbolism, he will not suggest desirable things about his intelligence. The speaker who is frustrated because he has not been appreciatively understood may find it difficult to reflect good will. The speaker, finally, who does not try to understand others or who is not interested in them for their own sake may have some difficulty suggesting that he is a man of good character. On the other hand, the speaker who has increasingly satisfied these primal needs will be able to express his true individuality with all the charm, freshness, and force which an uninhibited individual carries.

The second relation between rhetoric and ethics appears in a mutual need of persuasion and ethics for each other. We have already pointed out that persuasion needs ethics; ethics also needs the service of persuasion. In order for the kind of interchange to occur which creates appreciative understanding as we have defined it, certain physical, biological, psychological, social, and historical conditions must be met. At the simplest physical level, air must be free of smog and radioactivity. Slums must be cleared because conditions there make less possible the kind of interchange which creates appreciative understanding. Disease likewise hinders this interchange. The list runs almost without end, but if the human being is to be developed so that he is sustained and transformed into the best that he can become, these threats must be met. Plainly, the art of persuasion is indispensable to the moral law, for without persuasion the air will not be kept pure nor the slums cleared nor programs for the abolition of disease discussed and adopted. Nor will men attempt mutual understanding without persuasion and exposition that will enable them to realize the significance of this ethical doctrine. Finally one will find that if one is to be understood appreciatively by others, the skills of rhetoric will be aids, if not indispensable tools.

The concept of constitutive needs should be significant for rhetoric, thirdly, because of its ethical significance. Rhetoric, if it is to be ethical, must create conditions favorable to expansion of symbolism and mutual understanding and control. We would define ethical rhetoric, therefore, as *the discovery of the means of symbolism which lead to the greatest mutual understanding and mutual control.* Our analysis of the significance of symbolism and mutual understanding enforces the conclusion, therefore, that *ethical rhetoric has the promise of creating those kinds of communication which can help save the human being from disintegration, nourish him in his growth toward uniquely human goals, and eventually transform him into the best that he can become.*

# 7 Speech Criticism

The student who learns to listen carefully to the speeches he hears and to analyze them with a view to finding out what made them effective or ineffective has discovered a useful tool for helping him to improve his own speeches—rhetorical criticism. The more speeches he reads, the more speeches he listens to, the more he becomes conscious of the elements of effective speechmaking. In the first selection in this section, Wilbur Schramm gives some of the answers modern communication researchers have found for the question: "How does communication have an effect?" These answers provide general insights into what a communicator has to do to achieve an effect. Schramm's chief concern is the message itself. Thus, one criterion for judging a speech is the extent to which its message conforms to "the conditions of success in communication" as listed by Schramm.

In the second selection, Marie Hochmuth Nichols deals specifically with evaluating speeches in terms of their persuasiveness. Although she concerns herself with the great speeches of both past and contemporary speakers, the criteria which she sets up can be usefully applied to classroom speeches as well. Not until the speaker considers his speeches in the classroom more than a series of exercises through which he must go to fulfill a requirement or to get a grade does the rhetorical experience become a meaningful part of preparing him to participate actively in the decision making of a free society.

In the last selection, Donald C. Bryant and Karl R. Wallace provide a "Pattern for the Study of a Speech." Their outline will serve as a guide for evaluating speeches both in and out of the classroom.


## HOW COMMUNICATION HAS AN EFFECT

### WILBUR SCHRAMM

The chief reason we study this process is to learn something about how it achieves effects. We want to know what a given kind of

From *The Process and Effects of Mass Communication*, ed. Wilbur Schramm. Copyright 1954 by the University of Illinois. By permission of the University of Illinois Press.

communication does to people. Given a certain message content, we should like to be able to predict what effect that content will have on its receivers.

Every time we insert an advertisement in a newspaper, put up a sign, explain something to a class, scold a child, write a letter, or put our political candidate on radio or television, we are making a prediction about the effect communication will have. I am predicting now that what I am writing will help you understand the common everyday miracle of communication. Perhaps I am wrong. Certainly many political parties have been proved wrong in their predictions about the effects of their candidates' radio speeches. Some ads sell goods; others don't. Some class teaching "goes over"; some does not. For it is apparent to you, from what you have read so far, that there is not such thing as a simple and easily predictable relationship between message content and effect.

Nevertheless, it is possible to describe simply what might be called the conditions of success in communication—by which we mean the conditions that must be fulfilled if the message is to arouse its intended response. Let us set them down here briefly, and then talk about them:

1. *The message must be so designed and delivered as to gain the attention of the intended destination.*

2. *The message must employ signs which refer to experience common to source and destination, so as to "get the meaning across."*

3. *The message must arouse personality needs in the destination and suggest some ways to meet those needs.*

4. *The message must suggest a way to meet those needs which is appropriate to the group situation in which the destination finds himself at the time when he is moved to make the desired response.*

You can see, by looking at these requirements, why the expert communicator usually begins by finding out as much as he can about his intended destination, and why "know your audience" is the first rule of practical mass communication. For it is important to know the right timing for a message, the kind of language one must use to be understood, the attitudes and values one must appeal to in order to be effective, and the groups standards in which the desired action will have to take place. This is relatively easy in face-to-face communication, more difficult in mass communication. In either case, it is necessary.

Let us talk about these four requirements.

1. *The message must be so designed and delivered as to gain the attention of the intended destination.* This is not so easy as it sounds. For

one thing, the message must be made available. There will be no communication if we don't talk loud enough to be heard, or if our letter is not delivered, of if we smile at the right person when she isn't looking. And even if the message is available, it may not be selected. Each of us has available far more communication than we can possibly accept or decode. We therefore scan our environment in much the same way as we scan newspaper headlines or read a table of contents. We choose messages according to our impression of their general characteristics—whether they fit our needs and interests. We choose usually on the basis of an impression we get from one cue in the message, which may be a headline, a name in a radio news story, a picture, a patch of color, or a sound. If that cue does not appeal to us, we may never open our senses to the message. In different situations, of course, we choose differently among these cues. For example, if you are speaking to me at a time when I am relaxed and unbusy, or when I am waiting for the kind of message you have (for instance, that my friends have come to take me fishing), then you are more likely to get good attention than if you address me when noise blots out what you say, or when all my attention is given to some competing message, or when I am too sleepy to pay attention, or when I am thinking about something else and have simply "tuned out." (How many times have you finished speaking and realized that your intended receiver had simply not heard a word you said?) The designing of a message for attention, then, involves timing, and placing, and equipping it with cues which will appeal to the receiver's interests.

2. *The message must employ signs which refer to experience common to both source and destination, in order to "get the meaning across."* We have already talked about this problem of getting the receiver in tune with the sender. Let us add now that as our experience with environment grows, we tend to classify and catalog experience in terms of how it relates to other experience and to our needs and interests. As we grow older that catalog system grows harder and firmer. It tends to reject messages that do not fit its structure, or distort them so that they do fit. It will reject Einstein, perhaps, because it feels it can't understand him. If an airplane is a completely new experience, but a bird is not, it may, as we have said, interpret the plane as a large, noisy bird. If it is Republican it will tend to reject Democratic radio speeches or to recall only the parts that can be made into pro-Republican arguments; this is one of the things we have found out about voting behavior. Therefore, in designing a message we have to be sure not only that we speak the "same language" as the receiver, and that we don't "write over his head," but

also that we don't conflict too directly with the way he sees and catalogs the world. There are some circumstances, true, in which it works well to conflict directly, but for the most part these are the circumstances in which our understandings and attitudes are not yet firm or fixed, and they are relatively few and far between. In communicating, as in flying an airplane, the rule is that when a stiff wind is blowing, one doesn't land crosswind unless he has to.

3. *The message must arouse personality needs in the destination and suggest some way to meet those needs.* We take action because of need and toward goals. In certain simple situations, the action response is quite automatic. When our nerves signal "pain-heat-finger" we jerk our fingers back from the hot pan. When our optic nerve signals "red traffic light" we stop the car. In more complicated situations we usually have more freedom of choice, and we choose the action which, in the given situation, will come closest to meeting our needs or goals. The first requisite of an effective message, therefore (as every advertising man knows), is that it relate itself to one of our personality needs—the needs for security, status, belongingness, understanding, freedom from constraint, love, freedom from anxiety, and so forth. It must arouse a drive. It must make the individual feel a need or a tension which he can satisfy by action. Then the message can try to control the resulting action by suggesting what action to take. Thus an advertisement usually tells you to buy, what, and where. Propaganda to enemy troops usually suggests a specific action, such as surrender, subversion, or malingering. The suggested action, of course, is not always the one taken. If an easier, cheaper, or otherwise more acceptable action leading to the same goal is seen, that will probably be selected instead. For instance, it may be that the receiver is not the kind of person to take vigorous action, even though that seems called for. The person's values may inhibit him from doing what is suggested. Or his group role and membership may control what action he takes, and it is this control we must talk about now.

4. *The message must suggest a way to meet those needs which is appropriate to the group situation in which the destination finds himself at the time when he is moved to make the desired response.* We live in groups. We get our first education in the primary group of our family. We learn most of our standards and values from groups. We learn roles in groups, because those roles give us the most orderly and satisfying routine of life. We make most of our communication responses in groups. And if communication is going to bring about change in our behavior, the first place we look for approval of this new behavior is to

the group. We are scarcely aware of the great importance our group involvements have for us, or of the loyalties we develop toward our several groups and institutions, until our place in the group or the group itself is threatened. But yet if our groups do not sanction the response we are inclined to make to communication, then we are very unlikely to make it. On the other hand, if our group strongly approves of a certain kind of action, that is the one we are likely to select out of several otherwise even choices.

You can see how this works in practical situations. The Jewish culture does not approve the eating of pork; the Indian culture does not approve the slaughter of cows, and the eating of beef. Therefore, it is highly unlikely that even the most eloquent advertisement will persuade an orthodox Jewish family to go contrary to their group sanctions, and buy pork; or an orthodox Hindu family, to buy beef. Or take the very simple communication situation of a young man and a young woman in a parked automobile. The young man communicates the idea that he wants a kiss. There isn't much likelihood of his not gaining attention for that communication or of its not being understood. But how the young woman responds will depend on a number of factors, partly individual, partly group. Does she want to be kissed at that moment? Does she want to be kissed by that young man? Is the situation at the moment—moon, soft music from the radio, a convertible?—conducive to the response the young man wants? But then, how about the group customs under which the girl lives? If this is a first date, is it "done" to kiss a boy on a first date? Is petting condoned in the case of a girl her age? What has she learned from her parents and her friends about these things? Of course, she won't knowingly have a little debate with herself such as we have suggested here, but all these elements and more will enter into the decision as to whether she tilts up her chin or says, "No, Jerry. Let's go home."

There are two things we can say with confidence about predicting communication effects. One is that a message is much more likely to succeed if it fits the patterns of understandings, attitudes, values and goals that a receiver has; or at least if it starts with this pattern and tries to reshape it slightly. Communication research men call this latter process "canalizing," meaning that the sender provides a channel to direct the already existing motives in the receiver. Advertising men and propagandists say it more bluntly; they say that a communicator must "start where the audience is." You can see why this is. Our personalities—our patterns of habits, attitudes, drives, values, and so forth—grow very slowly but firmly. I have elsewhere compared the process to the slow, sure, ponderous growth of a stalagmite on a cave floor. The stalagmite builds up from the calcareous residue of the water dripping on it from the cave roof. Each drop leaves only a tiny residue, and it is very seldom that we can detect the residue of any single drop, or that any single drop will make a fundamental change in the shape or appearance of the stalagmite. Yet together all these drops do build the stalagmite, and over the years it changes considerably in size and somewhat in shape. This is the way our environment drips into us, drop by drop, each drop leaving a little residue, each tending to follow the existing pattern. This personality pattern we are talking about is, of course, an active thing—not passive, like the stalagmite—but still the similarity is there. When we introduce one drop of communication into a person where millions of drops have already fallen and left their residue, we can hardly expect to reshape the personality fundamentally by that one drop. If we are communicating to a child, it is easier, because the situation is not so firmly fixed. If we are communicating in an area where ideas and values are not yet determined—if our drop of communication falls where not many have fallen before—then we may be able to see a change as a result of our communication.

But in general we must admit that the best thing we can do is to build on what already exists. If we take advantage of the existing pattern of understanding, drives, and attitudes to gain acceptance for our message, then we may hope to divert the pattern slightly in the direction we want to move it. Let's go back to elections again for an example. It is very hard to change the minds of convinced Republicans or Democrats through communication, or even to get them to listen to the arguments of the opposing party. On the other hand, it is possible to start with a Republican or Democratic viewpoint and slightly modify the existing party viewpoints in one way or other. If this process goes on for long enough, it may even be possible to get confirmed party-men to reverse their voting pattern. This is what the Republicans were trying to do in the 1952 election by stressing "the mess in Washington," "time for a change," "the mistakes in Korea," and "the threat of Communism," and apparently they were successful in getting some ordinarily Democratic votes. But in 1952, as in every campaign, the real objectives of the campaigning were the new voters and the undecided voters.

The second thing we can say with confidence about communication effects is that they are resultants of a number of forces, of which the communicator can really control only one. The sender, that is, can shape his message and can decide when and where to introduce it. But the message is only one of at least four important elements that determine what response occurs. The other three are the situation in which the communication is received and in which the response, if any, must occur; the personality state of the receiver; and his group relationships and standards. This is why it is so dangerous to try to predict exactly what will be the effect of any message except the simplest one in the simplest situation.

Let us take an example. In Korea, in the first year of the war there, I was interviewing a North Korean prisoner of war who had recently surrendered with one of our surrender leaflets on his person. It looked like an open and shut case: the man had picked up the leaflet, thought it over, and decided to surrender. But I was interviewing him anyway, trying to see just how the leaflet had its effect. This is what he told me.

He said that when he picked up the leaflet, it actually made him fight harder. It rather irritated him, and he didn't like the idea of having to surrender. He wasn't exactly a warlike man; he had been a clerk, and was quiet and rather slow; but the message actually aroused a lot of aggression in him. Then the situation deteriorated. His division was hit hard and thrown back, and he lost contact with the command post. He had no food, except what he could find in the fields, and little ammunition. What was left of his company was isolated by itself in a rocky valley. Even then, he said, the morale was good, and there was no talk of surrendering. As a matter of fact, he said, the others would have shot him if he had tried to surrender. But then a couple of our planes spotted them, shot up their hideout, and dropped some napalm. When it was over, he found himself alone, a half mile from where he had been, with half his jacket burned off, and no sign of any of his company. A couple of hours later some of our tanks came along. And only then did the leaflet have an effect. He remembered it had told him to surrender with his hands up, and he did so.

In other words, the communication had no effect (even had an opposite effect from the one intended) so long as the situation, the personality, and the group norms were not favorable. When the situation deteriorated, the group influence was removed, and the personality aggression was burned up, then finally the message had an effect. I tell you this story hoping it will teach you what it taught me: that it is dangerous to assume any simple and direct relationship between a message and its effect without knowing all the other elements in the process.

# THE CONSTITUENTS OF THE RHETORICAL ACT

### MARIE HOCHMUTH NICHOLS

The criticism of speeches must proceed from a clear conception of the nature of a speech. Whereas a speech may be easily differentiated from the graphic and visual arts on the basis of media and means, it is less easily differentiated from other verbal arts like poetry and prose writing generally. Traditionally the speech has functioned both as an end in itself and as a means to other ends. Thus, Greek and Roman orators perfected the speech as a verbal form serving its own ends. On the other hand, the historian Thucydides employed written forms of speeches in recording the political opinions of the day. Homer, Milton, Shakespeare, and numerous others have employed speeches as techniques for achieving particular effects within larger frameworks of verbal activity. Historically, the prose of the public speech was earliest to achieve artistic perfection; hence, the methods of the speech could be and sometimes were carried over into other forms of literary activity. All of this has been a source of confusion among critics who, at times, have mistaken the verbal record of the speaking event for the speech itself, and who just as often have applied the criteria of poetic to the evaluation of verbal activity demanding other criteria.

Two broad questions pertaining to the speech as a form have been traditional: Is the speech an art form? Is the verbal record of a speech to be considered literature? To the first question we may apply the ancient explanation that things come into being by luck, by nature, by spontaneity, or by art.[1] The records of speech-making indicate that principles and practices have entered into the making of speeches; speeches do not come into being by nature, nor are they typically the results of chance. More akin to architecture than to music as an art, the speech is primarily a practical art form. Just as the architect usually has functional ends primarily in mind in the construction of houses, office buildings, and

From *History and Criticism of American Public Address*, Vol. III, edited by Marie Hochmuth. Used by permission of David McKay Company, Inc.

Marie Hochmuth Nichols is Professor of Speech at the University of Illinois, and a past editor of the *Quarterly Journal of Speech*.

[1] Aristotle *Metaphysica* in *The Works of Aristotle*, VIII, Λ.3.1070ᵃ.

even churches, occasionally he achieves far more than merely functional ends in a Cathedral of Chartres or of Cologne.

To the question: Are speeches literature? the answer, of course, depends on the breadth of definition. If we define literature as a "nation's mind in writing," obviously all verbal activity which is recorded is literature. If we define it as a qualitative factor in verbal activity, then the speech may or may not be literature. If we restrict the term to verbal activity whose primary purpose is to induce immediate pleasurable response, then the speech is clearly not primarily a literary form, although as an incidental aspect it may produce pleasurable response. In our age, the committee for awarding the Nobel Prize for literature chose Sir Winston Churchill in preference to Ernest Hemingway, Graham Greene, and other contenders for the award in literature for his "historical and biographical presentations and for the scintillating oratory in which he has stood forth as a defender of eternal human values."[2] Thus, he takes his place beside Kipling, Shaw, Galsworthy, T. S. Eliot, and others as a "literary" figure.

I am concerned here with evaluating that which the Greeks called rhetoric. One need be under no illusion about the difficulties involved in using the term. Modern critics use it in a variety of ways.[3] Some use it to refer only to the "purple patches." Its use often does not reflect any clear effort to come to grips with the term. Thus, the literary historian, Vernon L. Parrington, writes of Lincoln: "Matter he judged to be of greater significance than manner. Few men who have risen to enduring eloquence have been so little indebted to rhetoric. Very likely his plainness of style was the result of deliberate restraint, in keeping with the simplicity of his nature."[4] Here rhetoric seems to be correlated with "manner," particularly with a style which is not plain. It presupposes a clean division between matter and manner, as if thought and the manner of expressing it were completely separate entities. On the other hand, the literary scholar and editor of Lincoln's speeches, Roy Basler, writes of Lincoln: "It would be difficult to find in all history a precise instance in which rhetoric played a more important role in human destiny than it

---

[2] *The New York Times*, October 16, 1953, p. 25, cols. 2, 3, 4.

[3] Donald C. Bryant, "Rhetoric: Its Functions and Its Scope," *Quarterly Journal of Speech*, 39 (December 1953), 402–7.

[4] Vernon Lee Parrington, *The Romantic Revolution in America* in *Main Currents in American Thought* (New York: Harcourt, Brace and Co., 1927–30), p. 158.

did in Lincoln's speeches of 1858."[5] The meaning of the term here is not clear. It appears to mean something "in" the speeches—but not necessarily the speeches themselves. Such a confusion leads two critics to come to completely opposite conclusions in evaluating Lincoln's indebtedness to rhetoric. At a pole opposite from many attempts to correlate rhetoric with style, lies the recent observation of Duhamel: "Cicero's style was influenced by his rhetoric."[6] Here rhetoric is a cause of style, not correlative with it.

Because of this troublesomeness, I. A. Richards has recommended that we "would do better just to dismiss it to Limbo,"[7] unless the term can be revived to mean a "study of verbal understanding and misunderstanding. . . ."[8] Kenneth Burke, on the other hand, recommends that a strong arm be used to reclaim a traditional province, once perfectly clear, but usurped by other disciplines.[9]

Doubtless no contemporary interpretation of the term throws more light on its proper use than that of the classical systematizers of the art. "Rhetoric may be defined as the faculty of observing in any given case the available means of persuasion," observed Aristotle. The ancients included in the term all the ingredients of persuasion, the impelling fact, the reasoned argument, the stategic ordering of details, no less than the well-wrought phrase. The art of rhetoric was the art of discovering arguments, adapting them, ordering them, expressing them in clear and proper words, and of using one's personal qualities to enhance the whole to the end of achieving persuasion in an audience. It was the whole rationale of persuasive discourse.[10] The term was so used by Cicero, and Quintilian, and by vigorous eighteenth- and nineteenth-century theorists, George Campbell, Richard Whately, and others. It is also used in this way by the contemporary critic, Burke, by the Chicago school of

---

[5] *Abraham Lincoln: His Speeches and His Writings* (Cleveland: The World Publishing Co., 1946), p. 28.

[6] P. Albert Duhamel, "The Function of Rhetoric as Effective Expression," *Journal of the History of Ideas*, 10 (1949), 346.

[7] I. A. Richards, *The Philosophy of Rhetoric* (New York: Oxford University Press, 1936), p. 3.

[8] *Ibid.*, p. 23.

[9] Kenneth Burke, A *Rhetoric of Motives* (New York: Prentice-Hall, Inc., 1950), Introduction, xiii.

[10] See Donald C. Bryant, "Rhetoric: Its Functions and Its Scope," *op. cit.*, 401–24.

critics, and generally by critics whose writings regularly appear in the *Quarterly Journal of Speech* and in *Speech Monographs*.

I use the term "rhetoric," then, to apply to verbal activity primarily concerned with effecting persuasion, whether it be done by writing or speaking. Rhetoric operates in the area of the contingent, where choice is to be made among alternative courses of action. Its concern is with substance as well as with form, if any arbitrary distinction is to be made. In this essay I am concerned with evaluating persuasive efficacy as it manifests itself in *oral* verbal activity, the speech. "Typically, a speech is an utterance meant to be heard and intended to exert an influence of some kind on those who hear it," remarks Wayland M. Parrish. "Typically, also the kind of influence intended may be described as persuasion."[11]

If we do not press the analogy too far, we may compare the speech with a multi-celled organism, whose units consist of speaker, audience, place, purpose, time, and form. In order to evaluate the speech, all these elements, verbal and nonverbal, must be examined.

*First,* consider the position of a speaker in the persuasive situation. In every instance, some specific "I" is doing the speaking. He may be familiar to us or quite unknown. If he is known, he may be known favorably or unfavorably. To the South during the Civil War, Lincoln was a "guerrilla"; to the North, in part, at least, he was "Honest Abe." Let us note for a moment the significance of the specific "I" in the speaking situation by referring to Emerson's characterization of Disraeli:

> Disraeli, the chiffonier, wastes all his talent on the House of Commons, for the want of character. He makes a smart cutting speech, really introduces new and important distinctions. . . . But he makes at last no impression, because the hearer asks, Who are you? What is dear to you? What do you stand for? And the speech and the speaker are silent, and silence is confession. A man who has been a man has foreground and background. His speech, be it never so good, is subordinate and the least part of him, and as this man has no planet under him, but only his shoes, the hearer infers that the ground of the present argument may be no wider.[12]

---

[11] Wayland M. Parrish and Marie Hochmuth, *American Speeches* (New York: Longmans, Green & Co., 1954), p. 3.

[12] *Journals of Ralph Waldo Emerson*, eds. Edward Waldo Emerson and Waldo Emerson Forbes (Boston: Houghton Mifflin Co., 1912), VII, 503.

Whether Emerson's judgment of Disraeli is or is not vindicated by history is not in question. The point is that when one listens to speeches, the individual "I" is an element in the situation. It may matter little in the judgment of "The Last Supper" who painted it, or of the "Moonlight Sonata," who composed it, or of *Pisan Cantos* whether the poet was or was not a traitor, but there is no gainsaying the fact that when speeches are being evaluated the speaker is of paramount importance. One asks the question, then: What are the predispositions, if any, toward the man who is giving the speech? This is a cell in the organism; it may be healthy or in some way defective. Either because of previous acquaintance or because of signs during the speech itself, the audience comes to some conclusion about the speaker, and this plays a part in the judgment. In the political campaign of 1952, Adlai Stevenson, scarcely known at all at the beginning of the campaign, was being compared with a rival candidate whose name was favorably known to millions. This could hardly fail to be a factor in the ultimate decision. Not only the speaking, but the *man* who spoke was a factor. The critic needs to note and assess the persuasive effect of "echoes and values" attaching to the person and character of the speaker. Rarely is this a simple matter, for the man is not always to be seen as a single individual having his own merits only. Men and women derive force from the symbolic relations in which they stand among others. Thus, Eisenhower became the "man of action" speaking for a nation proud of its ability to "get things done"; Clarence Darrow, according to Maloney in a study in this volume, became a champion for the downtrodden, the underdog, and spoke as the representative of a class. Thus, the impetus given to ideas set in motion by the speaker is not merely the impetus deriving from the force of one man's character, but often from the whole class which he images.

*Next*, let us consider the audience as a cell in this complex organism. Audiences neither come from a vacuum nor assemble in one. They come with pre-established systems of value, conditioning their perceptions. As Susanne Langer has observed, "Every society meets a new idea with its own concepts, its own tacit, fundamental way of seeing things; that is to say, *with its own questions, its peculiar curiosity*."[13] We are not without knowledge in regard to the role of perception. We know that perception is selective; we both see and hear with a previously established set of

[13] Susanne K. Langer, *Philosophy in a New Key* (Mentor Books; New York: The New American Library, 1948), p. 4.

values, theoretical, economic, aesthetic, social, political, and religious.[14] Not only do we have general sets of values that predetermine our responses, we often also have specific predispositions regarding the subject being discussed. The rhetorician discovers his potentials for persuasion in a wise regard for the prevailing attitudes in the audience. Although he need neither compromise his integrity, nor bow in subservience to an audience, he does need to understand the operating forces in the audience and select arguments that induce persuasion. He must remember that his choices are conditioned by the audience. The poem may be written with the audience thrice-removed from the creator, for the poet creates from his experience with his subject. But the speechmaker must compose his speech from the available potentials in his audience. He aims to link his propositions to their value systems, and value systems differ with age, sex, educational development, economic class, social strata, political heritage, specialized interest, and so on. The speaker is a selecter. He must exclude certain arguments and include others. He must decide how to order details and the thought patterns into which material is to be cast. All this is determined by the audience for which the speech is designed. The critic who attempts to discriminate among values without reference to the audience is doing what a rhetorical critic really cannot do. Since the audience conditioned the speaker's choices in selecting the arguments, ordering them, and expressing them, the critic must inevitably consider whether the speaker chose wisely or ill in relation to the audience. The critic's necessary tool, then, is not personal whim but clear perception of the role of choice. He must know the mood of the audience. Was it hostile, neutral, or partisan? What tensions, if any, were to be released? Was it keyed up for any particular occasion? Daniel Webster long ago called attention to the significance of occasion and audience-tone in persuasion: "True eloquence, indeed, does not consist in speech. It cannot be brought from far. Labor and learning may toil for it, but they will toil in vain. Words and phrases may be marshalled in every way, but they cannot compass it. It must exist in the man, in the subject, and in the occasion."[15] Let the critic know, then, the audience for which the speech was intended.

---

[14] Charles E. Osgood, *Method and Theory in Experimental Psychology* (New York: Oxford University Press, 1953), p. 292ff.

[15] *A Discourse in Commemoration of the Lives and Services of John Adams & Thomas Jefferson, Delivered in Faneuil Hall, Boston, August 2, 1826* (Boston: Cummings, Hilliard & Co., 1826), p. 34.

*Third*, we must consider the function of *place*. Place, of course, is not merely a physical condition. It is also a metaphysical condition, an ideological environment. We hear much of the "industrial" East, the "conservative" Midwest, the "progressive" Far West, "rumor-ridden" Washington. Speeches take place in halls, to be sure, but halls are "sacred halls," "smoke-filled rooms," places "hallowed by the memory of the sacred dead." The church is an "atmosphere" as well as a place. Place conditions both the speaker's method and the audience's reaction. People do not react in a smoke-filled room the way they do in the restrained atmosphere of the Senate gallery.

I do not intend to minimize the purely physical aspect of place, for this is sometimes important, of course. Comfort and discomfort, audibility or inaudibility may take on considerable proportions. Webster, with 100,000 people milling over Bunker Hill, could not have been expected to be talking to all of them, and an inaugural crowd in a chill wind is not likely to be giving itself completely to the speaker no matter how superlative his genius. No one would expect the playing of a concerto to produce the same effect in a run-down basement room of an apartment-hotel as it does in Carnegie Hall. And no one believes that a painting hung on just any wall will look well. In evaluating speeches, the aspect of place must be recognized as a conditioning factor. "The world will little note, nor long remember what we say here, but it can never forget what they did here," Lincoln observed at Gettysburg, and generations have murmured the words as they have explored the grounds.

*Fourth*, is the consideration of purpose. After examining the debates in the Constitutional Convention of 1787, the historians Samuel Eliot Morison and Henry Steele Commager concluded that "the main, central and determining consideration that appears throughout the debates, is to erect a government that would be neither too strong nor too shocking to popular prejudices for adoption, and yet be sufficiently strong and well-contrived to work."[16] This analysis highlights the significant role that *purpose* plays in evaluating speech-making. At the outset, it indicates that the finished Constitutional product did not represent anyone's notion of the perfect constitution, but what the Constitutional fathers thought they could get accepted. Presumably all language is uttered with some purpose, whether it be the salutation, "Good morning," or the frankly evangelistic sermon on Sunday. These purposes control choices

[16] Samuel Eliot Morison and Henry Steele Commager, *The Growth of the American Republic* (3rd ed.; New York: Oxford University Press, 1942), I, 281.

of materials. Whatever the end the speaker has in mind, his specific purpose is to speak with persuasive effect toward that end; his available resources for persuasion are those which can be directed toward fulfillment of purpose.

The consideration of purpose undoubtedly misleads the critics more often than any other aspect of speaking. In an age oriented toward quick and tangible evidences of success, the critic has tended to make the specific accomplishment of ends the test of rhetorical effectiveness. The number of votes in the ballot box, the amount of money collected as a result of a promotion campaign are taken to be the measure of effectiveness. They are taken to represent the fulfillment of purpose. James Hadley noted the trend in the nineteenth century and expressed concern: "Some have a simple test, and that is persuasiveness; the best oration is the most persuasive, and *vice versa*, the most persuasive is the best; for it best fulfils the end of eloquence, which is persuasion." With shrewd good sense and discrimination, Hadley continued: "The eloquence of Mike Walsh has an effect as persuasive on the collective blackguardism of New York as the eloquence of Daniel Webster has on the collective dignity and learning of the Senate or the Supreme Court. Should we therefore decide that one is no higher than the other? Now persuasiveness . . . is indeed an indispensable element in true eloquence. But there is another element . . . and that is artistic perfection. . . ."[17] In other words, the purpose of the speaker is to discover the available means of persuasion and the appropriate questions are: Did he discover them? What is their quality?

The critic who makes the fulfillment of specific purpose the only test of eloquence is not merely misguided, he is indeed attempting the impossible. As Leonard Bloomfield has observed, "persuasive and . . . powerful [as] . . . effect may be, it is nearly always uncertain."[18] He further observes: "In the long run, anything which adds to the viability of language has also an indirect but more pervasive effect. Even acts of speech that do not prompt any particular immediate response, may change the predisposition of the hearer for further responses: a beautiful poem, for instance, may make the hearer more sensitive to later stimuli. The general refinement and intensification of

[17] James Hadley, "Is Ancient Eloquence Superior to Modern?" *Essays, Philosophical and Critical* (New York: Holt & Williams, 1873), p. 349.

[18] Leonard Bloomfield, "Linguistic Aspects of Science," *International Encyclopedia of Unified Science*, Vol. I, No. 4, pp. 16, 17.

human response requires a great deal of linguistic interaction. Education or culture, or whatever name we choose to give it, depends upon the repetition and publication of a vast amount of speech."[19]

Clearly, the speaker should not be judged by the fulfillment of specific purpose alone. Who can know how many sinners were "almost" saved as a result of a revival service of Billy Graham? The function of the preacher is to use his talents toward this end, and it is by the talents, not by the accomplishment of the end merely that he should be judged. The odds against the accomplishment of a specific end may be insurmountable. Was Lincoln's First Inaugural rhetorically inferior because it did not prevent the Civil War? The eye of the critic must be focused on the methods used by the speaker and not merely on the ends achieved. It is reason and judgment, not a comptometer, that make a man a critic.

*Fifth*, is the factor of time and timing. Just as civilizations rise, develop, and decline, so too problems rise, grow in dimension, yield to solution, and eventually give way to other problems. Time represents a stage in the life of problems. It reflects itself in both the proposition of the speaker and in his mode of handling the problem. It likewise represents a stage in the life of feelings toward a proposition. Anyone knows that he is more susceptible to argument and discussion at one time than at another. A man who has just had lunch is not likely to become excited over the promise of release from hunger. A solution presented either prematurely or tardily will be found wanting. The man with an answer at the time when people are searching for an answer is in a much more effective position rhetorically than the man who gives an answer after doubt has already been resolved, or who offers one before the problem has become acute.

But not only are the substance of a speech and the feelings of an audience conditioned by *time*, the mode of handling data is likewise conditioned. Mode of handling is a product of a culture at a given time. The critic who tends to write off the florid style of the nineteenth century is in effect saying that according to his "more enlightened" twentieth-century taste, the nineteenth-century mode of handling was inferior. Not many of us look with undimmed eyes upon the glories of nature and describe what we see. We look with eyes conditioned to see in terms of the language habits we have inherited. The ornate language of the nineteenth century was shared by a multitude of people in the

---

[19] Leonard Bloomfield, *Language* (New York: Henry Holt & Co., 1938), p. 41.

century, and there is little reason to suppose that it was not as persuasive as the language of the twentieth century. Tastes vary with the times. The real question for the critic is: Does the mode of handling represent the tastes of the time? Is it adjusted to the intellectual development and the habits of the hearer? Is it in harmony with aesthetic values of the time? In the poetic age of the translators of the King James Version of the Bible, the translators wrote in God's description of the battle horse to Job:

> Hast thou given the horse strength? Hast thou clothed his neck with thunder? . . . The glory of his nostrils is terrible. . . . He saith among the trumpets, Ha, Ha.

Twentieth-century translators, heeding the injunction to produce a Bible "written in language direct and clear and meaningful to people today" write as follows:

> Do you give the horse his might? Do you clothe his neck with strength? . . . His majestic snorting is terrible. . . . When the trumpet sounds, he says, 'Aha![20]

In both cases, presumably, we have the language of the people, designed to have an impact on the readers in their own centuries. Does anyone really believe the new rendering of the passage is superior? A rhetorical critic may note differences in quality, to be sure, but the scale by which one determines persuasive effect must be a scale adjusted to the time in which the product was made.

In our discussion so far we have, in the main, been concerned with a consideration of the extra-verbal aspects of persuasion. We come now to the verbal instrument itself. According to George Campbell, astute eighteenth-century rhetorical theorist and practitioner of the art of rhetoric, "there are two things in every discourse which principally claim our attention, the sense and the expression; or in other words, the thought and the symbol by which it is communicated. These may be said to constitute the soul and the body of an oration. . . ."[21]

Both ancient and contemporary thought might question the dichot-

---

[20] See Dwight MacDonald, "The Bible in Modern Undress," *The New Yorker* (November 14, 1953), pp. 179, 187.

[21] *The Philosophy of Rhetoric* (New ed., with the Author's Last Additions and Corrections; Edinburgh: Neill & Co., for Archibald Constable & Co., and John Fairbairn, Edinburgh; and T. Cadwell & W. Davies, London, 1816), I, 82, 83.

omy between "the sense and the expression" as indicated by Campbell. From Aristotle to modern times competent critics have recognized that "there can be no distinction drawn, save in reflection, between form and substance. The work itself *is* matter formed. . . ."[22] The contemporary philosopher, Jordan, notes that "At the point of the abstract ultimate what is said . . . and the way it is said . . . may be the same thing. . . ."[23] Experience, of course, reveals that so united are matter and form that when a speaker struggles to make his thoughts clear but fails, he in fact says something else.

Recognizing the inseparability of matter and form in any art, we may, nevertheless, in "reflection," consider the work in terms of constituents, arguments, broad structural pattern, and particular stylistic features.

Let us first look at the substance of a speech. Persuasion requires choices among alternatives. The speech presumably will consist of persuasions to induce acceptance of the speaker's point of view. Presumably this point of view is directed toward some ultimate Good. Hence, the speaker's persuasions represent directly or by implication his philosophic outlook and commitment. These persuasions will be revealed verbally in statements of fact and of opinion. "Facts cannot be selected without some personal conviction as to what is truth,"[24] observes the historian, Allan Nevins. Likewise, Karl Wallace notes: "Truth is a word I shall use to describe the moment of certainty, or commitment, or decision which signals the resolution of doubt. The decision is revealed verbally as a statement of opinion or value, or as a statement of fact."[25] Accordingly, Richard Weaver remarks: "there is no honest rhetoric without a preceding dialectic,"[26] that is, without an attempt to discover truth. Thus, the critic is brought face to face with the necessity of understanding and discriminating among the ideas or the truths to which

[22] John Dewey, *Art as Experience* (New York: Minton, Balch & Co., © 1934), p. 109.

[23] E. Jordan, *Essays in Criticism* (Chicago: University of Chicago Press, 1952), p. 193.

[24] Allan Nevins, *The Gateway to History* (Boston: D. C. Heath & Co., 1938), p. 38.

[25] Karl R. Wallace, "The Field of Speech, 1953: An Overview" (A Speech, Delivered July 17, 1953, Summer Speech Conference, University of Michigan, Ann Arbor, Michigan [MS University of Illinois, Department of Speech]), p. 10.

[26] Richard M. Weaver, *The Ethics of Rhetoric* (Chicago: Henry Regnery Co., 1953), p. 25.

the speaker has committed himself. But to evaluate the speaker's philosophy involves the critic in a discrimination of ethical values. The warning of Baskerville is well taken: ". . . today's critic often side-steps inquiry into the basic soundness of the speaker's position, offering the excuse that truth is relative, that everyone is entitled to his own opinion, and that the rhetorical critic's task is to describe and evaluate the orator's skill in his craft and not to become entangled in complex ethical considerations."[27]

The simple fact is that audiences do not respond alike to any and every opinion, that whereas the critic may think it not his function to tangle with the problem of truth and the weight of ideas, audiences which determine the degree of persuasion do so involve themselves with these matters. Ideas are a means of persuasion. Emerson responding to Webster's 7th of March speech was keenly aware of Webster's philosophic position: "Nobody doubts that there were good and plausible things to be said on the part of the South. But this is not a question of ingenuity, not a question of syllogisms, but of sides."[28] For Emerson there was always "the previous question: How came you on that side? Your argument is ingenious, your language copious, your illustrations brilliant, but your major proposition palpably absurd. Will you establish a lie?"[29] In evaluating a sermon of an American churchman, a critic recently observed: "His arguments were specious, but his rhetoric was good." That rhetoric can consist of specious arguments as well as sound ones no one will question. But that the validity and the truth of the argument has nothing to do with pronouncing the rhetoric "good" is, indeed, dubious.

The critic's function is to examine the speaker's premises, stated or implied, and to examine the truth of those premises. Inevitably he must ask such questions as: Does the orator argue from an abiding concept of the "nature of things"? from a conception of expediency? from the authority of history? from similitude? from transcendental grounds?

There are conventional means for evaluating the quality of premises. Does the premise presented "correspond" to data which may be revealed to the senses of observers? Does the truth of a premise yield to a

[27] Barnet Baskerville, "Emerson as a Critic of Oratory," *The Southern Speech Journal*, 18 (March 1953), 161.

[28] *The Complete Works of Ralph Waldo Emerson*, ed. Edward Waldo Emerson (Centenary ed.; Boston: Houghton Mifflin & Co., 1903), XII, 225.

[29] "Eloquence," *ibid.*, VIII, 131.

pragmatic test? Is the truth of a premise "believed" by the many? Is the truth of a premise "self-evident"?[30] However much the critic may wish to escape discriminating among values, as an effective rhetorical critic he cannot do so.

This may not be the place to argue for any of the particular criteria of truth used through the ages. One may say that great and good men have from time to time used all of these tests, depending upon their general philosophic position. We do not ask too much when we ask a critic to reveal his philosophic position by his choice of criteria for evaluating premises. In fact, we may be paving the way for critical commentary vastly richer and more cogent than if the bases of evaluation were ignored.

Nor is the argumentative substance of the speech the critic's only concern. Persuasion represents deliberate manipulation of symbols. Symbols contain not only rational meanings. They contain experience also and represent attempts to create and release emotional tensions. Woven into the substance of argument are directives to action, terms of interpretation and valuation. Persuasion recognizes men to be creatures of desire; it also recognizes that desire provides a basis for action. Hence, the speaker's persuasions represent techniques for awakening and satisfying desire. Furthermore, within every culture are values that have authority. Thus, "virtue" was the ultimate Good for the Greeks; "courage," an ultimate Good for the Romans; "duty," an ultimate Good in early American Christian civilization. The critic examines the texture of persuasive compositions for those symbols of authority designed to evoke response. The perceptive critic must observe that since motives are not fixed, these authoritative symbols change from age to age. Whereas an early Christian civilization responded to appeals to action, presented in the name of "duty," a later civilization is activated to a greater degree by the promise of earthly "progress." On an ethical scale, we may find considerable difference between the lowest motive and the highest motive to which men will respond. The discerning critic must not only assess both extremes but he must locate the center of gravity. He need not deny the persuasive value of low motives, but he has no moral obligation to sanction the use of such motives under the label of "good" rhetoric.

---

[30] See C. J. Ducasse, "Propositions, Truth, and the Ultimate Criterion of Truth," *Philosophy and Phenomenological Research*, 5 (September–June, 1943, 1944), 317–40.

"The most minute study, the widest experience in the investigation of human actions and their motives," says Gamaliel Bradford, "only make us feel more and more the shifting, terrible uncertainty of the ground under our feet."[31] The difficulty of the task gives no warrant to the critic to shirk his responsibility. Surveying the rhetoric of Hitler's *Mein Kampf*, Kenneth Burke notes: "Here is the testament of a man who swung a great people into his wake. Let us watch it carefully, and let us watch it, not merely to discover some grounds for prophesying what political move is to follow Munich, and what move to follow that move, etc.; let us try also to discover what kind of 'medicine' this medicine-man has concocted, that we may know, with greater accuracy, exactly what to guard against, if we are to forestall the concocting of similar medicine in America."[32] Such an observation suggests the responsibility of the critic. His place should be in the vanguard, not in the rear—wise-after-the-fact. He should be ready to alert a people, to warn what devices of exploitation are being exercised, by what skillful manipulations of motives men are being directed to or dissuaded from courses of action. James G. Randall asks: Was the willful manipulation of men's minds by the wily a factor in the cause of the Civil War? Is it a factor in most wars?[33] The careful examination of motives must not merely furnish an amusing pastime for the critic; it is his urgent responsibility.

Pursuing our examination of aspects of form, we turn "in reflection" to the aspect of structure. Literary art, like all art, observes Daiches, "communicates significance through patterns."[34] A tragedy unravels through a pattern of exposition, complicating circumstances, climax, and denouement. A detective story lays down premises and takes its deductive course. The speech also is a structured organism and this structure must be a concern of the critic. By structure we mean, as Whitehead has suggested, "that eye for the whole chessboard, for the bearing of one set of ideas on another."[35] In speech-making this has traditionally been

[31] Cited in Allan Nevins, *op. cit.*, p. 327.

[32] "The Rhetoric of Hitler's 'Battle,'" in his *The Philosophy of Literary Form* (Baton Rouge, Louisiana: Louisiana State University Press, 1941), p. 191.

[33] J. G. Randall, "A Blundering Generation," in his *Lincoln, The Liberal Statesman* (New York: Dodd, Mead & Co., 1947), pp. 36–64.

[34] David Daiches, *A Study of Literature for Readers and Critics* (Ithaca, New York: Cornell University Press, 1948), p. 77.

[35] A. N. Whitehead, *The Aims of Education & Other Essays* (New York: The Macmillan Co., 1929), p. 18.

called *dispositio*. Aristotle defined it as "the arrangement of that which has parts, in respect of place, or of potency or of kind."[36]

Probably all people need forms, for "We take delight in recognition."[37] Whether we speak a word, a sentence, or a whole speech, intelligibility depends on form. To borrow an ancient illustration, we recognize a bronze pitcher only after it has taken form from a mass of bronze and *become* a bronze pitcher.[38] In the laboratory, speech takes on a visual shape, as is shown by spectograph readings. In ordinary communication, meanings are in part determined by organization. Thus, "an rhetoric art is" yields intelligibility by assembling the elements: Rhetoric is an art.

The critic must observe the contribution made by thought pattern to the effectiveness of the whole. A thought pattern is something more than external manifestation of a beginning, a middle, and an end. It is a functional balancing of parts against each other, a determination of the relative strength of arguments. It is reflected in proportion and placing. The speaker who sandwiches weak arguments between strong arguments has at least considered force as a factor in persuasion. Structure reveals the speaker's assessment of his audience in the placement of parts, whether they are partisans, neutrals, or opponents, or are a significant mixture of two or more. To that extent, at least, it represents the psychology of the audience rather than the psychology of the speaker.[39]

We come finally to that most elusive of all aspects of the speaking act—style, still another aspect of form. Thonssen and Baird, referring to a rhetorical critic of the last century, have remarked, "Jebb is more deeply concerned with the orator's style than are most present-day critics. In this regard, he is, perhaps, less the rhetorical and more the literary critic."[40] Rhetorical critics unfortunately tend to be less interested in style than they ought to be, for, as Lasswell has noted, "style is an indispensable feature of every configuration of meaning in any process of communication."[41]

---

[36] *Metaphysica, op. cit.*, Δ. 19. 1022[b].

[37] Donald A. Stauffer, "Introduction: The Intent of the Critic," *op. cit.*, p. 24.

[38] Aristotle *Metaphysica*, Λ. 3. 1070[a].

[39] See Kenneth Burke, "Psychology and Form," in *Counter-Statement* (2nd ed.; Los Altos, California: Hermes Publications, 1953), p. 31.

[40] Lester Thonssen and A. Craig Baird, *Speech Criticism* (New York: Ronald Press, 1948), p. 257.

[41] Harold Lasswell, Nathan Leites, and Associates, *Language of Politics* (New York: George W. Stewart, Publishers, Inc., 1949), p. 38.

Partly because of the difficulty, and partly because of confusion with the function of literary critics, contemporary rhetorical critics have given the matter little attention. Preoccupation with trying to distinguish written from oral style has often yielded results both fruitless and misleading. "Not only are contemporary critics . . . unable to distinguish oral from written style," observes Schrader, "but they are also confused as to the nature of style itself."[42] "Their statements are often based on untenable assumptions, and their conclusions are even contradictory."[43]

If, as Wichelns has remarked, the problem of the orator is "so to present ideas as to bring them into the consciousness of his hearers,"[44] the neglect of style becomes serious, and mistaken notions about it equally hazardous.

It is significant that the two living orators who have achieved greatest distinction for their oratory are both sensitive stylists. Churchill has a feeling for the nobility of the English sentence, and Stevenson's style became a campaign issue in the election of 1952. In general, the style of our orators has been so undistinguished as to escape the notice of listeners, but this may in part account for the lack of impact that many speakers have had on their age. It does not justify the neglect of style by rhetorical critics. If the testimony of the centuries to the importance of style needed support, we could find it in an unsuspected source—from one of the great atomic scientists of the twentieth century. Said J. Robert Oppenheimer:

> The problem of doing justice to the implicit, the imponderable and the unknown is, of course, not unique to politics. It is always with us in science, it is with us in the most trivial of personal affairs, and it is one of the great problems of writing and of all forms of art. The means by which it is solved is sometimes called style. It is style which complements affirmation with limitation and with humility; it is style which makes it possible to act effectively, but not absolutely; it is style which, in the domain of foreign policy, enables us to find a harmony between the pursuit of ends essential to us, and the regard for the views, the sensibilities, the aspirations of those

[42] Helen Wheatley Schrader, "A Linguistic Approach to the Study of Rhetorical Style" (Ph.D. dissertation, Northwestern University, 1949), p. 17.

[43] *Ibid.*, p. 15.

[44] Herbert A. Wichelns, "The Literary Criticism of Oratory," in *Studies in Rhetoric and Public Speaking in Honor of James Albert Winans* (New York: The Century Company, 1925), p. 190.

to whom the problem may appear in another light; it is above all style through which power defers to reason.[45]

Thus, in its simplest manifestation, style is a mode of "ingratiation";[46] in its most complex aspect it is the "ultimate morality of mind."[47] It is an "aesthetic sense" says Whitehead, "based on admiration for the direct attainment of a foreseen end, simply and without waste." It is an index of a preference for "good work."[48]

That audiences have value systems pertaining to style is well known. Two thousand years ago Aristotle called attention to reaction tendencies of listeners in regard to stylistic matters: "The effect which lectures produce on a hearer depends on his habits; for we demand the language we are accustomed to, and that which is different from this seems not in keeping but somewhat unintelligible and foreign because of its unwontedness. . . . Thus some people do not listen to a speaker unless he speaks mathematically, others unless he gives instances, while others expect him to cite a poet as a witness. And some want to have everything done accurately, while others are annoyed with accuracy, either because they cannot follow the connexion of thoughts or because they regard it as pettifoggery."[49]

Aristotle's statement has been proved valid by the test of centuries. The language of persuasion must be conditioned by the needs of the audience, and the needs of the audience differ considerably. As we remarked earlier, the ideals of any age, regarding style, may differ. The late John Livingston Lowes said of the King James Version of the Bible: "Its phraseology has become part and parcel of our common tongue— bone of its bone and flesh of its flesh. Its rhythms and cadences, its turns of speech, its familiar imagery, its very words, are woven into the texture of our literature, prose and poetry alike. . . . The English of the Bible . . . is characterized not merely by a homely vigour and pithiness of phrase, but also by a singular nobility of diction and by a rhythmic quality which is, I think, unrivalled in its beauty."[50] The twentieth-

---

[45] "The Open Mind," *The Bulletin of the Atomic Scientists*, 5, No. 1 (January 1949), 5.

[46] Kenneth Burke, *Permanence and Change* (New York: The New Republic, 1935), p. 71.

[47] A. N. Whitehead, *op. cit.*, p. 19.

[48] *Ibid.*, p. 19.

[49] *Metaphysica*, a. 3. 995ᵃ.

[50] "The Noblest Monument of English Prose," in his *Essays in Appreciation* (Boston: Houghton Mifflin Co., 1936), pp. 3–5, *passim*.

century revisers of the Bible were enjoined to "combine accuracy with the simplicity, directness, and spiritual power" of the King James Version, as well as to make it "more readable for the American public of today."[51]

Style is in no sense magic. It is rather a manifestation of a speaker's or writer's temper and outlook. It has the capacity to name objects, to evaluate them, and to incite feelings toward them. In its objective manifestations it pertains to the selection of words and the ordering of them, and in this a preference for "good work" may be shown.

"Style to be good must be clear," notes Aristotle, "as is proved by the fact that speech which fails to convey a plain meaning will fail to do just what a speech has to do."[52] Beyond clearness, of course, lie other properties: appropriateness, distinctive language constructions, rhythm. All of these have concern for the analyst of rhetorical style, for they are means by which the orator reaches the minds of the listeners. They are means by which he seeks identification and ingratiation.

For want of better methods, the rhetorical critic sometimes satisfies himself with a simple enumeration of stylistic devices of the speaker. Unless the enumerations are particularizations of the pervasive tones and effects sought by the speaker, such enumeration probably serves little purpose. We need to ask: What is language doing to further the end of ingratiation or identification? If, for instance, the prevailing tone of a speech is "humorous," we might expect language to behave in such a way as to produce humor. Hence, the rhetorical critic would look to language constructions, the diction, the characteristics of rhythm which contribute to the prevailing tone. If style is the man himself, then a close scrutiny of the details of style should tell us what manner of man is doing the speaking, and in what relationship he conceives himself to be with his audience. If it is style which "complements affirmation with limitation and with humility"; if it is style which "makes it possible to act effectively, but not absolutely"; if it is style which "in the domain of foreign policy, enables us to find a harmony between the pursuit of ends essential to us, and the regard for the views, the sensibilities, the aspirations of those to whom the problem may appear in another light"; if it is style "through which power defers to reason"—then, to look to style for manifestations of the groundswells and tensions of our times, for manifestations of healthy states and unhealthy ones must become the

[51] Dwight MacDonald, *op. cit.*, p. 175.
[52] *Rhetorica*, iii. 2. 1404[b].

imperative task of the critic concerned with the implications of his art for the nation and the world. May not the simple metaphor be the harbinger of death and destruction, or the cock's crow of an era of good feeling as well as a literary tool in the grammar books?

These are the ingredients of the rhetorical situation which must be examined for their contribution to the persuasive efficacy of the whole. As one may observe, some of them are verbal aspects, others are nonverbal. Just as in drama many elements are harmonized to give delight to an audience, so too in the rhetorical situation many elements contribute to the end of persuasion. The total organism is the concern of the critic.

## PATTERN FOR THE STUDY OF A SPEECH

DONALD C. BRYANT
KARL R. WALLACE

The following scheme . . . may provide a convenient guide for making a study of a speech and for writing up the results. The outline is suggestive in detail, not inclusive . . . The student will supplement and omit as the circumstances of the individual speech suggest, but he should probably give consideration to each of the principal items at least.

### How the Speech Is Made

I. Kind and purpose
   A. General: Informative, persuasive, or other
   B. Particular: Purpose and reason for this speech
      1. In the occasion and circumstances
      2. In the audience
      3. In the speaker
      4. In the subject

From *Fundamentals of Public Speaking* by Donald C. Bryant and Karl R. Wallace. Copyright © 1953, 1960 by Appleton-Century-Crofts, Inc. Reprinted by permission of Appleton-Century-Crofts.

Donald C. Bryant is Professor of Speech at the State University of Iowa. Karl R. Wallace is Head of the Department of Speech and Theatre Arts at the University of Illinois.

II. Condition, source, authenticity, and reliability of the text

III. Thought-and-idea-content
   A. The Subject
      1. General—particular
      2. Ostensible—real
   B. Underlying assumptions and background reasoning
   C. Governing idea (subject sentence or proposition) and supporting ideas
      1. Explicitly stated
      2. Implicitly presented
   D. Over-all plan and structure
      1. Pattern of organization: Time, space, topical, cause-to-effect, disease and remedy, etc.
      2. Logical-chronological outline
      3. Departures from consistent plan
         a. Introduction of extraneous matter, for what reason and with what effect
         b. Use of structural digressions, for what reason and with what effect
         c. Failure to follow through
      4. Establishing and maintenance of unity
         a. Sustained mood or attitude
         b. Connective and transitional methods
         c. Structural emphasis
         d. Kind and function of introduction and conclusion

IV. Development: Amplification and Support
   A. Methods, techniques, and materials of amplification
      1. Methods: example, information, comparison, definition, etc.
      2. Techniques: restatement, repetition, quotation, etymology, etc.
      3. Use of laws and principles of interest: perennial interests, human interest, humor, variety, activity, familiarity, novelty, laws of attention
   B. Methods of argument and persuasion
      1. Evidence and logical support
      2. Motives and basic lines of thought
      3. Suggestion
      4. Involvement of feelings, desires, likes and dislikes of audience

C. Predominant or characteristic methods of development: reasons, effects

V. Style: the use of language
   A. Qualities of the vocabulary
      1. Clearness, appropriateness, interest, impressiveness
      2. Size, sources of words, net effect
   B. Qualities of the connected language
      1. Clearness: length of sentences, structure of sentences, coherence and emphasis, idiomatic usages
      2. Propriety
         *a.* To speaker, occasion, audience, subject
         *b.* Correctness, conventionality of forms
      3. Interest and attractiveness
         *a.* Movement and variety
         *b.* Strength and beauty
         *c.* Wit and humor
      4. Impressiveness
         *a.* Memorable coinages of phrases and slogans
         *b.* Vividness of images and figures
         *c.* Rhythms and harmonies
   C. Apparent total effects or general characteristics; how achieved

VI. Delivery: speech and action
   A. General characteristics
      1. Loud—weak
      2. Fast—slow
      3. Intelligible—unclear
      4. Pleasant—unpleasant
      5. Appropriate—inappropriate
   B. Factors meriting special comment
      1. In voice
      2. In pronunciation
      3. In vocal rhythm and movement: phrasing, pause, changes of pace, inflection, etc.
      4. Gesture, facial expression, bodily movement
   C. Basis of description of delivery
      1. Primary sources: face-to-face, recording, radio-TV, etc.
      2. Secondary sources: various accounts of witnesses and others
   D. Apparent total effects or general characteristics; how achieved

## How the Speech Works

I. Who the audience is
   A. As people in general
      1. Old—young
      2. Prosperous—unprosperous
      3. Urban—rural
      4. Educated—uneducated
      5. Men—women
      6. Business, professions, trades, etc.
   B. As these people in particular
      1. Relation of audience to speaker's subject and particular purposes
         a. Special knowledge and interests
      2. Economic, political, racial, religious, geographical, domestic allegiances
      3. Special desires, needs, susceptibilities, preoccupations, prejudices, preferences
   C. As affected by the ideas, materials, methods, structure, style, etc. of the speech in
      1. Holding attention
      2. Informing
      3. Convincing
      4. Enlisting feelings, tastes, emotions
      5. Releasing motives and impulses to believe and to act
   D. Probable (or actual) responses of audience; how brought about

II. Who the speaker is
   A. From outside the speech
      1. His family educational, social, religious, economic, political, professional background so far as relevant to this occasion
      2. His habits of thought, opinions, knowledge, experience, temperament
      3. His relation to the subject, to the occasion, and to the audience
      4. His reputation as known to this audience at this time, especially as a man likely to speak truly and wisely
         a. As a man of intelligence, knowledge, and sound opinion
            (1) In general
            (2) On the current subject

        *b.* As a man of sound morality
           (1) Honesty
           (2) Truthfulness
           (3) Firmness
        *c.* As a man of good will
           (1) Friendliness
           (2) Regard for the welfare of his listeners

B. From the speech
    1. What the speaker says and does which may affect the audience's opinions of him as a man of "good sense, good morals, and good will"
        *a.* Explicitly in the material and language
        *b.* Implicitly in the content and style
        *c.* In the delivery
    2. The speaker's conception of himself in relation to the audience and in relation to the picture of himself which he gives to the audience
C. Relation of what the speaker shows himself to be in the speech to what the audience "knows" him to be beforehand
D. Probable (or actual) responses of the audience to the speaker's character and personality; how brought about

### Appraisal and Judgment

I. Quality of the speech in terms of the speaker's skill
  A. Value of the material presented
    1. Thoroughness and soundness of the speaker's knowledge
    2. Scope and quality of his thinking and judgment
    3. Significance of his purpose and governing idea
  B. Skill of the presentation
    1. Discovery of available resources of subject, audience, and circumstances
    2. Use of resources discovered
        *a.* Speaker's special excellences
        *b.* Speaker's weaknesses
           (1) Seen in things done
           (2) Seen through omissions
         *c.* Sources of speaker's strengths
        *d.* Sources of speaker's weaknesses
           (1) Limitations of his capacities
           (2) Faults of ethics and sense of responsibility

C. Determinable effects of speech
D. Relation of quality of speech as speech to determinable results; reasons

II. Quality of speech in terms of its social consequence
   A. Value to this audience
      1. Because of ideas and information presented and opinions and actions sought
      2. Because of means and methods used to affect audience's minds and feelings
   B. Value to society generally
      1. At present
      2. In the future

III. Composite estimate of the worth of the speech; reasons
   A. "A good man speaking well" in the public interest
   B. Or something less

# Bibliography

Below are listed some materials in both books and journals so that the interested reader may continue his reading. This list is far from comprehensive. Rather, it attempts to *indicate* the depth and scope of work that has been done in the area of rhetoric and public speaking.

## The Nature of Communication

Berlo, David K., *The Process of Communication*. New York: Holt, Rinehart & Winston, Inc., 1960.

Chase, Stuart, *The Proper Study of Mankind*. New York: Harper and Brothers, 1948.

Cherry, Colin, *On Human Communication*. New York: The Technology Press of M.I.T., 1957.

Eisenson, Jon, J. Jefferey Auer, and John V. Irwin, *The Psychology of Communication*. New York: Appleton-Century-Crofts, 1963. See especially "The Communicative Process: Schema and Design," pp. 131–65.

Hartley, Eugene L., and Ruth E. Hartley, *Fundamentals of Social Psychology*. New York: Alfred A. Knopf, Inc., 1952. See especially "Communication—The Basic Social Process," pp. 15–195.

Hovland, Carl I., Irving Janis, and Harold H. Kelley, *Communication and Persuasion*. New Haven: Yale University Press, 1953.

Katz, Elihu, and Paul Lazarsfeld, *Personal Influence*. Glencoe, Illinois: The Free Press, 1955.

Schramm, Wilbur, ed., *The Process and Effects of Mass Communication*. Urbana: University of Illinois Press, 1954. See especially "How Communication. Urbana: University of Illinois Press, 1949.

Shannon, Claude, and Warren Weaver, *The Mathematical Theory of Communication*. Urbana: University of Illinois Press, 1949.

## Invention

Andersen, Kenneth, and Theodore Clevenger, Jr., "A Summary of Experimental Research in Ethos," *Speech Monographs* (June 1963), pp. 59–78.

Ball, V. C., "The Moment of Truth: Probability Theory and Standards of Proof," *Vanderbilt Law Review* (1961), pp. 807–30.

Berlo, David K., and Halbert E. Gulley, "Some Determinants of the Effect of Oral Communication in Producing Attitude Change and Learning," *Speech Monographs* (March 1957), pp. 10–20.

Bormann, Ernest G., "An Empirical Approach to Certain Concepts of Logical Proof," *Central States Speech Journal* (Winter 1961), pp. 85–91.

Cathcart, Robert S., "An Experimental Study of the Relative Effectiveness of Four Methods of Presenting Evidence," *Speech Monographs*, (August 1955), pp. 227–33.

Ehninger, Douglas, "The Classical Doctrine of Invention," *Gavel*, (March 1957), pp. 59–62, 70.

―――― and Wayne Brockriede, *Decision by Debate*. New York: Dodd, Mead & Co., 1963. See especially "Unit of Proof and its Structure," pp. 98–109.

Hargis, Donald E., "The Forms of Support," *Western Speech*, (March 1950), pp. 18–22.

Hartely, Eugene L., Ruth E. Hartely, and Clyde Hart, "Attitudes and Opinions" in *The Process and Effects of Mass Communication*, ed. Wilbur Schramm. Urbana: University of Illinois Press, 1954.

Hovland, Carl I., and Walter Weiss, "The Influence of Source Credibility on Communication Effectiveness," *Public Opinion Quarterly* (Winter 1951), pp. 635–50.

――――, Irving L. Janis, and Harold H. Kelley, *Communication and Persuasion*. New Haven: Yale University Press, 1953. See especially "Group Membership and Resistance to Change" and "Personality and Susceptibility to Persuasion."

James, Fleming, Jr., "Burden of Proof," *Virginia Law Review* (1961), pp. 51–70.

Katz, Daniel, ed., *Public Opinion Quarterly* (Summer 1960), special issue on "Attitude Change."

Pence, Orville L., "Emotionally Loaded Argument: Its Effectiveness in Stimulating Recall," *Quarterly Journal of Speech* (October 1954), pp. 272–76.

Ruechelle, Randall C., "An Experimental Study of Audience Recognition of Emotional and Intellectual Appeals in Persuasion," *Speech Monographs* (March 1958), pp. 49–58.

Utterback, William E., and Harold F. Harding, "Some Factors Conditioning Response to Argument," *Speech Monographs* (November 1955), pp. 303–8.

Wallace, Karl R., "The Substance of Rhetoric: Good Reasons," *Quarterly Journal of Speech* (October 1963), pp. 239–49.

## Organization

Coleman, E. B., "Improving Comprehensibility by Shortening Sentences," *Journal of Applied Psychology* (April 1962), pp. 131–34.

Crane, Loren D., "Toward a Theory of Arrangement," *Ohio Speech Journal* (1962), pp. 11–17.

Darnell, Donald K., "The Relationship between Sentence Order and Comprehension," *Speech Monographs* (June 1963), pp. 97–100.

Gulley, Halbert E., and David K. Berlo, "Effect of Intercellular and Intracellular Speech Structure on Attitude Change and Learning," *Speech Monographs* (November 1956), pp. 288–97.

Hovland, Carl I., Irving L. Janis, and Harold H. Kelley, *Communication and Persuasion*. New Haven: Yale University Press, 1953.

———, and others, eds., *The Order of Presentation in Persuasion*. New Haven: Yale University Press, 1957.

Knower, Franklin H., "Studies in the Organization of Speech Material," *Journal of Educational Research* (November 1945), pp. 220–30.

Monroe, Alan H., *Principles and Types of Speech*, 5th ed., pp. 235–329. Chicago: Scott, Foresman and Co., 1962.

Parker, John P., "Some Organizational Variables and Their Effect upon Comprehension," *Journal of Communication* (March 1962), pp. 27–32.

Smith, Raymond G., "An Experimental Study of the Effects of Speech Organization upon Attitudes of College Students," *Speech Monographs* (November 1951), pp. 292–301.

Thistlethwaite, Donald L., Henry DeHaan, and Joseph M. Kamenetzky, "The Effects of 'Directive' and 'Nondirective' Communication Procedures on Attitudes," *Journal of Abnormal and Social Psychology* (July 1955), pp. 107–13.

Walter, Otis M., and Robert L. Scott, *Thinking and Speaking: A Guide to Intelligent Oral Communication*, pp. 57–82. New York: The Macmillan Company, 1962.

Wilson, John F., and Carroll C. Arnold, *Public Speaking as a Liberal Art*, pp. 191–224. Boston: Allyn and Bacon, Inc., 1964.

## Language and Style

Berlo, David K., *The Process of Communication*, Chapter 8, "Dimensions of Meaning." New York: Holt, Rinehart & Winston, Inc., 1960.

Blankenship, Jane, *Public Speaking: A Rhetorical Perspective*. Englewood Cliffs, N.J.: Prentice-Hall, Inc., 1966. See the Chapters "Style: Some Theoretic Considerations" and "Style: Some Practical Applications."

———, "A Linguistic Analysis of Oral and Written Style," Quarterly *Journal of Speech* (December 1962), pp. 419–22.

Bryant, Donald C., "Of Style," *Western Speech* (Spring 1957), pp. 103–10. Association," *Quarterly Journal of Speech* (October 1950), pp. 326–32.

———, "Aspects of the Rhetorical Tradition: Emotion, Style, and Literary

———, and Karl R. Wallace, *Fundamentals of Public Speaking*, 3rd ed.,

Chapter 16, "The Language of the Speech." New York: Appleton-Century-Crofts, 1960.

Cooper, Lane, ed., *Theories of Style*. New York, 1907. Reprinted as *The Art of the Writer*. Ithaca, New York: Cornell University Press, 1952. Contains, for example, Buffon's "Discourse on Style" and Swift's "A Letter to a Young Clergyman."

Gleason, Henry Allan, Jr., *Introduction to Descriptive Linguistics*. New York: Henry Holt and Co., 1955. A good introduction to the study of language in terms of its internal structure.

Hughes, John P., *The Science of Language*. New York: Random House, Inc., 1962.

Jakobson, Roman, and Morris Halle, *Fundamentals of Language*. The Hague: Mouton and Co., 1956.

Middleton, Murry J., *The Problem of Style*. Oxford: Oxford University Press, 1925.

Nebergall, Roger, "An Experimental Investigation of Rhetorical Clarity," *Speech Monographs* (November 1958), pp. 243–54.

Quirk, Randolph, *The Use of English*. New York: St. Martin's Press, 1962.

Thomas, Gordon L., "Oral Style and Intelligibility," *Speech Monographs* (March 1956), pp. 46–54.

Ullmann, Stephen, *Language and Style*. New York: Barnes and Noble, Inc., 1964. Advanced reading but very rewarding.

Whatmough, Joshua, *Language: A Modern Synthesis*. New York: St. Martin's Press, 1956.

Wimsatt, W. K., Jr., "Verbal Style: Logical and Counterlogical," *Publications of the Modern Language Association* (March 1950), pp. 5–20.

### Delivery

Allport, Gordon W., and Philip E. Vernon, *Studies in Expressive Movement*. New York: The Macmillan Company, 1933.

Birdwhistell, Ray L., *Introduction to Kinesics*. Washington, D.C.: Foreign Service Institute, 1952.

Black, John W., and Wilbur Moore, *Speech: Code, Meaning, and Communication*, pp. 231–254. New York: McGraw-Hill Book Company, 1955.

Bryant, Donald C., and Karl R. Wallace, *Fundamentals of Public Speaking*, 3rd ed., pp. 189–248. New York: Appleton-Century-Crofts, 1960.

Critchley, MacDonald, *The Language of Gesture*. London: Edward Arnold, 1939.

Diehl, Charles F., Richard C. White, and Kenneth W. Burk, "Rate and Communication," *Speech Monographs* (August 1959), pp. 229–232.

Harwood, Kenneth A., "Listenability and Rate of Presentation," *Speech Monographs* (March 1955), pp. 57–59.

Hildebrandt, Herbert W., and Walter W. Stevens, "Manuscript and Extemporaneous Delivery in Communicating Information," *Speech Monographs* (November 1963), pp. 369–72.

Krout, Maurice H., "The Social and Psychological Significance of Gestures," *Journal of Genetic Psychology* (December 1935), pp. 385–411.

Miller, Gerald R., and Murray A. Hewgill, "The Effect of Variations in Nonfluency on Audience Ratings of Source Credibility," *Quarterly Journal of Speech* (February 1964), pp. 36–44.

Monroe, Alan H., *Principles and Types of Speech*, 5th ed., pp. 47–130. Chicago: Scott, Foresman & Company, 1962.

Ruesch, Jurgen, and Weldon Kees, *Nonverbal Communication*. Berkeley: University of California Press, 1956.

Walter, Otis M., and Robert L. Scott, *Thinking and Speaking*, pp. 93–103. New York: The Macmillan Company, 1962.

Wilson, John F., and Carroll C. Arnold, *Public Speaking as a Liberal Art*, pp. 286–322. Boston: Allyn & Bacon, Inc., 1964.

### Ethics of a Speaker

Aronson, Elliot, Judith A. Turner, and J. Merrill Carlsmith, "Communication Credibility and Communication Discrepancy as Determinants of Opinion Change," *Journal of Abnormal and Social Psychology* (July 1963), pp. 31–36.

Bryant, Donald C., and Karl R. Wallace, *Fundamentals of Public Speaking*, 3rd ed., pp. 287–300. New York: Appleton-Century-Crofts, 1960.

Flynn, Lawrence J., "The Aristotelian Basis for the Ethics of Speaking," *Speech Teacher* (September 1957), pp. 179–87.

Haiman, Franklyn S., "Democratic Ethics and the Hidden Persuaders," *Quarterly Journal of Speech* (December 1958), pp. 385–92.

———, "A Re-examination of the Ethics of Persuasion," *Central States Speech Journal* (March 1952), pp. 4–9.

Lillywhite, Harold, "Standards of Ethical Communication in Contemporary Society," *Gavel of Delta Sigma Rho* (January 1963), pp. 21–24, 30.

Murphy, Richard, "Preface to an Ethic of Rhetoric," in *The Rhetorical Idiom*, ed. Donald C. Bryant. Ithaca, New York: Cornell University Press, 1958. Pp. 125–43.

Rogge, Edward, "Evaluating the Ethics of a Speaker in a Democracy," *Quarterly Journal of Speech* (December 1959), pp. 419–25.

Schrier, William, "The Ethics of Persuasion," *Quarterly Journal of Speech* (November 1930), pp. 476–86.

Weaver, Richard M., *The Ethics of Rhetoric*. Chicago: Henry Regnery Co., 1953.

Weinberg, Harry L., "An Ethics for Public Speaking: A Semantic Approach," *Pennsylvania Speech Annual* (June 1955), pp. 7–12.


### Speech Criticism

Baird, A. Craig, and Lester Thonssen, "Methodology in the Criticism of Public Address," *Quarterly Journal of Speech* (April 1947), pp. 134–138.

Black, Edwin, *Rhetorical Criticism: A Study in Method*. New York: The Macmillan Company, 1965.

Brigance, William Norwood, ed., *History and Criticism of American Public Address*, Vols. I and II. Reprint edition. New York: Russell & Russell, Inc., 1960. Originally printed in 1943. Vol. III, ed. Marie Hochmuth. New York: Longmans, Green and Co., 1955.

Cleary, James W., and Frederick W. Haberman, eds., *Rhetoric and Public Address: A Bibliography, 1947–1961*. Madison and Milwaukee: University of Wisconsin Press, 1964. Check index under name of particular speaker and under heading of "Criticism."

Croft, Albert J., "The Function of Rhetorical Criticism," *Quarterly Journal of Speech* (October 1956), pp. 283–98.

Hochmuth, Marie, "Lincoln's First Inaugural," in *American Speeches*, eds., Wayland Maxfield Parrish and Marie Hochmuth. New York: Longmans, Green and Co., 1954. A good example of speech criticism.
———, "The Criticism of Rhetoric," in *A History and Criticism of American Public Address*, Vol. III, ed., Marie Hochmuth. New York: Longmans, Green, and Co., 1955.

Nichols, Marie Hochmuth, *Rhetoric and Criticism*. Baton Rouge: Louisiana State University Press, 1963.

Parrish, Wayland Maxfield, "The Study of Speeches," in *American Speeches*, eds., Wayland Maxfield Parrish and Marie Hochmuth. New York: Longmans, Green and Co., 1954.

*Quarterly Journal of Speech*. A publication sponsored by The Speech Association of America, often containing speech criticism and articles on the nature of criticism.

Reid, Loren D., "The Perils of Rhetorical Criticism," *Quarterly Journal of Speech* (December 1944), pp. 416–22.

Thonssen, Lester, and A. Craig Baird, *Speech Criticism: The Development of Standards for Rhetorical Appraisal*. New York: The Ronald Press Company, 1948.